The Right and the Righteous

Religious Forces in the Modern Political World

General Editor Allen D. Hertzke, The Carl Albert Center, University of Oklahoma at Norman

Religious Forces in the Modern Political World features books on religious forces in politics, both in the United States and abroad. The authors examine the complex interplay between religious faith and politics in the modern world, emphasizing its impact on contemporary political developments. This new series spans a diverse range of methodological interpretations, philosophical approaches, and substantive concerns. Titles include:

God at the Grass Roots: The Christian Right in the 1994 Elections (1995) edited by Mark J. Rozell, Mary Washington College, and Clyde Wilcox, Georgetown University

Let Justice Roll: Prophetic Challenges in Religion, Politics, and Society (1996) edited by Neal Riemer, Drew University

Churches of the Poor: The Pentecostal Church in Central America (1996) by Anne M. Hallum, Stetson University

The Right and the Righteous: The Christian Right Confronts the Republican Party (1996) by Duane Murray Oldfield, Knox College

Religion and the Culture Wars: Dispatches from the Front (1996) by John C. Green, Bliss Institute of Applied Politics, University of Akron; James L. Guth, Furman University; Corwin E. Smidt, Calvin College; and Lyman A. Kellstedt, Wheaton College

The Fullness of Time: Toward an Understanding of the Protestant Movement in Central America (1996) by Anne M. Hallum, Stetson University

The Christian Democrat International (1996) by Roberto Papini, Trieste University, translated and with a foreword by Robert Royal, Ethics and Public Policy Center

The Right and the Righteous

The Christian Right Confronts
the Republican Party

Duane Murray Oldfield

ROWMAN & LITTLEFIELD PUBLISHERS, INC.

Lanham × Boulder × New York × London

ROWMAN & LITTLEFIELD PUBLISHERS, INC.

Published in the United States of America
by Rowman & Littlefield Publishers, Inc.
4720 Boston Way, Lanham, Maryland 20706

3 Henrietta Street
London, WC2E 8LU, England

British Cataloging in Publication Information Available

Library of Congress Cataloging-in-Publication Data

Oldfield, Duane Murray.
The right and the righteous : the Christian Right confronts the
Republican Party / Duane Murray Oldfield.
p.   cm. — (Religious forces in the modern political world)
Includes bibliographical references and index.
1. Christianity and politics—United States—History—20th
century. 2. Conservatism–Religious aspects—Christianity—
History—20th century. 3. Conservatism—United States—
History—20th century. 4. Republican Party (U.S. : 1854–)
5. United States—Politics and government—1945–1989. 6. United
States—Politics and government—1989– 7. United States—Church
history—20th century. I. Title. II. Series.
BR526.057 1996   322'.1'097309045—dc20   96–14647   CIP

ISBN 0–8476–8190–4 (cloth : alk. paper)

Printed in the United States of America

 The paper used in this publication meets the minimum requirements of American National Standard for Information Sciences—Permanence of Paper for Printed Library Materials, ANSI Z39.48-1984.

Contents

Tables

Acknowledgments

This project was a long time in the making. During that time I received invaluable assistance from a wide variety of people and institutions. Without their help this book could not have been completed.

My first thanks go to the many activists and scholars who gave their time to be interviewed in the course of my research. I was consistently surprised by their hospitality and willingness to make room in their own busy schedules. Even when they are not cited directly, they should know that their contributions helped shape my thinking on the issues discussed here.

My thanks also go to fellow scholars who read and listened to my arguments in their various stages of completion. Paula Consolini, Taylor Dark, Gus DiZerga, Jo Freeman, John Gerring, Judith Gruber, David Hadwigger, Allen Hertzke, Kristin Luker, Marissa Martino-Golden, Beth Reingold, Michael Rogin, Arun Swamy, Joe White, the members of the Media Research and Action Project, and an anonymous reader at Rowman & Littlefield provided me with valuable advice and forced me to rethink my less supportable conclusions.

The late Aaron Wildavsky provided assistance far beyond the call of duty. Aaron's enthusiasm, curiosity, and love of learning provided intellectual stimulation even when we disagreed—which we often did. I know that I am just one among many scholars who miss him terribly.

At Boston College and at Knox College I have found supportive environments in which to develop my ideas and my teaching. At Boston College, a series of graduate student research assistants helped move this project along. I am deeply grateful for their assistance.

Fellowships from the Brookings Institution and the Institute for Governmental Studies helped finance this project. During my stay in Washington, D.C., Brookings provided an excellent working environment. Other institutions were helpful as well. Chatham House allowed

ix

me to draw on my previously published material in chapter 6. My employment with the Washington Center's programs at the 1988 and 1992 Republican conventions gave me access to valuable research opportunities. A travel grant from Boston College financed follow-up research. The process of gathering information on the far-flung and often confusing events discussed in this work would have been much harder without the resources of the Data Center in Oakland and Political Research Associates in Cambridge. I would also like to thank the staff of the lobbying group People for the American Way for allowing me to utilize its extensive files.

My parents, Martha and Bruce Oldfield, wondered at times whether this book would ever be finished. Now it is and I want to thank them for standing by me through a long process. Finally, my deepest debt is to Karen Kampwirth. Her love, support, intelligent commentary, and toleration of a grumpy writer were the key factors in bringing this work to its conclusion.

Introduction

From its "family values" rhetoric to Pat Buchanan's declaration of "cultural war," the 1992 Republican convention provided a national showcase for the Christian Right. The convention illustrated the powerful role the Christian Right plays within the Republican party and laid to rest rumors that the movement was dead. The defeat of George Bush, the candidate that that convention nominated, did little to slow the movement's momentum. Membership in movement organizations skyrocketed and the Christian Right was soon able to claim credit for the sweeping Republican congressional victories of 1994. Major candidates for the 1996 Republican presidential nomination vied with each other to demonstrate their fealty to the movement. The Christian Right may or may not help the Republicans, but there is little doubt that the movement is a force to contend with.

The significance of the Christian Right's foray into party politics goes well beyond current headlines. A central theme of this book is that the Christian Right is not a transitory phenomenon. It has survived, and will continue to survive, the repeated death sentences pronounced by outside observers. The movement is deeply rooted in the American social structure, drawing its strength from a vibrant, well-politicized religious constituency and from that constituency's impressive organizational infrastructure. The religious constituency and the movement have adapted well to the "modern" trends that many believed would lead to their demise. The issues the movement addresses are real ones and struggles over them will continue to play a key role in shaping our culture. In short, the Christian Right will not go away.

Nor will the Christian Right leave the Republican party. The movement has already played a key role in a process that, over the last few decades, has redefined both the Democratic and Republican parties. With the Christian Right's help, the two parties have come to divide more and more clearly over issues such as abortion, homosexu-

1

ality, and women's rights. As this has happened, the Christian Right and its constituency have become more and more closely tied to the GOP. As the threat of "exit" from the party has declined, the Christian Right has invested heavily in augmenting its voice *within* the party. It now controls an estimated eighteen state Republican parties and is a significant force in thirteen more.[1] The movement, and particularly its leading organization, the Christian Coalition, are not likely to give up that investment. The Christian Right does not fit neatly into the Republican party, but it is likely to remain uneasily lodged there for some time to come. The Republican party's identity will be intertwined with that of the Christian Right for the foreseeable future.

If the Christian Right is going to be with us—and with the Republican party—for a long time to come, we need to understand how the movement and the party came to their current situation. That is, obviously, a task of the book as a whole. One event, however, can provide a useful introduction. The 1994 National Religious Broadcasters (NRB) Convention did not receive the media attention accorded to the national party conventions, Pat Robertson's presidential campaign, or the 1994 elections, but it was an important event in its own right and provides a window into many of the themes of the rest of this book.

NRB Present and Past

From 29 January to 2 February 1994, four thousand people crowded the Washington Sheraton for the fiftieth anniversary convention of the NRB. In many ways it was a typical business convention. Products ranging from color-coded Bibles to recording equipment and super screen televisions were on display. Publishers distributed catalogues and brought in authors for book signings. Religious cartoons, talk shows, music videos, and movies competed with more traditional programming (preaching and Bible discussion shows) for the attention of broadcasters and access to the nation's airwaves. Workshops provided tips for broadcasters attempting to reach Hispanic audiences, deal with federal regulations, and select the right software system. Participants mingled in halls and hotel restaurants, making contacts and cementing deals. The convention had the feel of a business convention for a simple reason: religious broadcasting is a very big business, with nearly 1,600 radio and 274 television stations spending over a billion dollars a year on the purchase of airtime alone.[2]

Yet this convention was more than just a business meeting. Prayers, gospel music, and testimonies of salvation left no doubt that this was a distinctly religious gathering. Evangelism was the focus as speakers exhorted their listeners to witness to the young, to the inner cities, and to the many nations of the world. A workshop provided advice for dealing with the "world challenge" of Islam. Speakers called upon the nation to repent of its sins in a "National Day of Prayer."[3]

The NRB convention was also about politics. Interspersed among the commercial and religious exhibits were the booths of political groups such as the Family Research Council, Concerned Women for America, National Right to Life, and Pat Robertson's Christian Coalition. Conventiongoers gathered to launch a new political organization, the Alliance Defense Fund, designed to provide support for "Christian legal organizations and volunteer attorneys on the front line of the civil war of values."[4] Prominent political figures including William Bennett, Jack Kemp, former attorney general Edwin Meese, Senator Dan Coats of Indiana, and Virginia Senate hopeful Oliver North were among those who addressed the assembled delegates. As I mingled among the crowds of this my third NRB convention, the conversations I overheard were political as often as they were religious.

A complex mix of business, evangelism, and politics, NRB conventions provide a window onto much larger phenomena: the growth, political mobilization, and shifting political alignments of America's evangelical Protestant population. To properly gauge the significance of what happened at the 1994 convention, however, one needs to take a look backward.

In the early 1980s, the modifier "New" usually preceded the term "Christian Right." The movement today has been around long enough that the modifier has begun to disappear, but it is important to remember what a new—and unexpected—development the Christian Right was. The 1960s and early 1970s generated a variety of new movements, but few observers at the time foresaw the rise of a movement from among conservative evangelicals. When Americans thought of religiously based political activism, the images that came to mind were likely to be those of figures on the left: Martin Luther King, Jr., or antiwar priests such as Daniel Berrigan. Thus the rapid rise of the Christian Right in the late 1970s caught opponents—and even some supporters—by surprise.

To illustrate the social and political changes that the emergence of the Christian Right entailed, a return visit to the National Religious Broadcasters Convention is in order. The 1994 convention, as mentioned earlier, marked the fiftieth anniversary of the NRB. Over those fifty years, the evangelical mission of the broadcasters remained constant, but their societal position and political orientation shifted dramatically. Over those years, evangelical Protestants saw their denominations and religious institutions grow dramatically. At the same time, evangelicals moved from political withdrawal to political activism, and from Democratic to Republican allegiance. Closer examination of these three moves will remind us of the changes that have taken place and will show why the Christian Right is likely to be with us for some time to come.

Religious Growth

The NRB was organized in 1944 as a means of winning more airtime for evangelical Protestants. Radio networks resisted selling airtime to religious broadcasters. When they gave out free airtime as a public service, they turned to the mainline Protestant denominations affiliated with the Federal Council of Churches.[5] Several evangelical programs, such as Charles Fuller's "Old Time Revival Hour," found airtime and an audience, but evangelical radio, and later television, faced numerous obstacles. Over the next several decades, buoyed by the deep pockets of their audiences and a favorable ruling by the Federal Communications Commission, evangelicals chipped away at the public service monopoly of their rivals.[6]

Today, the conservative evangelicals who gather at NRB conventions dominate the airwaves. Paid religious programming has displaced free public-service airtime and the vast majority of these paid programs are evangelical.[7] Steve Bruce estimates that 75 percent of religious radio and television is evangelical or fundamentalist.[8] Evangelical broadcasting provides a powerful base for the Christian Right to draw upon. Televangelists (Jerry Falwell, Pat Robertson) and radio personalities (James Dobson) are key movement leaders. Massive religious broadcasting empires disseminate the movement's message, mobilize citizens across the nation, and raise very large sums of money.

The evangelical success has not been limited to the realm of broadcasting. As evangelical broadcasters were experiencing success, so too was evangelical religion in general. When the NRB formed, American Protestantism was dominated by the Methodists, Presbyterians, Episcopalians, and other denominations affiliated with the Federal Council of Churches. Progressive, prestigious, and flush with members, their dominant position appeared secure. However, as evangelical churches continued their steady growth, membership in the mainline denominations stagnated and then began a precipitous decline. Evangelicals have now pulled to a rough numerical equality with their mainline counterparts. As part of what Robert Wuthnow labels a "restructuring" of American religion, evangelicals have moved from an isolated, minority status to center stage.[9]

The success of evangelical religion, like the success of evangelical broadcasting, supplies a critical base of support for the Christian Right. Evangelical Protestantism provides the movement with a large pool of potential recruits, the culture and values that define it, and, ultimately, with powerful organizational resources. As Mancur Olson has pointed out, it often makes little economic sense for individuals to join together to promote common political ends.[10] One way around the "collective action" problem is to utilize organizations built for non-political ends, tapping resources that could never have been gathered for solely political endeavors. Few human activities have elicited such outpourings of time, money, and effort as organized religion. If even a fraction of these resources can be utilized for political ends, the results are likely to be dramatic. The value of religious broadcasters' resources has been mentioned already, but also important are the resources of more traditional religious organization in the form of local churches and denominations. Local churches can provide political movements with access to attentive, well-organized constituencies. Pat Robertson—and Jesse Jackson, for that matter—found that local congregations made very effective building blocks for a presidential campaign.[11] Higher-level church organization can play a political role as well. America's largest Protestant denomination, the 15.5-million-member Southern Baptist Convention (SBC), has been taken over by conservatives who have not hesitated to support the Christian Right. The multidenominational National Association of Evangelicals has also swung into action on behalf of Christian Right causes.[12]

From Withdrawal to Activism

Evangelical religion and broadcasting provide potentially powerful resources, but these resources need not be used for political purposes. Evangelicals have long been torn between political involvement and an exclusive focus on saving souls. At the time of the NRB's founding, the balance leaned heavily toward soul saving. In the first quarter of this century, religiously conservative Protestants, some labeled "fundamentalist" after a series of pamphlets entitled *The Fundamentals*, had waged battle with their more liberal, "modernist" counterparts. The conservatives lost. The major northern denominations remained in liberal hands and, as symbolized by the Scopes "Monkey Trial," fundamentalist arguments lost much of their credibility in the broader society. Fundamentalists withdrew from societal involvement and built their own institutions, hoping to protect the faith and insulate themselves from the corruption of the surrounding world.

The National Association of Evangelicals (NAE), which helped found the NRB, pursued a more moderate strategy than the fundamentalists. The NAE attempted to engage the broader society rather than separate from it, but the political content of this engagement was quite limited. The NAE sought to make evangelical Protestantism socially and intellectually respectable again. It formed the NRB to fight for access to the nation's airwaves. However, respectability and airtime were means primarily toward the religious goal of spreading the faith. Throughout the 1950s and 1960s, studies found that evangelical Protestants exhibited low levels of political participation.[13]

In recent years, NRB conventions have reflected a far-reaching politicization of the evangelical community. Congressional leaders, presidential candidates, and presidents themselves address the delegates. Religious and political themes have become more and more closely intertwined. In my research, as I listened to "Christian" radio, watched televangelists, went to conventions and rallies, and read movement literature, I soon found the themes expressed extremely repetitive and predictable. While this predictability can lead to boredom on the part of the outside observer, it is a sign that a common political worldview has come to animate and motivate what had been a fragmented and apolitical constituency. Tune in to a Christian radio station anywhere in the country and you will hear similar themes: the dangers posed by abortion, pornography, educational bureaucrats, and homosexuals, with all these perceived problems linked to the denial of our nation's Christian roots and the rise of a secular humanist worldview.

This common political ideology is deeply rooted; I see little reason to believe it will be reversed in the near future. It helps insure that evangelical leaders will continue to devote a considerable portion of the resources at their disposal to the promotion of political ends. It motivates the prodigious grassroots volunteer efforts of the Christian Right's rank and file. And as this ideology has taken hold, evangelical voting rates have risen.[14]

From Democrats to Republicans

Not only have evangelicals gained new resources and a new political ideology, they have also adopted a new political party. When the NRB was formed fifty years ago, white evangelicals tended toward conservatism and anticommunism but were, for the most part,

Democrats. The 1994 convention presented a striking contrast. In an unusual twist, the staunchly anticommunist group commended the ex-communist and president of Russia, Boris Yeltsin.[15] No such commendation was given American Democrat Bill Clinton. Notwithstanding the fact that Clinton is himself a Southern Baptist, the NRB broke with tradition and publicly refused to issue a presidential invitation. An NRB press release declared, "we cannot give a platform to a leader who so aggressively supports and puts forth policies and positions which are blatantly contrary to scriptural views."[16]

This snub was by no means the only sign of a Republican tilt to the convention. The major political speakers were Republicans, as were the vast majority of those in attendance. One man, a representative of a Washington, D.C., urban ministry, discretely admitted to me that he was, in fact, a Democrat. While clearly enthusiastic about religious aspects of the convention, he found its political tone disquieting. Any Democrat would. Speakers, books, radio shows broadcasted live from the convention, all contributed a steady stream of attacks upon Democratic leaders and the social movements affiliated with the party. If the Republicans were not quite portrayed as God's party, there was little doubt as to which party was the devil's.

The Republican tilt of the NRB convention represents an extreme version of what is happening in white evangelical circles more generally over the last two decades. Anti-Democratic from its founding, the Christian Right has developed closer and closer ties to the GOP. Evangelical religious leaders shifted their party allegiance.[17] Evangelical voters moved more slowly, but there too a clear pattern emerged. Once Democratic loyalists, white evangelicals are now solidly in the Republican camp. While George Bush could manage only 37 percent of the overall vote in 1992, he won 62 percent of the vote of white evangelicals. Among white evangelicals who attend church regularly, Bush's level of support rose to 72 percent.[18]

Strengths, Weaknesses, and a Look Forward

The Christian Right is rooted in the changes that the National Religious Broadcasters, and American evangelicals more generally, have undergone. Where once there was a marginal, apolitical, Democratic constituency, a resource-rich, politically motivated, increasingly Republican movement has emerged. Spreading the faith and building up a powerful array of institutions, evangelicals created a formidable resource base. As evangelicals developed a common political ideology, they provided the justification for an aggressive reentry into the nation's political life and, more specifically, into the Republican party. The Christian Right looks like it will be a key feature of the American political scene for many years to come.

In highlighting the deep roots and strengths of the Christian Right, I do not mean to deny its weaknesses. The Christian Right by no means has the support of all evangelicals (if it did, Jimmy Carter, Bill Clinton, and Al Gore would be counted among its members). Religious differences within the evangelical community continue to undermine movement organizing efforts. The imperatives of appealing to an evangelical constituency and building up religion-based institutions often conflict with those of alliance building and operating successfully in a broader, more secular political world. And, of course, the Christian Right's opponents, including many within the Republican party, are not without powerful resources of their own.

This study will examine the Christian Right's strengths and weaknesses, the partisan political terrain on which it operates, and the development of its relationship with the Republican party. The chapter summary below provides the reader a sense of the overall framework before plunging into the details.

The Christian Right is a religion-based movement; to properly understand it requires attention to the religious history underlying the movement. In chapter 1 I show that this history leaves a mixed legacy for the Christian Right. On the one hand, American evangelicalism has shown impressive private vitality, providing the movement with a very sizable potential constituency. On the other, evangelicalism's public credibility is often limited. A century of generally losing encounters with modern intellectual and social trends has undermined evangelicals' standing in the broader society. The Christian Right often must choose between approaches that appeal to the religious sentiments of its evangelical constituency and those that will be influential with outsiders. Furthermore, it inherits serious religious divisions within its evangelical base. These divisions continue to present difficulties for movement organizing.

Chapter 2 puts the preceding history into theoretical perspective and provides an explanation for the resurgence of political activism among the evangelical community within the last twenty years. Too often, the Christian Right is analyzed in terms of faulty theories of status politics and "modernity." I will critique these theories and their tendency to dismiss the movement's motivations and concerns as irrational. My alternative formulation argues that the Christian Right can be better understood as rooted in real social conflicts. As evangelicals have found it harder and harder to isolate their subculture from the broader society, the Christian Right has emerged as a movement focused on those institutions—churches, schools, the media, and the family—that pass on subcultural values in a hostile world. A proper understanding of the Christian Right's relation to modernity can explain both the movement's internal dynamism and its lack of credibility with outsiders.

With the historical and sociological origins of the Christian Right laid out, chapter 3 moves on to the political terrain upon which the movement must operate—specifically the American party system. Changes in the presidential nominating process over the last thirty years have altered the prospects for social movement influence and the resources needed to exert that influence. Using the concepts of exit, voice, and loyalty developed by Albert Hirschman, one can distinguish between different methods by which movements can influence party behavior. In particular, the use (or threat) of "exit" from a party contrasts with the exercise of "voice" within a party.

Chapters 4 through 6 document the confrontation between the Christian Right and the shifting structures of the American party system. Arguments from the first two chapters—on the movement's motivations, divisions, and limitations—together with chapter 3's analysis of the possibilities the party system leaves open to it, are combined to study the long and conflictual record of Christian Right/party interaction.

Chapter 4 analyzes the institutional origins of the Christian Right and the development of its relations with the party system through the mid-1980s. From a largely unorganized evangelical swing constituency (with a strong possibility for exit from the GOP), conservative activists developed a well-organized movement aligned with the Republican party. It appears the emergence of the Christian Right was part of a far-reaching reshaping of the Democratic and Republican parties. As the Democrats became ever more firmly the party of social liberalism and the Republicans the party of social conservatism, the Christian Right and, more slowly, evangelical voters grew more firmly tied to the GOP. With exit a less plausible option, incentives for the Christian Right to exercise its voice within the Republican party grew stronger, as did the resources it had available to pursue such a course.

Chapter 5 looks at one of the most prominent attempts of the Christian Right to exercise its voice within the Republican party, the 1988 presidential campaign of televangelist Pat Robertson. The Robertson campaign was a turning point for movement/party relations. It demonstrated the political potential of Christian Right resources, brought the movement into internal party affairs, and laid the foundation for the most important Christian Right organization of the contemporary era, the Christian Coalition. Nonetheless, Robertson lost. His loss illustrated many of the problems that continue to undermine movement efforts to exert influence within the party, including serious religious differences within the movement and the contradictory demands of mobilizing the movement's core constituency while successfully appealing to broader audiences. Robertson's campaign also demonstrated that the Christian Right's resources are far more effective in some aspects of party affairs (caucuses, state party meetings) than in others (primary elections).

Chapter 6 brings the account up to the present, focusing on Christian Right activism at the state party level, the 1992 and 1994 campaigns, and the rise of the Christian Coalition. The Christian Right has experienced a powerful grassroots mobilization in recent years. This mobilization has resulted in movement gains, and relations with the GOP have grown even closer. Nonetheless, the problems described in chapter 5 remain and chapter 6 describes the movement's uneven success in dealing with them.

The current situation of the party and the movement is illustrated by the Republican party's Contract with America and the Christian Coalition's Contract with the American Family. The politics surrounding the two contracts are indicative of the movement's power within, and close cooperation with, the GOP. The social issue realignment described in chapter 4 is now very well advanced. Nonetheless, the Christian Right remains a distinctive bloc within the party. Years of experience have not been sufficient to overcome the basic dilemmas the movement faces as it attempts both to mobilize its base constituency and to build the outside alliances necessary to effectively exercise its voice within the party.

My concluding remarks include a prediction, namely that the Christian Right will neither succeed nor go away. The movement's characteristic dilemmas will help define the political tensions of the Republican party for some time to come.

Data

First, the reader should have a sense of the research upon which these arguments are based. Primary sources included over seventy formal interviews, which ranged from thirty minutes to over five hours in length and were conducted in the period 1989 to 1994. Interview subjects ranged from local Robertson activists to the chairman of the liberal lobbying group, People for the American Way. I talked with leaders of major Christian Right groups, Republican party officials, and national staff members of Pat Robertson's presidential campaign. Since the information I wanted to gather from the interviewees varied widely, no standard interview format was used.

In addition to formal interviews, I attended the 1988, 1989, and 1994 meetings of the National Religious Broadcasters convention, the 1989 Conservative Political Action Conference, the 1988 Washington for Jesus events, state and county Republican party conventions, and the 1988 and 1992 Republican National Conventions. I listened to "Christian" radio, read movement literature, and watched a wide variety of televangelists. This informal exposure to movement and party culture is not always referred to directly, but nonetheless played a central role in shaping my thinking.

Finally, this work is based upon a wide array of scholarly works and journalistic accounts of events. The rise of the Christian Right has helped spur further inquiry into the history and nature of American evangelicalism. My debt to this literature is substantial in chapter 1. While this book is, in part, a response to the lack of literature specifically on Christian Right/Republican party relations, related topics have been well studied. Fine accounts of the rise of the movement, the activities of televangelists, and the voting patterns of evangelicals have helped put my own research into proper perspective. This study has benefited from the fine efforts of journalists and investigative reporters. Presidential contests, nasty partisan infighting, religious controversies and scandals—all are prime attractions for the press corps and led to a wealth of coverage of the events related here.[19] I was happy to utilize the eyes and ears of hundreds of reporters to supplement my own investigative efforts.

Chapter 1

Setting the Stage for the Christian Right: Evangelicals and American Society

American evangelicals inhabit a paradoxical world. The United States, they believe, is a "Christian nation," a country founded on faith and the stronghold from which the gospel will be spread across the globe.[1] Yet at the same time evangelicals feel besieged at home. They see their faith and values under increasing attack from secular and humanist forces. As they describe the corruption of American society, comparisons are often made to the decadent latter years of the Roman Empire. And, paradoxically, both sets of views are often held by the same people, at the same time.

As this paradox illustrates, evangelical perceptions of American society are complex and not easily characterized. To properly understand the place of evangelicals within American society, their understanding of that place, and the political activity (or nonactivity) that this understanding leads them to, historical perspective is necessary. For while the Christian Right is a relatively new movement, evangelical Protestantism has a long history in the United States.

This chapter will not provide a comprehensive religious history.[1] Instead it focuses on those aspects of the historical legacy that shape and limit today's Christian Right. The story told here is one of evangelicalism's displacement from its nineteenth-century position in the mainstream of American cultural intellectual and political life. A variety of strategies were used by evangelicals to deal with that displacement; and critical religious differences have developed *within* the evangelical camp. This chapter documents the post–World War II growth that has taken place in evangelical ranks and discusses the difficulties of measuring the evangelical constituency. (For the moment it is important to remember that the category "evangelical" is a loose one whose boundaries have shifted somewhat over time. Unless specifically noted otherwise, "evangelical" will be used to refer to historically white denominations such as the Southern Baptists and the Assemblies of God.) Many of the dilemmas of the Christian Right were inherited from its evangelical past.

In the Mainstream

In the United States, Christian sects are infinitely diversified and perpetually modified; but Christianity itself is an established and irresistible fact, which no one undertakes either to attack or defend. The Americans, having admitted the principle doctrines of the Christian religion without inquiry, are obliged to accept in a like manner a great number of moral truths originating in it and connected with it.

—Alexis de Tocqueville

In 1870 almost all American Protestants thought of America as a Christian nation. Although many Roman Catholics, sectarians, skeptics, and non-Christians had other views of the matter, Protestant evangelicals considered their faith to be the normative American creed. Viewed from their dominant perspective, the nineteenth century had been marked by the successive advances of evangelicalism, the American nation, and hence the kingdom of God.

—George Marsden

The observations of Alexis de Tocqueville and George Marsden capture a critical feature of American religious life. America lacks an established state religion; church and state are officially separate. Yet the country has been marked throughout much of its history by the cultural hegemony of the Christian faith and the "moral truths" associated with it. The late nineteenth century described by Marsden marked a high point for American evangelicalism, as the progress of church and nation appeared to go hand in hand. At that time, evangelicalism was closely allied with the forces of science and higher learning. It was widely believed that objective study of the Bible and of the empirical facts of the natural world would lead to similar conclusions. Faith was widespread that education would further the causes of religion, material progress, and democracy. This faith was symbolized both by the immensely popular McGuffey's readers, which interwove religious and moral lessons with training in the basics of literacy, and also by the close connections between colleges, universities, and their church sponsors.

American Protestantism in this period was generally democratic and optimistic. Denominations stressing basic appeals to the common people grew rapidly in the nineteenth century, the most notable examples being the Baptists and the Methodists.[2] The gloomy Calvinist doctrine of predestination receded in importance. In its place came increasing emphasis on salvation as dependent on an exercise of free will, as a choice open to all who would accept Christ into their life. Optimism extended to the nation as well. America was seen as playing a special role in God's plan, a role vindicated by the nation's rapid expansion and economic growth. This Protestant nationalism helped tie religious doctrine to more secular themes of progress. For it was America's democracy, education, and industrial know-how—as well as its religious vitality—that separated the country from the traditional, superstitious, and corrupt societies of Europe. The progress of Christian civilization and the progress of the American nation were seen to be one.

The picture painted above is a simplification. Not all Americans were evangelical Protestants. Furthermore, Protestant evangelicalism was, and remains, a complex phenomenon consisting of numerous contradictory elements. Many evangelicals of the time saw serious problems in American society. They were active in movements to remedy perceived evils, playing prominent roles in the Prohibition, feminist, prison reform, and abolitionist movements. Those who had lived through the horror and carnage of the American Civil War—particularly those who had lost that war—necessarily had doubts concerning God's unique blessing of America. By 1870, stirrings of conflict between science and biblical authority had arisen with Darwin's theory of evolution. Philosophers and theologians, particularly in Europe, were coming to question key aspects of the Christian faith. Nonetheless, taking these qualifications into account, we still see a situation in marked contrast with the one that exists today. Most evangelicals felt comfortably in the mainstream of national culture. Scientific and philosophical doubts, for the most part, affected a limited elite audience. The identity of evangelical and national progress was, if not convincing to all, at least plausible for many.

From the Mainstream to Marginality

It is in the collapse of the evangelicals' mainstream position that the religious origins of the contemporary Christian Right are to be found. As the nineteenth century drew to a close, evangelicals came to face serious challenges from a number of different directions. As evangelicals were forced into a defensive position, their movement and their place within American society changed dramatically.

Intellectual Challenges

One set of challenges was intellectual. Darwinism did not go away. Instead its influence spread and brought into question previous assumptions concerning the compatibility of scientific observation and biblical authority. Given American faith in science, this was a troubling development for evangelicals. Equally troubling was the challenge presented by new forms of biblical criticism. Liberal theologians were coming to treat the Bible itself as a historical document, subjecting it to the same rigorous scrutiny applied to other texts. This involved the tracing of contradictions between various sections of the text, examining historical influences upon it, and even questioning the authenticity and authorship of certain gospels. This was a profoundly subversive enterprise. Treating the Bible like other ancient writings and the Christian faith like other world religions were new approaches that threatened the very bases of authority in the evangelical community. For it was belief in the Bible—and in the ability of the common person to understand its meaning directly—that provided the bedrock of evangelical faith.[3]

How were evangelicals to deal with conflicts between biblical authority and secular intellectual trends? One solution was to revise religious messages to a form more in keeping with intellectual respectability. Religious liberals took this course, abandoning biblical literalism in favor of approaches that stressed basic ethical imperatives and made their peace with Darwin and higher biblical criticism. Some became advocates of the "Social Gospel," calling on Christians to become active in efforts to ameliorate the dislocations caused by capitalist economic development. Starting in the late nineteenth century, religious liberalism began making inroads in the theological seminaries and leadership of major Protestant denominations, including those of distinctly evangelical origins such as the Northern Baptists and Methodists.

The roots of the Christian Right are to be found among those who, in the face of the social and intellectual challenges that had swayed their liberal counterparts, held fast to biblical literalism. Central to the resistance to liberalism was a movement that eventually came to be known as fundamentalism. (The name is derived from a series of twelve widely distributed pamphlets that appeared in the years from 1910 to 1915 and were collectively entitled *The Fundamentals*.) Fundamentalism, like theological liberalism, came in a dizzying array of particular forms that cannot adequately be examined here. However, I do want to focus on one aspect of the movement that is critical to an understanding of the contemporary Christian Right.

That is, fundamentalism was dramtically displaced from the center to the fringes of American religious and intellectual life. Fundamentalists argued, with some justification, that they were the defenders of the mainstream Protestant religious, cultural, and moral heritage. Religious liberals, they argued, were subversive interlopers, embarked on a course that would undermine American faith and American democracy. Fundamentalists remained strong in many of the largest Protestant denominations through the First World War, and as late as the 1920s militant fundamentalists were vying seriously for control of the Northern Baptist and Presbyterian denominations. While liberalism made its first inroads among intellectual elites, fundamentalists could still boast of academically prominent defenders, most notably within Princeton Seminary.

By the 1930s all this had changed. The fundamentalist struggle to control the major northern denominations had ended in failure. Separatist strategies became the norm. Instead of trying to recapture wayward denominations, fundamentalists broke away to form a myriad of small—but doctrinally pure—churches that spent much of their energy feuding with each other. As the battle was lost in the North and in establishments of higher learning, the movement's center of gravity shifted. Fundamentalism became a more rural, southern, and anti-intellectual movement. Moderate Protestants began to withdraw their support. The movement's tone grew more shrill and its assumptions found less and less acceptance within educated society. Fundamentalists had moved from the mainstream to the margins of their society.

The defeat of fundamentalism was symbolized most dramatically in the Scopes "monkey trial" of 1925. Technically, this was a fundamentalist victory. Biology teacher John Scopes was found guilty of the crime of teaching evolution in the Tennessee public schools. However, the trial was a public relations disaster for fundamentalism and for one of its leading figures—William Jennings Bryan, who volunteered his services to the prosecution. Defense lawyer Clarence Darrow interrogated Bryan mercilessly on the issue of biblical literalism. As Bryan fell into a morass of contradiction and confusion, he—and the movement he represented—became the laughingstock for much of the American public. A serious contender for the presidency and a once-respectable religious philosophy had both become objects of ridicule.

The Challenge of Diversity

In the latter half of the nineteenth century, what had been an over-whelmingly Protestant nation absorbed several waves of non-Protestant immigrants. At midcentury came an influx of Irish Catholics. Then, in the period from 1880 to 1915, the country absorbed over twenty million immigrants, the majority of whom were Jews and Catholics from Southern and Eastern Europe.[4] The identity of Protestantism and the nation became harder to maintain. The problem was not simply one of religious differences. Catholic immigrants were seen as a threat to Protestant social norms of sobriety, thrift, and self-control. This helped reenforce the doubts many Americans felt about rapid urbanization. The rise of large urban centers, with their anonymous masses free of community moral controls, was a troubling development to those Americans who, following Jefferson, equated Republican virtue and agrarianism. That these anonymous masses were often Catholic only added to the perceived problem. In the view of many evangelicals, the sins of Europe were increasingly coming to infect the United States.

Responses to these demographic challenges often ran parallel to the responses to the intellectual challenges discussed previously. Many Protestants, particularly theological liberals, were willing to adapt and accept a more pluralist social order. Others, particularly fundamentalists, were unwilling to surrender their position without a fight. Two movements are worth consideration in this regard: the second birth of the Ku Klux Klan and the temperance movement.

The original Klan emerged as a vigilante response to the limited gains made by southern Blacks in the Reconstruction period. In 1915 the organization was reborn with a new agenda. The organization was still racist; the glorification of the original Klan in D. W. Griffith's *The Birth of a Nation* was a key recruiting tool. However, as the organization developed, its prime targets shifted. The new Klan focused its attacks on Catholics and Jews. At first, the organization grew slowly. Then, with new leadership and a receptive political climate, the movement grew at an explosive pace in the early 1920s. At its height the Klan could boast of several million members and played a key role in the political life of states as far apart as Indiana and Oregon. The Klan in the 1920s was not an exclusively fundamentalist movement but there was a significant overlap in membership.[5] Against the erosion of evangelical hegemony, the KKK represented the period's most prominent attempt to reassert a linkage between Protestantism and Americanism.

This attempt failed. The Klan collapsed as rapidly as it arose. Its leaders, the sworn defenders of Protestant morality and Christian womanhood, turned out to be a collection of swindlers and molesters. In state after state, the movement was discredited by scandal, the greatest blow coming with the conviction of Grand Dragon D. C. Stephenson in a case involving both rape and murder. By the late 1920s, the movement had essentially collapsed. The campaign to reassert Protestant dominance failed along with it. In 1924, a powerful Klan contingent in the Democratic party was able to block the presidential nomination of the Catholic governor of New York, Al Smith. President Coolidge, the Republican candidate that year, refused to condemn the Klan. Yet in 1928, Smith became the first Catholic to receive a major party nomination. In 1932, as economic disaster overrode nativist concerns, FDR was swept into office as the leader of America's new majority coalition, a coalition in which Catholics and Jews were prominent members.

Protestants fought not just to preserve the predominance of their religion, many also battled to enforce the moral norms associated with it. The fight for Prohibition was the most important of these battles. The movement gained support up through its greatest triumph, the passage of the Eighteenth Amendment in 1919, but like fundamentalism as a whole, the movement for Prohibition had grown more socially marginal as time went on. In the nineteenth century, the temperance crusade drew heavily from the ranks of established professionals and was closely linked to a number of progressive reform movements.[6] In the early twentieth century, the movement grew stronger but its composition changed. Its links to other reform causes eroded and its social base began to resemble those of fundamentalism and the Klan, with which it came to be closely associated. (Al Smith was anathema to the Klan not simply because he was Catholic but also because he was a wet.) Like the Klan, Prohibition's triumph was short lived. By 1933, the amendment was repealed, its backers largely discredited.

Dealing with Marginality

Defeated on a variety of fronts, evangelical Protestants persevered. Although their doctrines were no longer intellectually fashionable and their values no longer dominated public discourse, their denominations survived and even grew. The movement's doctrinal and organizational adaptations to a more marginal societal position are critical to an understanding of the contemporary Christian Right. A key doctrinal change (a move from postmillennial to premillennial eschatology) cut across religious lines within evangelicalism. Other adaptations, however, have served to divide evangelicals and helped to define religious differences within the evangelical community.

The Millennium: Evangelicals' Place in This World and the Next

As evangelicals fought their intellectual, religious, and cultural battles with those who would question the faith, the content of that faith began to shift as well. This was most notable in their eschatological leanings. Shifting views of the endtime, important in themselves, also reflected and influenced evangelicals' relations with their society.[7] In the midnineteenth century, American evangelicals tended to take a *post*millennialist position. Through the late nineteenth and early twentieth centuries, *pre*millennialist positions found increased support, particularly within the fundamentalist movement. (Religious liberals tended to deemphasize or drop concern for biblical prophecy.) The conflict between the "pre" and "post" millennialist positions concerns the timing of the second coming of Christ and of the thousand-year age of Christ's reign on earth. Postmillennialists, as the name implies, believe that Christ will return at the end of this thousand-year period; premillennialists believe that Christ's return will be the event that ushers in this new era.

The importance of this debate went well beyond theology. Positions on this issue were, and continue to be, closely linked to social and political outlooks. The postmillennial view was an optimistic one, stressing possibilities for the redemption of society through human efforts. Some even argued that the nineteenth-century advance of Christianity in America marked the beginning of the millennial era. As evangelicals faced the challenges of Darwinism, Catholicism, and religious modernism, postmillennial optimism grew harder to sustain.

The move to premillennialism reflected and reenforced increasingly pessimistic evaluations of American society. Premillennialists did believe that Christ's reign was at hand but emphasized the radical discontinuity between the present and the millennial ages. They contended that human society was irredeemably flawed and could not be reformed through human effort. The transition to the new age would be accomplished through the intervention of supernatural forces, and through the fulfillment of biblical prophecies of death and destruction. The emphasis on the supernatural provided a ready explanation for evangelical failure and a strong incentive to give up projects of societal reform. If this world was a sinking ship, as premillenialists claimed, the role of Christians was not to repair it but to get souls into the lifeboats as soon as possible. Thus, as evangelicals faced defeat on multiple fronts, premillennial eschatology helped encourage a strategy that restricted itself to soul winning, a strategy that remained dominant through the 1960s.

Diverse Approaches: Religious Definitions and Differences

While all evangelicals have had to respond to the intellectual and cultural challenges that have arisen since the midnineteenth century, they have not all agreed on the proper response. The evangelical camp has long been internally divided and these divisions have played a significant role in the development of the Christian Right. It is now time to move beyond the loose definition of "evangelical" with which this chapter began. Three main groups within contemporary evangelicalism are worth particular attention: fundamentalists, neoevangelicals, and charismatics/Pentecostalists.

Fundamentalism
The original fundamentalist movement was a broad based one, with a strong presence in the mainline Protestant denominations such as the Northern Baptists and Presbyterians. In the wake of fundamentalism's defeat within these denominations, the movement began to lose its social and intellectual respectability. Fundamentalists withdrew both from mainline denominations and from societal involvement; a narrower and more sectarian fundamentalism was the result. The emphasis was upon separatism. Newer and purer denominations were formed, denominations that would not compromise on issues of biblical inerrancy and proper moral behavior. A watchful eye was kept on any behavior that might indicate contamination by a sinful society. Cooperation with the contaminated was to be avoided. With such an emphasis on theological and moral purity, it is not surprising that schism ran rampant. Groups that had split from mainline denominations soon split themselves and then split yet again.

The result has been an extremely complex institutional legacy of independent Bible churches and Bible institutes. One of the most important fundamentalist organizations has been the American Council of Christian Churches. Founded by Carl McIntire in 1941, the ACCC was designed as a fundamentalist counterpart to the World Council of

Churches (WCC). McIntire was a strident voice, railing against the evils of ecumenism, communism, and the WCC. Independent Bible institutes such as Bob Jones University, which turn out new generations dedicated to the preservation of an unsullied faith, are also important.[8] Today's most prominent fundamentalist is independent Baptist minister Jerry Falwell. While his willingness to work with others despite religious differences is seen as heretical by some, Falwell continues to define himself as a fundamentalist.

Neoevangelicalism

There is no sharp dividing line that separates neoevangelicals from fundamentalists.[9] Indeed, neoevangelicals can be seen as the heirs of the more moderate wing of the original fundamentalist movement. Neoevangelicals, like fundamentalists, believe the Bible to be literally true, emphasize the need to be "born again," and argue that one must witness one's faith to others. The differences are to be found in the intransigence of their opposition to a sinful society. Whereas fundamentalists seek to separate themselves from dangerous societal influences, neoevangelicals hope to participate in and influence the society in which they live. Thus neoevangelicals are more willing to associate with those who differ and are less likely to quarrel over narrow points of theological difference.

The contemporary neoevangelical movement can be traced to the founding of the National Association of Evangelicals (NAE) in 1942. Its founders wanted to establish an alternative to the liberalism of the World Council of Churches but felt that the fundamentalism of McIntire's ACCC was not an adequate response. Uncomfortable with the negativism and schism characteristic of fundamentalism, they hoped to create a more positive, inclusive organization. One measure of the NAE's more moderate approach was its willingness to admit as members Pentecostal denominations that fundamentalists would view as heretical. Of equal importance to the neoevangelical movement was the figure of Billy Graham. The phenomenal success of Graham's crusades reestablished a societal presence for evangelicals and provided an alternative to the social isolation of fundamentalist separatism.[10] While Graham was sufficiently conservative to appeal to fundamentalists as well as neoevangelicals, his willingness to deal with the mainline churches led to numerous fundamentalist attacks upon him. In the 1980s, Graham expressed doubts about the stridency of the Christian Right and supported better relations with the Soviet Union. As a revered senior figure, Graham now faces few direct assaults, but his toleration of more liberal political and theological views places him a good distance from the spirit that animates fundamentalism.

Pentecostalists/Charismatics

While Pentecostalists have been accepted within the neoevangelical movement, their distinctive doctrines set them apart. Like the other two groups, Pentecostalists emphasize the authority of the Bible and the need to be "born again." What sets them apart are their beliefs concerning the Holy Spirit. In the days of the Pentecost, the Bible says that Christ's disciples were filled with the Holy Spirit and thereby empowered to heal the sick and speak in the tongues of many nations.[11] Whereas other Protestants believe these gifts manifested themselves only in the days of the early church, Pentecostalists believe that these gifts are available to the believer today. The "gift" of the Holy Spirit is, for Pentecostalists, an experience a step beyond that of being born again. Glossolalia (speaking in tongues) and faith healing are the most common forms that gift takes. These practices are viewed with extreme suspicion by fundamentalists, who see them as misguided enthusiasm or, worse, evidence of demonic possession.

The American Pentecostalist movement began in the early years of this century. Pentecostal denominations grew but were shunned by other Protestants and generally appealed to a lower-class constituency. In the last few decades, Pentecostalism and a related charismatic movement have grown at a phenomenal rate, gaining wider acceptability and a more diverse following. Pentecostal denominations have reported extremely rapid membership increases. The largest Pentecostal denomination, the Assemblies of God, has more than quadrupled its membership in the last thirty-five years.[12] In addition, a powerful charismatic movement is spreading through non-Pentecostal denominations. While charismatics continue to be active in their original denominations, they typically attend additional meetings in which the gifts of the Holy Spirit are emphasized. The charismatic movement has brought the Pentecostal message to a new and more diverse audience, including significant numbers of Catholics. (The reader should note that popular usage of the term "charismatic" varies. Often it is used to refer to both Pentecostalists and charismatics.)

Pentecostalists and charismatics have been particularly prominent on America's airwaves. Many of the leading televangelists have been from these groups, from pioneers of the medium such as Oral Roberts and Rex Humbard to a younger generation that included Jimmy Swaggart, Jim and Tammy Bakker, and presidential candidate Pat Robertson. Their predominance may be due, in part, to the televisual appeal of Pentecostal/charismatic practices, particularly with regard to faith healing. Whatever the causes of their success, their presence on the nation's airwaves is of particular political importance. Televangelists have played a key role in broadcasting the social, theological, and political messages of the evangelical world to outside audiences. In addition, the resources of televangelists' media empires are well suited for conversion to political ends.[13]

Growth and Characteristics

In the wake of their failed cultural and intellectual struggles, evangelicals suffered from a lack of public credibility. They embraced premillennialism and were internally divided. But they did not go away. Evangelicalism's public weakness coincided with striking private vitality. If evangelicals lacked the social respectability of their mainline Protestant rivals, they could, at least, outrecruit them.

A brief review of denominational growth patterns will help illustrate evangelical vitality and establish the necessary groundwork for later discussion of evangelical political mobilization. In the aftermath of World War II, American religions prospered. The generation that returned from the war to establish families returned to church as well. In virtually all denominations church attendance rose dramatically during the late 1940s and the 1950s. A building boom took place as church facilities, put on hold during the depression and the war, were at last constructed. But this generalized growth was not to last. By the 1960s, growth in the mainline Protestant denominations came to an end. In the next few decades, these denominations suffered large declines in membership, declines that look even more dramatic in the context of an expanding population. Yet evangelical denominations continued to grow and a broad-based charismatic movement gained support from many who remained in the mainline denominations (and in the Catholic Church).

Table 1.1 illustrates these trends nicely. The Presbyterians, Episcopalians, and Methodists, flagship denominations of mainline Protestantism, benefit from a post–World War II religious resurgence but by 1960 their membership has peaked and a steady decline begins. Yet the fundamentalist/neoevangelical Southern Baptists show continuous, rapid growth to the present day, surpassing the Methodists to become far and away the largest denomination within American Protestantism. Although beginning from a lower base, the growth of the Pentecostal Assemblies of God and Church of God is even more dramatic. Between 1940 and 1993, membership in both denominations increased more than tenfold.

Table 1.1
Denominational Growth and Decline (in millions)

	1940	1960	1980	1988	1993
Mainline Protestants					
Episcopal Church	2.0	3.3	2.8	2.5	2.5
Presbyterian Church in the U.S.	2.7	4.2	3.4	2.9	2.7
United Methodist	8.0	10.6	9.5	9.1	2.7
Evangelical Denominations					
Assemblies of God	0.20	0.51	1.1	2.1	2.3
Church of God (Tenn.)	0.06	0.17	0.44	0.58	0.70
Southern Baptist	4.9	9.7	13.6	14.8	15.4

Source: For 1940–1988 numbers, see Mark Noll, *A History of Christianity in the United States and Canada* (Grand Rapids: Eerdmans, 1992), 465. For 1993, see National Council of the Churches of Christ, *Yearbook of American and Canadian Churches 1995,* ed. Kenneth B. Bedell (Nashville: Abingdon Press, 1995).

With the growth of the evangelical constituency, the legitimacy of the mainline churches as the spokespersons for American Protestantism was now open to question. Immediately after World War II, the mainline churches, with their superior numbers and their more educated and wealthy members, were considered the representatives of American Protestantism. Fundamentalists, Pentecostalists, charismatics, and, to a lesser extent, neoevangelicals were often considered fringe elements, relics of a bygone age. When the media wanted to allot public service airtime to Protestant spokespersons, they turned to the National Council of Churches.[14] Today, with evangelicals roughly matching mainline Protestants in numbers, such attitudes are harder to maintain.

Religious trends are difficult to predict, but a number of factors suggest that evangelicals are well positioned for future growth. Wade Clark Roof and William McKinney examined a number of factors linked to denominational growth, among them age of members, fertility, retention of existing members, and recruitment of outsiders.[15] The authors found a significant move toward the "no religious preference" category among the young. But in the face of this trend, it was the evangelicals ("conservative Protestants" in Roof and McKinney's terminology) who did the best job of holding their members. After reviewing the plight of liberal and moderate Protestants, they described evangelical prospects in the following manner:

> Protestant conservatives, in contrast, fare better. Fewer of them are now switching to liberal denominations, and they hold on to more of their younger members. Their death rates are lower, and their birth rates are higher—a winning combination in the game of religious growth. Compared with other Protestants, they gain the most committed converts, retain the most committed members, and lose those who are least likely to be regular participants and supporters.[16]

Political scientists Lyman Kellstedt, John Green, James Guth, and Corwin Smidt provide a measurement of the shifting fortunes of evangelical and mainline Protestants and of the current size of the evangelical constituency. In 1960, they estimate, 41 percent of white Americans were mainline Protestants and 26 percent were evangelicals. By 1988, the mainline percentage had dropped to 27 percent, while the evangelical percentage remained at 26 percent. The relative position of evangelicals looks even stronger if we take church attendance into account. In 1960, there were 50 percent more regularly attending mainline Protestants than there were regularly attending evangelicals. In 1988, there were 50 percent more regularly attending evangelicals.[17]

While the figures mentioned above show evangelicals' position strengthening relative to that of mainline Protestants, they do remind us not to oversell evangelical growth. Since 1960, evangelicalism's success has consisted of holding its own in a religious marketplace that has dealt serious blows to its rivals. Its share of the (white) market has been a steady 26 percent.[18]

This 26 percent of the white population translates into over 20 percent of the United States' overall population, a quite sizable constituency. We should not assume, however, that this represents the segment of the population readily available for mobilization by the Christian Right. There are two reasons for caution. First, many white evangelicals do not support the political positions advocated by the movement and, even when they do, that does not necessarily translate into support for the movement itself. While the Christian Right draws its backing heavily from white evangelicals, it by no means has their undivided support. Second, measuring the evangelical share of the population is a complicated and inexact science. This point is worth examining in further detail.

Two survey strategies are commonly used to determine the number of evangelicals.[19] One, used in the Kellstedt, Green, Guth, and Smidt study mentioned above, classifies individuals by denomination. Respondents who identify themselves as members of the Assemblies of God, the Southern Baptist Convention, and so on, are placed in the evangelical category. The denominational method is useful because denominational data going back in time are widely available and because this method is closely linked to church organization. A key factor in the mobilization of the Christian Right was the utilization of church organizational resources. Particularly important has been the capture of the leadership of the fifteen million member Southern Baptist Convention by conservative forces sympathetic to the movement. Unless otherwise noted, the denominational method will be the one utilized in the remainder of this book. Nonetheless, the denominational method has its problems. Some denominations are not easily classified. Furthermore, this method includes as evangelicals members of evangelical denominations who are not religiously active or who do not hold to evangelical religious beliefs. It misses the many members of nonevangelical denominations (including charismatics) whose religious beliefs are evangelical in nature.

A second approach is a doctrinal one. To be labeled "evangelical," respondents must hold the proper religious beliefs. What, however, are the religious beliefs one must hold to qualify as "evangelical"? Loose doctrinal measures can produce a seemingly enormous evangelical constituency. In a 1984 Gallup survey, 40 percent of Americans answered yes to a question asking if they had had a "born-again" experience.[20] Results like this have often been used to indicate the existence of an enormous evangelical constituency, potentially open for mobilization by the Christian Right. However, when Black respondents are separated out, and further restrictions are added to the definition of "evangelical," the constituency shrinks markedly.[21] A three-step definition is commonly employed. In addition to proclaiming themselves "born again," respondents must also profess a belief in the literal truth of the Bible and have encouraged others to believe in Christ to qualify as an evangelical. (Unfortunately, surveys have varied in their exact wording, making comparisons between surveys difficult.) These more restrictive doctrinal measures come to estimates of the evangelical population roughly similar to the denominational measures discussed earlier, from 18 percent of the white population to 20 percent of the overall population.[22]

While the various measures often come to similar estimates of the number of evangelicals, they do not put exactly the same people inside and outside that category. This points to an important fact: the boundaries of the evangelical category are not clear cut. The fit between denominational and doctrinal evangelicalism is by no means perfect; quite a few members of mainline churches come out as "evangelicals" based on their responses to survey items whereas a significant portion of the members of "evangelical" denominations do not.[23] This fact has implications for Christian Right organizing. For example, despite their affiliation with an evangelical denomination whose leaders are closely tied to the Christian Right, some Southern Baptists may not even share evangelical religious beliefs with the movement. Conversely, a significant proportion of mainline Protestants, African-American Protestants, and Catholics professes evangelical beliefs. Christian Right groups such as the Christian Coalition have attempted to build coalitions on the basis of these shared beliefs.

Having considered the size of the evangelical constituency that the Christian Right inherited, it is now time to consider briefly the composition of that constituency. Who are evangelicals? Table 1.2 shows that the answer to that question depends, in part, on whether we use a denominational or doctrinal measurement strategy. Whereas denominational evangelicals are overwhelmingly southern, doctrinal evangelicals have a stronger midwestern presence. Doctrinal evangelicals are also older and more female than their denominational counterparts. Compared with their nonevangelical counterparts, both sets of evangelicals are poorer, less well educated, more likely to be born in a rural area, more likely to be from the South, and more likely to be housewives.

The political mobilization of the Christian Right has been shaped by the nature of its evangelical constituency. As the movement became active within the Republican party, it brought in a set of supporters quite different from those who made up the traditional base of Republican activists. This has been both a source of the Christian Right's value to the party and a source of movement/party tensions.

Evangelicalism at the Dawn of the Christian Right

A Potential Constituency

By the 1970s, evangelicalism, with its fundamentalist, neoevangelical, Pentecostal, and charismatic components, had regrouped from

Table 1.2
Who Are Evangelicals? (whites only)

	Doctrinal evangelicals %	Denominational evangelicals %	Nonevangelicals %
Education			
Less than high school	23	26	16
Some college	38	26	50
Income			
Less than $15,000	41	30	26
Over $50,000	10	15	19
Region			
South	32	75	20
Midwest	39	17	31
Other			
Female	68	52	51
Housewife (women)	29	26	19
Rural born	47	44	25

Source: Clyde Wilcox, *God's Warriors* (Baltimore: John Hopkins University Press, 1992), 46. The figures are derived from the 1988 American National Election Study (ANES) survey.

its earlier defeats and was showing impressive vitality at the private level. Liberal Protestant denominations had stopped growing and, in most cases, had begun to lose members; evangelical denominations continued their steady, and in some cases spectacular, growth. The neo-evangelical and charismatic movements spread evangelicalism beyond the narrow base responsive to the doctrinally rigid, sectarian message of hard-core fundamentalism. Evangelical preachers expanded from the radiowaves to television. By the late 1960s, mainline Protestant and Catholic broadcasts were becoming less common and evangelicals were coming to dominate religious broadcasting.[24] Evangelical schools, Bible institutes, and missionary organizations expanded as well.

Evangelicals thus constituted a quite sizable constituency, with extensive internal organizational resources. They lacked the capacity to dominate American society and, in fact, tended toward withdrawal from it. But if mobilized politically, they might represent a potent force. However, the political mobilization of this force was not a foregone conclusion. From the 1930s through the 1960s, evangelical resources tended not to be mobilized for political ends. Furthermore, any such mobilization would have to deal with some serious problems rooted in the historical legacy of evangelicalism.

Continuing Problems

Public Credibility

One problem can be traced back to the failure of the evangelical response to intellectual challenges represented by the theory of evolution, higher criticism of the Bible, and liberal Protestantism. Like Bryan at the Scopes trial, evangelicals have often been objects of ridicule. While evangelicalism continues to show popular vitality, it has lost its claims to intellectual respectability at the elite level. Within academia, the media, and political discourse, arguments based on evangelical biblical premises are deemed inappropriate and easily dismissable.[25]

Evangelicals today face a serious political dilemma. A large constituency with a distinct set of political interests, they nonetheless have difficulty gaining a hearing within the broader society. The language evangelicals utilize to express their interests, although central to the identities of those within the movement, undercuts acceptance of their positions among outsiders. This problem becomes more acute when separatist strategies are abandoned. For evangelicals (particularly fundamentalists) whose main goal was to successfully insulate themselves from the corruptions of the broader society, failure to gain a hearing within that society was a minor difficulty. Now that evangelicals are attempting to reassert their influence within the broader society, it is a serious problem indeed. Robert Dugan of the National Association of Evangelicals sums up the problem in the following manner: "Evangelicals face a tough assignment. Secular minds virtually dismiss biblical values as a legitimate basis for public policy. Some are openly hostile, gratuitously tolerating religious beliefs as innocuous enough when confined to the purely personal, but off limits in the 'real world.'"[26]

Christian Nation or Minority Rights?

A second set of problems is rooted in the evangelical encounter with cultural pluralism. Since the loss of their central position in American culture, evangelicals have struggled to define their relations with the broader society. One option was to simply give up on a depraved and sinful society and isolate oneself from it as best one could. This was a popular strategy. Fiercely independent fundamentalist churches and Bible institutes emphasized the need to abstain from such worldly temptations as dancing and motion pictures and from the corruptions of the political world. Such antipolitical attitudes continue to present serious obstacles to the mobilization of the Christian Right's constit-

uency. Thus Bob Jones, Jr., a leading fundamentalist educator, denounced Jerry Falwell's forays into politics. Jones called Falwell "the
most dangerous man in America," and urged his fellow fundamentalists to "turn their back on the Moral Majority and seek the soul-satis-
fying contentment of being a scriptural minority."[27]

Those evangelicals who ignore Jones' warnings and reenter the
political world face a difficult choice. Should they accept the marginal position to which they have fallen? On the one hand there are
appeals for a return to a lost dominance, for an acknowledgment that
this is, in fact, a "Christian nation." On the other hand, evangelicals
often portray themselves as a persecuted minority, their rights and
culture deserving of protection from the actions of an overbearing
majority. Both of these strategies can be seen at work in the contemporary Christian Right. The former line of argument grabs the headlines. When religious leaders proclaim their intentions to recapture state
and society, the gauntlet is laid down. Other groups take notice. While
it receives less attention, the second line of argument is equally important. Many evangelicals see their movement as a defensive one. In
their efforts to protect their schools and their families from hostile
influences, they often invoke a language of minority rights.[28]

In practice, these two approaches may maintain an uneasy coexistence. Many Christian Right groups and leaders will make both sets of
arguments without seeing any inherent inconsistency. Yet at a theoretical level, a fundamental tension exists between these two lines of
argument. This theoretical tension must eventually be dealt with and,
as we shall see in later chapters, the choice of argument to stress has
very real practical consequences. In its rejection of societal pluralism, the "Christian nation" argument is certain to bring conflict with
outsiders. The minority rights argument may avoid this problem; but
in the process, claims to the possession of a universally valid worldview are undermined. For the one true faith to admit to being one
minority among others is a serious concession indeed. Thus we will
see that Christian Right activists are often faced with a difficult choice:
approaches tailored to gain outside support versus those that uphold
the core religious doctrines that motivate its members.

Premillennialism
Another set of problems arises out of premillennial doctrine. As
evangelicals became more politically active, their premillennial beliefs
presented two main obstacles to organizing. First, premillennialism is
linked to a strong aversion to political involvement that persists to
this day among many evangelicals; overcoming this aversion has been

a serious problem for the contemporary Christian Right. After all, if a supernatural transformation of this world is foreordained and imminent, what role is left for the political activism of mere mortals? (It is interesting to note that, as evangelicals have abandoned separatist strategies and returned to the political arena, postmillennial theologies have made something of a comeback within movement circles.[29]) Second, premillennial doctrines, deeply embedded in the discourse of the evangelical community, are profoundly disturbing to outsiders. Speculation that intertwines endtime prophecy with contemporary conflicts in the Middle East and potential nuclear war does not travel well outside evangelical circles.[30] Pat Robertson found this out when his statements on biblical prophecy, which had been delivered to an appreciative evangelical audience on his "700 Club" program, were used against him in his presidential campaign.

Religious Divisions

The Christian Right must also deal with the problems created by intraevangelical religious differences. Evangelicalism is a broad and diverse movement. This diversity is a source of strength but it also can make political mobilization difficult. Distinctions between fundamentalists, neoevangelicals, Pentecostalists, and charismatics are critical to a proper understanding of Christian Right politics. Thus, for example, much coverage of the early Christian Right group Moral Majority took at face value leader Jerry Falwell's claims that his was a purely political organization, that it was an organization open to Catholics, Jews, and even nonbelievers. Technically this was correct; the fact that a self-proclaimed fundamentalist was willing to be this tolerant of doctrinal differences was certainly a noteworthy development. However, a close look at the Moral Majority reveals that almost all of its state leaders were ministers of independent Baptist churches.[31] A look at Pat Robertson's presidential campaign yielded similar results. Robertson's campaign stressed moral themes with broad appeal to evangelicals. Yet he had an extremely hard time getting votes beyond his Pentecostalist and charismatic base. Among the local Christian Right activists I interviewed, divisions between charismatics and fundamentalists often were cited in explanations of the battles surrounding the Robertson campaign.

Can doctrinal differences be overcome? The answer to this question will have a profound impact upon the future course of the Christian Right. A strong case can be made that denominational differences are losing their importance and that cross-denominational splits between religious liberals and conservatives are coming to replace them as the fundamental cleavages in American religious life. As the historical identities that separate denominations fade from view, questions of moral values and political ideology increasingly form the basis for religious cleavages. Americans, it is argued, are dividing into more distinct conservative and liberal camps; the religious center is not holding. This argument suggests that the doctrinal differences discussed above are fading and that cooperation in a crusade against liberal forces is likely. I find this line of argument—made by scholars such as James Davison Hunter, Wade Roof, William McKinney, and Robert Wuthnow—to be a compelling one.[32] As one watches cooperation between conservative evangelicals and Catholics on an issue such as abortion, culminating in a recent joint declaration by evangelical and Catholic leaders, it becomes clear that much has changed since 1960, when fundamentalists issued dire warnings concerning America's fate if a Catholic were elected president.[33]

Nevertheless, a reduction in the intensity of these doctrinal controversies does not mean that they have disappeared. While charismatics, Pentecostalists, and fundamentalists may now be willing to be in the same room with each other, this does not mean that they will be able to work together harmoniously on a common project. New Right leader Paul Weyrich has spent the last twenty years attempting to build coalitions among cultural conservatives; in my interview with him, Weyrich remarked on the continuing difficulties he faced in getting evangelical religious factions to work with each other. In fact, he said, they would much rather deal with a liberal Protestant, a Roman (or, in Weyrich's case, Eastern Rite) Catholic than with each other.[34] Weyrich's statement is significant for two reasons. First, it is a reminder that doctrinal differences must still be taken seriously in attempts to understand the dynamics of the Christian Right. Second, Weyrich's reference to the advantages of his own outsider's status has relevance beyond his personal situation. The Christian Right may well prove better able to unite around sympathetic outsiders (such as conservative Republican politicians) than around figures from within the movement (such as Pat Robertson), for outside figures do not tap into the heritage of doctrinal conflict in the way that insiders do.

The Historical Legacy

A statement by Karl Marx applies to movements of the Right as well as to those that claim to follow his teachings. He said, "Men make their own history, but they do not make it just as they please: they do not make it under circumstances chosen by themselves, but under circumstances directly encountered, given and transmitted from the past."[35] As the Christian Right emerged in the 1970s, it could not escape the implications of its history. The movement inherited a complex array of possibilities, limitations, and contradictions that shape its actions to this day.

The dilemmas that face the Christian Right today arise as the movement attempts to translate the private vitality of the evangelical subculture into political power and legitimacy. As evangelicals attempt to express their grievances within the broader society, they find that the discourse they are used to using among themselves—particularly insofar as that discourse involves prophetic themes—has little credibility in the media, the universities, or in political life. Furthermore, evangelicals must now deal with a troubling plurality of religious and moral perspectives, a plurality that is hard to accept without undermining the universalistic claims of their own doctrines. In each case, evangelicals vying for public influence must play a difficult balancing act: compromise is often necessary to build coalitions and gain their doctrines a wider hearing but those same compromises threaten to undermine the values and institutions of the evangelical subculture, the values and institutions that have mobilized the constituency upon which their political movements are based.

Private religious vitality has coincided with considerable religious diversity. Thus evangelicals vying for political influence must not only master the dilemmas of dealing with the broader society, they must also overcome serious divisions within their own constituency. Divisions between fundamentalists, neoevangelicals, Pentecostalists, and charismatics present a constant challenge to attempts at united action, as we shall see throughout this study.

Having followed the growth of an evangelical subculture, it is now time to see how—and why—that subculture has been mobilized to political action. In examining the factors that led to the rise of the Christian Right, I want to reflect at a more theoretical level upon the history presented in this chapter. What is the nature of the social forces that drove evangelicals from their mainstream position? Why do evangelicals persist in the face of these forces? Why was isolation from the larger society no longer viable? What accounts for the dramatic contrast between the movement's private vitality and its lack of public credibility? These critical questions have been central to academic—and popular—accounts of the politics of the Christian Right. Too often, however, they have been answered incorrectly. My answers are the subject of chapter 2.

Chapter 2

A Constituency Awakens

If the years from the 1930s through the 1960s can be characterized as a period of evangelical withdrawal from the political world, the last several decades have seen a renewed activism. What led to the political awakening of an evangelical constituency? How do the forces that led the constituency to mobilize continue to shape its activities today? In this chapter I will endeavor to answer these questions. In the process, I address some particularly common misperceptions of the Christian Right's origins. Emphasizing the irrational, antimodern character of the movement and its demands, these misperceptions are a hindrance to a proper understanding of the movement, its actual relation to "modernity," and the rootedness of its demands in very real social conflicts. Misperceptions cleared away, I provide an alternative explanation, one that accounts for both the movement's continued strength and its inherent weaknesses.

The development of a social movement such as the Christian Right is dependent upon a number of factors. The emergence of a politicized evangelical constituency, the forces that have shaped that constituency, and its political orientation are among them. But a constituency alone does not create a movement. Later chapters will deal in some detail with the mobilization of resources, the alliances, and the shifting structure of political opportunities that encouraged the Christian Right's development. Thus, while the present chapter has a great deal to say about the movement's origins and prospects, it is only a partial account.

The Politics of Status

The emergence of the Christian Right in the late 1970s baffled many, but one theory seemed well placed to explain the movement. Developed in the 1950s to explain the rise of McCarthyism, the status politics approach, pioneered by theorists such as Richard Hofstadter, Daniel Bell, and Seymour Martin Lipset, fit the new situation nicely.[1] The theory had been a mainstay in the explanation of previous movements of the radical right, some of which are historically linked to, or share constituencies with, the Christian Right. It is not surprising that observers tried to place Jerry Falwell within the framework that had been used to analyze Billy James Hargis's Christian Crusade in the 1950s and 1960s. Moreover, the theory focused on noneconomic motivations and attacks on societal elites, both of which were clearly observable in the politics of the Christian Right.[2]

While application of this framework was an obvious step, it was a mistaken one. A status politics approach to the Christian Right fundamentally misinterprets the movement's motivations and prospects for success. The status politics framework has been subjected to repeated criticism, both in its original formulation and in its application to the Christian Right.[3] Nonetheless, as late as 1989, Kenneth Wald et al. could declare; "In one form or another, the concept of 'status politics' remains at the heart of scholarly efforts to account for mass based moral reform movements."[4]

This may be an exaggeration, based in part on the authors' very loose definition of the term "status politics"; nonetheless, many of the theory's assumptions remain influential, particularly in popular accounts of movement activities.[5] To clear the way for analysis of the Christian Right's place within American cultural and political life, I will not only critique the assumptions of the status politics approach, I will also use this critique to establish the basic concepts that will guide the interpretation of the Christian Right that follows.

The status politics model begins with an examination of social/structural strain. The motive force in this analysis is the progress of a sophisticated, cosmopolitan industrial order. Industrialization displaces existing groups and generates new elites. It is the reaction to such change that forms the basis for status politics. Thus, Daniel Bell makes the following argument in his article "The Dispossessed":

> What the right as a whole fears is the erosion of its own social position, the collapse of its power, the increasing incomprehensibility of a world— now overwhelmingly technical and complex—that has changed so drastically within a lifetime.
>
> The right, thus, fights a rear guard action. But its very anxieties illustrate the deep fissures which have opened in American society as a whole, as a result of the complex structural strains that have been taking place in the last thirty years or so.[6]

In the status politics model, the "dispossessed" fight against the modern world in what is ultimately a losing battle (a rearguard action). They fail to accept or understand the emerging societal order and for that reason are held to be prone to irrational and potentially dangerous actions.

While industrialization has generated instability throughout the world, the political forms it has taken in the United States are seen to be unique. As developed by theorists such as Bell, Hofstadter, and Lipset, the status politics approach grew out of attempts to understand "American exceptionalism." Lacking Europe's feudal, hierarchical elites and revolutionary working-class movements, American politics, they argue, has operated largely within a liberal consensus. Americans' response to the difficulties of industrialization have rarely involved attacks on capitalism itself. This does not mean, however, that American politics has been without conflict. In addition to the interest-based bargaining characteristic of American pluralism, the system is marked by repeated outbreaks of status politics. Populism and McCarthyism are seen as the paradigmatic cases of status-based movements, but other examples would include the Ku Klux Klan, the John Birch Society, and—according to more recent theorists—the New Right.

The status approach emphasizes the irrational mindset of movement participants. It does this by making a fundamental distinction between interest and status politics. The former is characterized by "the clash of material aims and needs among various groups and blocs," while the latter deals with "projective aspirations arising from status aspirations and other personal motives."[7] Material interests are held to be rational; they can be discussed and compromises about them can be reached. "Normal" pluralist politics involves group bargaining over such interests. Status concerns, on the other hand, are described in irrational, psychological terms.[8] The stated goals of status-based movements, it is argued, should not be taken at face value. Demands that flow from personal insecurities often bear little relation to the social problems that spawned discontent. Hofstadter uses the analogy of a man who relieves his personal frustrations by kicking his cat. Status-based movements often target the socially prominent, for by tearing down prominent individuals their own status may be reaffirmed.[9]

Much emphasis is placed on the "paranoid style" supposedly characteristic of status-based movements. Marked by political moralism these movements view politics as a straightforward battle between good and evil. The moral and practical complexities of issues are denied as groups espouse simple solutions to national problems. These simple solutions generally involve the uncovering of conspiracies. The virtuous people can follow the wrong path only if deceived by the machinations of the few. For the Populists, the villains are the international money changers. McCarthyism focuses on internal Communist subversion. The John Birch Society revives the conspiracy of the Illuminati. The Christian Right puts forward conspiratorial accounts of the doings of secular humanists. The "paranoid style" is seen to pose a serious threat to interest-based pluralism. The moralistic political style is viewed as incompatible with the compromises and complexities inherent in democratic political life. If politics is viewed as a simple contest between good and evil, toleration of opposition is unlikely. The psychological characteristics of status-anxious individuals are held to be unpleasant; Adorno's *Authoritarian Personality* is often referred to. A status-based mobilization of these individuals is therefore believed to threaten the stability of democratic norms and the autonomy of elites who defend them.[10]

The application of these concepts to the early Christian Right was best exemplified by two influential works, Alan Crawford's *Thunder on the Right* and *The Politics of Unreason* by Seymour Martin Lipset and Earl Raab.[11] Crawford is more alarmed by the New Right and the Christian Right than are Lipset and Raab but the theoretical framework employed in both cases is very similar.[12] The New Right is seen as a status-based reaction against the trends of modernization and the societal elites who embody those trends. As such its demands can be explained in terms of the status anxieties of its members, and their irrational reaction against the complexities of the modern world.

Alan Crawford's view of New Right women provides an excellent example of a status-based analysis of the movement:

> The revolt of the New Right women is, clearly, a rear-guard action to arrest society's growing acceptance of views more liberal than their own. It is in this sense a status revolt. . . . These Americans resent the fact that many of the relevant social questions are being resolved by others. They sense a loss of their own social status, resulting in attitudes which Friedrich Nietzsche described in the late 19th century as *ressentiment*, a term now used to explain the social behavior of persons frustrated by their roles in society. . . . The New Right is such a symbolic movement, a movement of social protest whose preferred issues—the "hearth and home" issues of the New Right women—are often nonpolitical, fringe issues at best. They seek through victory to regain lost status, to embarrass or humiliate their enemies in the Eastern liberal establishment, and to regain control of the culture. It is a politics that is almost wholly reactionary.[13]

Here we find the classic elements of the status approach. A group being left behind by societal change is frustrated and disturbed. It takes out its resentments in an irrational attack on societal elites. Yet, if we look more closely, Crawford's own description provides ample material for alternate interpretations. Perhaps social trends are moving in destructive directions. Is "rear-guard" action then necessarily irrational? Shouldn't any reasonable political actors be upset if "relevant social questions" are being resolved by others who do not share their values? Those not working from within a status politics framework might question whether control of hearth, home, and culture is really a "fringe" issue. Crawford's comments illustrate the key deficiencies of the status politics approach.

First, the status framework fails to take cultural issues seriously in their own right. It reduces cultural concerns to surrogates for discontent with one's ranking in a hierarchical social order. A more straightforward interpretation of Christian Right motives is needed. Members of the movement express concern and mobilize around cultural issues because those issues are seen to be—and in fact are—important in their own right. The movement's opposition to abortion, homosexuality, and "secular humanism" is genuine and not simply a means for its members to tear down elites and regain lost status. This is not to say that evangelicals are not dismayed by the fact that they lack status. Many of the activists I interviewed were acutely aware that they were objects of ridicule in the broader society. Their main concern, however, was that their *values and culture* were being ridiculed. Status concerns were not separate from and prior to cultural concerns.

A second problem is the status framework's emphasis on the irrational nature of status politics. This problem is closely linked to the previous one. If cultural issues are mere surrogates for status discontent, it makes sense to analyze the expression of cultural concerns in psychological terms, as displaced expressions of frustration and rage rather than as rational attempts to pursue cultural goals.[14] However, this leads to serious misunderstanding of the Christian Right. I do not deny that psychological investigation of the highly charged symbolism of family, sexuality, faith, and sex roles employed by the Christian Right could uncover a wealth of suppressed anxieties and displaced fears; but beneath these anxieties and fears lies a rhetoric and program that is a rational response to real social changes. Thus, it is critical that the movement be understood in terms of these social changes and ongoing attempts to deal with them, rather than simply as the paranoid lashing out of those who are discontented with their status.

Behind the first two problems lies a third and more fundamental one: the status framework's understanding of modernity and modernization. Assumptions concerning modernization, mentioned earlier, are central to the status politics theory. It is opposition to modernity that is the thread that supposedly ties together such seemingly disparate movements as the Populists, McCarthyites, and Christian Right. The theory's approach to modernity is also closely linked to its analysis of movement psychology. It should come as no surprise that movements that can not come to terms with the modern world in which they live will develop a politics of irrational frustration.

The problem is not that an analysis of "modernization" fails to throw light on the politics of the Christian Right. The problem lies in the specifics of the analysis of modernity and in the links the theory makes between modernity and movement style. Status theorists—and many other commentators—tend toward a rather blunt dichotomy. On the one side, there lies an increasingly complex and cosmopolitan industrial (or, as is now common, postindustrial) society; on the other side are groups left behind by these changes (such as evangelical Protestants). Protest by groups such as the Christian Right can be seen as dramatic but ultimately futile attempts to hold back the tides of history. This interpretation is an appealing one and is popular well beyond the ranks of status theorists.[15] One reason for its popularity is its apparent fit with the history recounted in chapter 1. The evangelical descent from the societal mainstream can easily be interpreted as the steady marginalization of a group being left behind by the forces of modernity.

In the long run this analysis may be correct; perhaps the Christian Right will eventually be overcome by "modern" secularizing trends. There are, however, serious reasons to question such an analysis in the shorter term, not the least of which is that the "antimodern" evangelical constituency appears to be thriving in a supposedly hostile "modern" world. Chapter 1 was not just a story of evangelicals' public defeat; it was also a story of vitality in private life as evangelicals faced those defeats. The relationship between evangelicalism and modernity is more complex than a status framework would indicate.

One aspect of the data presented in chapter 1 appears to provide support to a status-politics explanation that sees the Christian Right as an irrational response to "modernity." If the cutting edge of modernity is to be found among the well educated and well-to-do, in the nation's cosmopolitan urban centers, this is not the place that one finds evangelicals. Evangelicals are poorer, more rural, and less well educated than the American population as a whole. Summing up his review of the evangelical constituency, James Davison Hunter concludes:

The collective interaction of these demographic factors clearly confirms the initial proposition that the evangelical community as a whole is—perhaps more than any other major American religious body—sociologically and geographically distant from the institutional structures and processes of modernity. The demographic evidence also suggests that secularists and nonChristians are the closest to these structures and processes.[16]

Hunter is correct. Evangelicals are not at the cutting edge of modernity. Thus, it does make sense to see the mobilization of the Christian Right as an attempt to fight the trends of "modernity." But opposition to modernity need not imply either that evangelicals are "declining" or that their "backlash" political mobilization is irrational.

Several factors should give pause to those willing to dismiss evangelicalism as a declining, ultimately doomed, antimodern movement. If evangelical Protestants are doomed to extinction, they show no inclination to accept their assigned fate. The denominations that form the constituency of the Christian Right display a surprising vitality, confounding analysts who have written them off as a throwback to an earlier age. In fact, it is the mainline Protestant churches, with their active efforts to remain "relevant" in the face of contemporary intellectual trends, that appear headed for extinction. Since the mid-1960s, denominations such as the United Methodists, the Episcopalians, and the United Presbyterians have suffered significant *absolute* membership losses. Over the same period, conservative Protestant denominations such as the Southern Baptists and the Assemblies of God have expanded at a rapid pace, matching or exceeding population growth. In addition to the growth of these denominations are other indicators of evangelical vitality: a flourishing charismatic movement within mainline Protestant denominations and the Catholic Church, active missionary-outreach programs, and a set of televangelists who constitute an important force in American religious and political life.[17] While evangelicals remain poorer and less educated than other Americans, the gap between evangelicals and the population as a whole in these areas has been gradually shrinking over the last few decades.[18] Rather than declining, the evangelical constituency is growing and assuming a less marginal societal position.

Evangelicals have also demonstrated quite a bit of flexibility as they adapt their message and organization to the demands of the modern world. While they may not be willing to accept the scientific theory of evolution, they are quite accepting of technology and industrial progress. Evangelicals have pioneered new methods of appealing to mass publics, utilizing the latest media techniques in their efforts. Even their moral doctrines, the "traditional" values many evangelicals so ardently defend, have been adapted to better fit a contemporary ethos of self-fulfillment.[19] These adaptations may indicate that the movement has been coopted, that it has compromised fundamental truths it professes to uphold; but they also provide evidence of the movement's ability to function, even thrive, in a supposedly hostile modern world.

Modernity and the Evangelical

Is there an alternative to the simplistic vision of evangelicalism and modernity put forward by status theorists, an alternative that can explain evangelicalism's current vitality as well as its many defeats? Indeed, "modernity" can simultaneously undermine evangelicalism's public credibility *and* help fuel its private vitality. The following section analyzes the particular social forces that helped lead a segment of the evangelical community to political activism. In the last few decades the American evangelical subculture has found it harder and harder to isolate itself from troubling aspects of the broader culture. As their subculture has been "invaded," many evangelicals have been moved to political action. The final section of this chapter analyzes the political motivations, possibilities, and limitations of the Christian Right's evangelical constituency.

Modernity

The concept of "modernity" has been the subject of endless debate. My purpose here is not to address—much less resolve—the debates that surround the concept of modernity or the process of "modernization." My goal is more modest: to provide a definition and a framework that make sense of the history and prospects of American evangelicalism.[20]

"Modernization" will henceforth be used to refer to a process of societal development marked by economic growth, technological innovation, and rationalization. "Modernity" will refer to the condition of societies in which this process is well advanced.[21] Perhaps the characteristic feature of the modern condition is change. Modern economic growth is based upon the continual introduction of new products and means of production. Dramatic scientific and technological advances become routine occurrences. This is not to say that nonmodern societies do not change; obviously they do. What sets modern societies apart is the rapidity of change and the degree to which change is institutionalized and esteemed. Modernity is a condition in which novelty and innovation assume unprecedented value. The rapid change characteristic of modernity leads to a fundamental reshaping of societal organization. Three aspects of this reshaping are of critical importance to the fate of evangelicalism: rationalization, cultural pluralism, and differentiation.

Rationalization

Rationalization has been central to the concept of modernity, at least since Weber. Modernity is marked by the spread of a calculating, instrumental rationality. Such a rationality is concerned not with choice among ends but rather with the most efficient means of achieving given ends. Its goal is the capability to better control and manipulate the natural and social environments. This rationality is generally abstract and calculating, and often expressed in mathematical form. Instrumental rationality, like mathematics, is not a modern invention. What is new in modernity is the degree to which whole areas of life come to be organized along instrumental lines, freed from the constraint of ethical and cultural controls. The process of rationalization has reshaped both the realm of ideas and that of societal organization.

In the realm of ideas, rationalization is seen in the increased legitimacy of science, economic analysis, and utilitarian value systems. These modes of thought are marked by their instrumental nature, their skepticism toward inherited beliefs, and their abstract modes of expression. As these modes of thought assume a more prominent position, those that come into conflict with them, that try to defend holistic, supernatural, or traditional systems of belief, face serious challenges.

Not only is rationalization a process privileging new systems of thought, it also involves the reshaping of societal organization in accord with that thought. In the words of one author, this entails "the infusion of rational controls through all spheres of human experience."[22] One form this "infusion" takes is a market system increasingly freed from the restrictions of religion and custom, in which land, labor, and capital become commodities, measurable and exchangeable through the abstract media of money. Another is the expansion of bureaucracies organized along instrumental lines, regulating ever broader areas of behavior. Even so basic a category as time is affected. What had once been gauged in terms of ritual, harvest cycles, and the like becomes subject to precise, abstract measurement.

Rationalization has generally been held to undermine the position of religious belief. Ritual, myth, belief in supernatural forces, all run counter to the calculating, instrumental spirit of the modern age. The hypothesized incompatibility of rationalization and religion has been a key factor leading social scientists to predict that the modern age will be an increasingly secular one. The story of American evangelicalism's descent from the cultural mainstream fits well with these predictions. The history presented in chapter 1 is, in large part, one of evangelicalism's failure and marginalization as it attempted to confront the force of rationalization. This marginalization can be seen in its most striking form in the fundamentalist crusade against Darwinism. Upholding the Bible against the forces of science, fundamentalists eventually found that they had lost credibility within academia, the media, and intellectual circles more generally. Nor was this their only such defeat. Fundamentalist insistence upon the reality of miracles, the literal truth of the Bible, and the immanence of the second coming all proved difficult to defend on scientific, instrumental grounds and led to their further marginalization.

Evangelicals suffered not just in their confrontation with the *ideas* associated with rationalization, they were marginalized also by the changes in social organization that went along with these ideas. Most important was the expansion of state bureaucracies to fulfill social roles that were once the province of the church. Religious influence in education and in the provision of social welfare waned as these areas came more firmly under the control of secular "experts" and the state. Universities threw off their denominational ties as a professionalized professorate and secular administrators supplanted religious authorities. Care for—and control of—the poor became less and less a function of religious institutions and came more firmly under the control of social-welfare, psychiatric, and criminal-justice professionals funded by state institutions.[23]

Cultural Pluralism

"Cultural pluralism" refers to the coexistence of subsocieties with distinctly different cultural values and histories. Increased mobility, urbanization, and mass communications lead to a situation in which individuals are much more likely to be exposed to values that differ significantly from their own. Exposure to alien values is not a new phenomenon in itself. What is new is the multiplicity of alien persons and messages that bombard the individual and the difficulty of escaping from the bombardment.

Like rationalization, cultural pluralism poses a distinct threat to religion. Religious worldviews, particularly monotheistic ones such as Christianity, tend toward universalist ambitions, making claims of ultimate meaning applicable to all times and all peoples. When a single such worldview is affirmed in all aspects of an individual's life, its plausibility is likely to be enhanced. Under conditions of cultural pluralism, however, the individual is constantly confronted by others expressing views and living lives incompatible with his or her supposedly universal values. Instead of being a given aspect of an all encompassing social world, religious systems become consumer objects, among which the individual is free to pick and choose.

American evangelicalism's descent from the mainstream was to a significant degree tied to its confrontation with the growth of cultural pluralism. The nineteenth-century cultural position of evangelicals, as we saw in chapter 1, could not survive a more diverse population that included large Catholic and Jewish minorities. Evangelicals were also confronted with the modernist doctrines that gained favor within liberal, "mainline" Protestantism. Now they must deal with increasingly prominent secular, Eastern, and new-age belief systems. Not only did evangelical Protestants have to deal with the fact that an increasing portion of the population was not in accord with their religious doctrines, they also faced mounting threats to the moral values associated with their religion. Evangelical attempts to restore their position through political means—from Prohibition to the crusade of the 1920s Ku Klux Klan—ended in failure. In a more religiously and morally pluralistic America, evangelical Protestantism became one faith among many, vying for support in the religious marketplace.

Diversity of faiths and values is common in the modern situation but it is not unique to it. Important as American diversity is, equally important are the changes that made isolation from this diversity difficult. Diverse religious communities, isolated in their own local subcultures, may coexist within a nation quite well insulated from the effects of cultural pluralism. But as the American population moved from rural villages to cosmopolitan urban centers, isolation and insulation proved more difficult. One was continually rubbing shoulders with those with whom one differed. Equally important was the rise of a national media bringing the nation's—and the world's—diversity to those in every corner of the country. First in print, then over the radiowaves, and, finally, onto TV screens across the nation came an ever-increasing cascade of images that conflicted with evangelical faith and moral values. Even the most isolated rural locations were exposed to the new-age doctrines of Shirley MacLaine, the provocative antics of Madonna, and a host of other nontraditional beliefs and lifestyles. Today's cultural pluralism is extremely difficult to escape in America.

Differentiation

"Differentiation," the third critical aspect of modernity, refers to the process whereby social functions, once closely intertwined, come to be separated, and carried out by their own relatively independent set of institutions. Perhaps the best example of this is the growing differentiation of the economic system from other aspects of social life. The production and exchange of goods, once tightly enmeshed in a web of familial, religious, and political restrictions, begins to operate more and more along an abstract market rationality of its own. Similarly, the family, state bureaucracies, and religious organizations develop according to their own logics. This is not to say that these different spheres of life are no longer interrelated; obviously they are. But it is to say that these realms are more independent than they used to be. The modern individual no longer is subject to an overarching moral order. Instead, he or she is likely to find one set of norms applying in the workplace, another in politics, and still others in church and family life.

In analyzing the fate of American evangelicalism, one aspect of differentiation is of utmost importance: the division of life into distinct public and private spheres, operating according to quite different logics. This division is linked to the expansion of instrumental rationality discussed above. As the public world of the market and state bureaucracies comes increasingly to be organized along formal and instrumental lines, affective ties and the creation of meaning are relegated to the private sphere, to the realm of family, friendship networks, and sexual identity.

Differentiation, and particularly the widening public/private division, has several implications for religion. First, religion can no longer be the basis for an overarching order pervading all areas of life. More and more of social life is organized around the pursuit of scientific knowledge, response to market incentives, or expert-driven bureaucratic attempts at social engineering. In these public realms, religious authority is limited. Second, to the extent that religion survives, it tends to be relegated to the private realm. It provides for the subjective needs of individuals: a sense of meaning, norms of family life, and personal behavior. When the individual steps into the public realm—on the job, for example—religious authority and legitimation are generally left behind. Third, the privatization of religion reenforces trends toward cultural pluralism. As religion comes to fulfill the subjective needs of individuals, it becomes, in effect, a consumer item, competing for allegiance in a religious marketplace. Individuals free to pick and choose among religious doctrines may satisfy their subjective needs in a myriad of different ways. And, with religion fulfilling these private, individual needs, it matters less and less that the needs are fulfilled by mutually incompatible doctrines.

The effects of differentiation and privatization can be seen in the story told in chapter 1. Evangelicals lost their nineteenth-century position of influence in the nation's political, social service, educational, and scientific institutions. Educational and scientific endeavors developed in accord with their own logics, leaving biblical and denominational authority behind. Social welfare became more and more the province of the state and of secular experts. Evangelicalism survived, but as a private phenomenon. It adapted to this situation by marketing itself aggressively to individual consumers, but its public credibility and influence was limited.

Continued Vitality

The consideration of modernity presented thus far helps explain why evangelicalism lost its former position; what then accounts for the continued vitality of American evangelicalism? Why do presumably less modern evangelical denominations continue to grow while liberal Protestant groups, willing to embrace modern trends, lose members at an alarming rate? How is evangelical growth possible in the face of rationalization, cultural pluralism, and differentiation? Two factors are critical. First, American evangelicalism has not been, and is not now, a strictly "antimodern" movement. Second, evangelicalism (even in its antimodern aspects) is attractive as a *refuge* from an atomistic and competitive modern society.

Modern Evangelicals?

Visiting America in the 1830s, de Tocqueville found that religion was allying itself with the forces of progress rather than reaction. He observed, "In France I had almost always seen the spirit of religion and the spirit of freedom marching in opposite directions. But in America I found that they were intimately united and they ruled in common over the same country."[24] Whereas the church in France was being pulled down by its alliance with a doomed aristocratic order, American religion faced no such encumbrances; adapting itself to the will of the people, religion in America flourished. De Tocqueville is only one of many who have attempted to understand the very divergent fates of the church in Europe and America. In the years since de Tocqueville wrote, religious institutions have fared quite differently on the two sides of the Atlantic. European churches have seen a steady decline in their influence and membership, neatly conforming to predictions that modernization and secularization would prove synonymous. Religion in America, however, has shown a stubborn persistence—church membership remains high, indeed it may even be higher than that of a century ago.[25] A profound gap exists between the religious orientations of American and European publics (table 2.1). Why has religion proved so persistent in one of the world's most developed and presumably modern nations? Part of the answer is to be found in the nature of American religion, in the qualities that have allowed it to adapt to the constraints of modernity.

One of the problems of those who assume a simple conflict between evangelicalism and modernity is that American evangelicalism can not be neatly categorized as an antimodern force. Nineteenth-century American evangelicalism, as described in chapter 1, felt itself to be allied with the forces of modernity, with science, economic expansion, higher learning, and the progress of the American nation. While it is true that these forces of modernity came into conflict with some aspects of evangelical religious doctrine by the end of the century, the previous alliance between evangelicalism and modernizing forces should not be forgotten. If fundamentalists came to do battle with modernity, they did so not in the name of some traditional social

Table 2.1
Religious Belief in Selected Countries

Country	Belief in God or Universal Spirit %	Religion "very important"* %	Affiliated with a Church %
United States	94	58	57
Italy	88	36	5
United Kingdom	76	23	22
France	72	22	4
West Germany	72	17	13

Source: Barry Kosmin and Seymour P. Lachman, *One Nation Under God* (New York: Crown Trade Paperbacks, 1993), 9. Columns one and two are from a 1979 Gallup Poll and the third column is from a 1981 Gallup Poll.

*Response to a question asking how important their religious beliefs were in their lives.

order; rather, they were at most defending a slightly earlier stage of modernity. Their attack upon modernity is selective; evangelicals remain ardent defenders of economic development (it is not from their ranks that critics of growth arise) and of those aspects of science and technology (the vast majority) that do not come into direct conflict with their religious doctrines.

Furthermore, modernization is too often equated with developments in elite culture. While American evangelicalism has come into conflict with aspects of science and with the worldview of well-educated elites in academia and the media, it is quite compatible with another aspect of modernity: the world of popular mass culture. In order to understand the interconnections between popular culture and evangelicalism, and to understand what this can tell us about evangelicalism's relation to modernity, it will be useful to consider briefly the origins of the popular style in American religion or—to follow the title of historian Nathan Hatch's recent work—to examine "the democratization of American Christianity."

In his brilliant study of American religion in the early years of the nineteenth century, Hatch provides a compelling portrait of the rise of popular religious movements of the era. Tracing the dramatic rise of groups such as the Baptists, Methodists, and Disciples of Christ, Hatch emphasizes the populist, democratic character of American popular religion. In the wake of the revolution, American Protestantism was dominated by relatively conservative, hierarchical denominations. With their well-educated clergy and sedate ceremonies, Congregationalists and Episcopalians were paragons of respectability. But just as the gentlemanly, deferential politics of the Federalists were supplanted by the democratic upsurges of Jeffersonianism and Jacksonianism, these denominations found themselves displaced by a movement featuring uneducated backwoods preachers and unseemly displays of public fervor.[26] Baptists, Methodists, Mormons, independent revivalists—all brought the gospel to the people in a popular, accessible language. Baptists and Methodists became the largest denominations in American Protestantism; established denominations began to adopt some of the popular style of the insurgents.

The story told by Nathan Hatch fits well with de Tocqueville's description of the same period: the forces of American religion advancing in alliance with those of a leveling democracy. And the popular religious movement described by Hatch is, both in terms of denomination and of culture, a predecessor of contemporary evangelicalism. Baptists—particularly Southern and independent Baptists—are at the heart of contemporary evangelicalism and a core component of the Christian Right's constituency. Television preachers continue the populist style; fervent and enthusiastic, often scandalizing educated elites, they remain responsive to the beliefs and culture of their mass audience. But what do these popular, democratic religious movements have to with the process of modernization discussed earlier? Hatch puts the case nicely and provides the basis for further analysis of the compatibility of modernity and American evangelicalism.

> This story also provides new insight into how America became a liberal, competitive, and market driven society. In an age in which most ordinary Americans expected almost nothing from government institutions and almost everything from religious ones, popular religious ideologies were perhaps the most important bellwethers of shifting worldviews. The passion for equality in those years equaled the passionate rejection of the past. Rather than looking backward and clinging to an older moral economy, insurgent religious leaders espoused convictions that were essentially modern and individualistic. . . . to achieve these visions of the common good, they favored means inseparable from the individual's pursuit of spiritual and temporal well-being. . . . religious movements eager to preserve the supernatural in everyday life had the ironic effect of accelerating the break-up of traditional society and the advent of a social order of competition, self-expression, and free enterprise.[27]

Hatch implies that religious populism had distinctly modern elements, or at least elements that were compatible with modernity. Let us look at some of these elements, both in the time Hatch describes and in our own.

A key aspect of American popular religion in both periods is its adaptability and responsiveness to its audience. From the handbill and the Methodist circuit rider to mass rallies, evangelizing "crusades," and programs on radio and television, evangelicals have spared no effort to bring their message to the masses. Then, as now, American evangelists were willing to speak the language of the people, crude and sensationalistic though it may be. The enthusiasm of the backwoods camp meeting, the theatrics of turn-of-the-century base-ball player/evangelist Billy Sunday, and the antics of televangelists Jim and Tammy Bakker have shocked the respectable but demonstrat-ed a continuing ability to connect with a mass audience. In the pro-cess, not only has the style of presentation adapted to audience demands, so too has the content of religious doctrine. In the words of one observer: "Religious styles constantly adapt and accept vulgar-ization in accordance with the stylistic tendencies of their various markets, sometimes in such a way as to weaken both content and in-tellectual articulation."[28]

The populist, market-oriented approach of American evangelicalism was suited to adjust to the terrain of modernity for several reasons:

1. Unlike so many European churches, the religious movements described by Hatch (and de Tocqueville) did not tie themselves politically to the doomed forces of aristocracy and reaction. Denominations were multiple and many of these were progressive. As they crafted messages to appeal to diverse audiences, churches fit themselves to every nook and cranny of the social structure. Those opposed to existing social or political arrangements could easily find a denomination sympathetic to their views. Thus, few Americans were forced to chose between religion and their politics.[29] Furthermore, American evangelicalism did not base its authority on the deference due educated, gentlemanly ministers. As social hierarchies of deference collapsed, religious authority did not collapse with it.

2. The populist, audience-centered style of evangelicalism is well suited to the competitive world of consumer capitalism. If increasing cultural pluralism leads religions to become commodities among which the individual can pick and choose, then few movements are better prepared to promote their wares than evangelicalism. Commentators, such as Laurence Moore in his book *Selling God*, have long noted similarities between the styles of the salesman and the evangelist. To the dismay of many observers, some evangelists have often embraced the comparison, declaring themselves "salesmen" for Christ. Some have gone even further, promoting Christ himself as the ultimate salesman. Pat Robertson's "700 Club" features short spots formatted to look exactly like advertisements to plug their religious "product." Over the years, American evangelists have been at the cutting edge of promotional, marketing, and communications techniques.[30] Dependent upon audience support for their survival, independent evangelists have proven quick to innovate.

3. The appeals of populist evangelicalism are individualist, and in many ways, modern. In part, this reflects a general tendency of Protestantism. Max Weber's *Protestant Ethic and the Spirit of Capitalism* is only the most famous of the many works emphasizing the compatibility between Protestantism and modern development. Whether or not the Protestant ethic in fact played the historical role attributed to it by Weber is a matter of some dispute. What is clearer are a number of affinities between Protestantism and modernity. The Reformation worked to greatly

accelerate the disenchantment of the world. Miracles, saints, and the role of ritual were all given less importance than in the world of Catholicism.[31] Instead, bypassing the mediation of church structure and societal ritual, what assumed central importance was a direct individual relationship with God. With the sacred limited to this realm, the way was open for other realms to come increasingly under the sway of secular, instrumental belief systems and organization. Protestantism thus proved compatible with differentiation of church functions from other aspects of social life and with the privatization of religion.

Moving from the general features of Protestantism that were the concern of Weber, the democratic religious movements described by Hatch extended the individualist nature of Protestantism. In keeping with a nation of independent, market-oriented small farmers, these movements stressed the values of individual autonomy and popular sovereignty. They railed against the learned church authorities who would interpose themselves between God and the believer; the individual armed with a Bible was to assume greater power. Attacking Calvinist doctrines of predestination, they emphasized that salvation was a matter of individual decision rather than preordained plan.

Evangelical individualism has developed further in this century. In keeping with more general societal trends,[32] evangelicals have begun to embrace an ethic of individual self fulfillment. Codes of discipline and denial have been weakening as evangelists put greater stress on the rewards that faith can bring in *this* life. Some television preachers promote a "gospel of prosperity," promising the viewer that faith (often manifested in the form of contributions) will be amply rewarded. Evangelical self-help manuals abound, promising to aid the reader in the pursuit of happiness, wealth, family harmony, and even a satisfying sex life (within the bounds of marriage, of course).[33] Incorporating therapeutic approaches to individual problems, contemporary evangelicalism has adopted many features of the self-expressive ethos of the "me generation."[34] An emphasis on this worldly fulfillment of individuals' private needs helps fit evangelicalism to the constraints of modern society.[35] Competing within the cultural pluralism of contemporary society, evangelicals can promote their doctrines as a tool in the promotion of private fulfillment.

Evangelical Refuge

If evangelicalism can survive because it has not tied itself to doomed reactionary forces, because it is willing to market itself, and because it has adjusted to individualism and the privatization of religion, we still have a difficult time explaining the recent growth of evangelical Protestantism. Adaptation may keep modernity from destroying the movement—but what is the movement's positive appeal? What is the attraction of the "product" evangelicals are so willing to promote? After all, evangelical religion is not alone in addressing private desires for fulfillment. Why would individuals not turn to secular doctrines or to liberal religions more in keeping with the ethos of modernity? In regard to secular doctrines, the answer is that they are. Therapists, consultants, self-help experts of all sorts do a booming business in today's society. But why are evangelicals outstripping their liberal counterparts? The answer to this question provides a crucial insight into evangelicalism's strength *and* into its political dilemmas.

A key to understanding evangelical growth is the refuge that churches can provide in a competitive, atomistic modern society. The instrumental rationality of bureaucracies and the marketplace may displace religious concerns from broad realms of life but instrumental rationality is not well suited to provide community or supply answers to questions of ultimate meaning. Religious institutions, with the fellowship of the congregation and their doctrines of transcendence, have the potential to fulfill these functions for the individual. But, again, why evangelicalism? Why wouldn't these functions be fulfilled by liberal churches more in keeping with the demands of modernity?

The problem for liberal churches is that the steps they have taken to adjust to the public institutions of the modern world *undermine* their capacity to serve as a private refuge from that world, to fulfill the functions mentioned above. Evangelical churches may be able to fulfill these functions precisely because they have resisted key adjustments to the "demands" of modernity. Dean Kelley's *Why Conservative Churches Are Growing* provides one of the fullest explications of this argument.[36] After providing figures on the declining membership of liberal Protestant churches that have done the most to maintain their "relevance" in the modern world, Kelley documents the rapid growth of their conservative counterparts. His argument is simple: the main function of religion is to provide an overarching system of meaning to individuals, a system that can explain and comfort in the face of failure, evil, and death.[37] Those churches that provide this system of meaning to individuals are likely to flourish; those that fail to do so, no matter how many other useful endeavors they perform, are likely to falter. But to provide such a system of meaning, Kelley argues, requires *strictness*.

Strict churches—including most evangelical denominations—make strong demands on their members.[38] They demand proper behavior and enforce that demand with peer pressure and sanctions. They insist that theirs is the one true faith, and resist ecumenicism. When liberal churches stress ecumenicism and their tolerance of a variety of opinions and behaviors, they are in essence signaling that their own doctrines and standards have no privileged place. While their tolerance and leniency may be admirable, Kelley claims that these traits undermine the church's ability to provide an overarching system of meaning. Individuals in trouble are searching for answers, not dialogue.

Liberal and conservative churches thus face quite distinct dilemmas in modern America. Having embraced a modern intellectual ethos that places all doctrines open to scrutiny and is tolerant of a variety of cultures and beliefs, liberal denominations have avoided some of the difficulties of their conservative counterparts. They have not put themselves on a collision course with scientific doctrines such as the theory of evolution. They are still respectable within the realm of academia and intellectual life. Their doctrines are not seen as intolerant or an embarrassment to the educated. Yet in achieving this public acceptability, liberal churches open themselves up to their own set of difficulties. Doubt and relativism undermine their private provision of meaning. And, while liberal Protestant ideas are acceptable in the realms of academia and intellectual discourse, they are not particularly influential. These realms do not operate according to religious precepts; religious authority grants one few privileges. In fact, liberal Protestants have gained acceptability precisely because they *do not* resort to religious authority. If an argument is put forward on scientific or social scientific grounds, they generally do not counter it by invoking the authority of Scripture. But where this is so, liberal Protestants often end up in the unenviable position of "amateur" scientists or social scientists, operating on terrain where the "professionals" are the true authorities.

Conservative evangelical churches face a very different dilemma. Strictness—the insistence on prophecy, revelation, and biblical literalism—provides a sense of meaning in a troubling world and has helped them grow while their liberal counterparts decline. But it is difficult to defend publicly. In academia, science, and the cosmopolitan world of the mainstream media, evangelical doctrines get little respect.

One solution to this dilemma would be for evangelical religion to restrict itself to the private realm, providing meaning and community for individuals who then "switch gears" to operate in the public worlds of work, politics, and communications. This division of labor has held in the past and may in fact prove feasible in the future. However, two factors are working to make this division an uneasy one. First, the strictness necessary to provide meaning tends to undermine such a division. If I insist that I am in possession of the one true faith, capable of providing an overarching system of meaning in the face of death, misfortune, and evil, it is hard to simply "switch off" that faith when I step out of the private realm. If the Bible is the inerrant word of God, then its authority should extend to all realms of life. Second, the developments of the last several decades of American history have made such a public/private division more difficult to maintain. The public forces of government, market, and media have not left a private world of faith untouched. As these public forces have invaded the evangelical subculture, evangelicals who have fought back have had to do so in the public domain of politics. There they have found that the strict doctrines that are their private source of strength are often a public source of weakness.

Invasion of the Evangelical Subculture

In an interview, Gary Bauer, head of the Christian Right organization the Family Research Council, described the motivation of his group's supporters in the following manner:

> Our opponents will often picture us attempting to exert our values on the rest of society. I think the people we work with see it as they were willing to go about their lives with a sort of separate but equal existence and that it's the culture that keeps pushing more into their homes and their schools and so forth. So they see what has happened in the last ten years as being more of a reaction of self defense than as an effort to violate American pluralism.[39]

Whether or not one agrees with Bauer's assessment of the Christian Right's respect for American pluralism, his statement does capture a critical element in the mobilization of the movement. The Christian Right's constituency was spurred to mobilize, in large part, by its growing inability to isolate itself from disturbing trends in the broader culture. From the 1930s through the 1960s, evangelicals had, for the most part, abstained from political activism. They built up their churches, evangelistic organizations, schools, and broadcasting empires. Evangelicals created a well-developed subculture within American society. They were moved to political action as that subculture found it harder and harder to insulate itself. Before detailing the "invasion"

of the evangelical subculture, we should first review the elements of
that subculture.

Subcultural Traits

Defining an evangelical subculture is no easy matter. Evangelicals
have long been divided. Fundamentalists, Pentecostalists, charismatics, and neoevangelicals have been battling for decades. Nonetheless,
amidst the doctrinal and personal clashes that mark the evangelical
world, a number of values are held in common, tending to distinguish
an evangelical subculture from the broader American society.

The core values are, not surprisingly, religious. Biblical literalism
is the foundation. The Bible is held to be the rock that holds the faithful steady against the temptations of modernism. Evangelicals tend not
to depend upon church hierarchies to interpret and apply doctrine. Each
individual—or more often each preacher—appeals directly to what is
claimed to be a commonsense understanding of Scripture. "Commonsense" interpretations come to widely varying conclusions (hence the
endless doctrinal disputes) but, these disputes notwithstanding, the Bible
is the source of authority that evangelicals of all types invoke. The
Bible provides the critical base for evangelicals in their disputes with
religious liberals, scientists, and secular experts of all sorts. Along with
defense of biblical authority come a number of doctrinal positions:
opposition to the theory of evolution, belief in millennial prophecies
(generally taking the form of dispensational premillennialism), and a
belief that God is active in historical developments.

Closely intertwined with evangelical religious doctrines is the evangelical vision of the family. Over the course of the post–World War II
period, "the family" has been assuming an ever more central
role within evangelical belief systems. Religious historian David Watt
states, "The importance evangelicals attached to the family in the 1960s
and 1970s can scarcely be exaggerated. In those decades evangelicals
talked about the family with the same regularity and nearly the
same passion with which the fundamentalists had discussed the Second Advent."[40]

Watt argues that the family has come to replace expectations of
the second coming as a source of hope in a hopeless world. While
evangelicals often portray the "traditional" family as a timeless entity
and a pillar of civilization throughout history, their vision of family
is specific to their time and culture. Their vision is one of patriarchal
authority, mothers inside the home, and children strictly disciplined.
This vision is, not surprisingly, suffused with religious images—fam-

ily Bible readings reenforcing the faith and passing it on to a new generation.

Closely tied to this vision of the family are stringent norms of sexual behavior. Sex is for marriage alone, closely tied to procreation, and, of course, heterosexual. Religion has traditionally been tied to the enforcement of sexual norms; as modernist liberals came to question received doctrines that stood in the way of human potential, restrictive sexual norms have been a key target of their assault. Evangelicals have held firm to older Christian standards.

Evangelicals also tend toward a fervent nationalism. They react enthusiastically to national symbols, rallying around the flag and offering strong support for the military. While evangelicals are concerned about what they see as the nation's moral drift, they continue to view the United States as the last best hope of a troubled world. In addition to their affection for the American social and political order, a specifically religious component helps fuel their nationalism. The United States is seen to have a key role in God's plan for world evangelism. Ed McAteer, president of Religious Roundtable, made the case in the following fashion:

> The United States has 7% of the world's land area, 6% of the world's population. Roughly 75% of mission dollars come from that 6%, 60% of missionaries from that 6%. . . . If this country falls to communism, who supplies that 75%? We must be sure that evangelism is supplied from here. . . . I understand the privilege and responsibility God has given to America.[41]

As McAteer indicates, evangelical nationalism has been closely tied to anticommunism. Communism is seen both as a threat to the nation and as an atheistic foe of religion.

Race plays an important—but difficult to capture—role within the evangelical subculture. Disproportionately Southern, evangelicals have been closely tied to that region's troubled racial history. White evangelicals have not, as a whole, been at the forefront of racial progress—although there have been many notable individual exceptions. Denominations such as the Southern Baptists have been intimately linked with the maintenance of white supremacy.[42] Great strides have been made in the last few decades; evangelical leaders now preach racial equality. Attitudes on contemporary race-related issues— affirmative action, South African sanctions—remain quite conservative among evangelical leaders (and followers).[43] The extent to which this reflects outright prejudice is not easy to determine.

Tables 2.2 and 2.3 illustrate some of the traits of the evangelical

Table 2.2

Evangelicals Compared to the U.S. Population as a Whole

	Evangelical Protestants %	National Sample %
Attend church regularly	5	46
Believe in life after death	89	77
Woman should take care of home (disagree)	52	68
Homosexuality not always wrong	11	27
Premarital sex not wrong	19	35
Opposed to laws against interracial marriage	42	66
Favor the right to speak of:		
Communists	37	57
Atheists	45	64
Homosexuals	44	66

Source: Wade Clark Roof and William McKinney, *American Mainline Religion* (New Brunswick: Rutgers University Press, 1987), chap. 6. The data is pooled from surveys conducted between 1972 and 1984. See their appendix for methodological details. In both the table and the text, I have substituted the term "evangelical" for their denomination-based "conservative Protestant" category.

subculture discussed above. Table 2.2, showing differences between evangelicals and the general public, finds these differences to be significant but not enormous. Two qualifications should be kept in mind in interpreting this table. First, the national figures in table 2.2 include large numbers of evangelicals. Thus the comparison tends to understate the differences between evangelicals and the rest of the population. Second, the denomination-based measure of evangelicalism that this table is based on includes many respondents who are only nominal church members. When sampling is narrowed to those active in their churches, evangelicals look even more distinct from the rest of the population.[44] Table 2.3 takes a slightly different set of questions and compares white evangelical Protestants with non-evangelical white Protestants and the unchurched. Disagreements become more apparent here. Taking the two tables together, the picture painted above—of a religiously, culturally, and racially conservative subcultural constituency—finds strong support. That having been said, it should also be pointed out that evangelicals are not a monolithic group. Although the subcultural traits I described are dominant, there are numerous exceptions, as can be seen in the significant segment of the evangelical population that takes the "liberal" position on many of the questions above. The Christian Right's agenda is not representative of the beliefs of *all* evangelicals. Jimmy Carter is as much an evangelical as Pat Robertson or Jerry Falwell.

Invasion

The "invasion" of the evangelical subculture can be seen, in part, as a continuation of the pressure of rationalization, cultural pluralism, and differentiation on a long beleaguered constituency. But modernity does not operate in the abstract; it manifests itself in concrete historical processes. Analyzing the specific forms of pressure evangelicals face is critical if we hope to understand the nature of the problems evangelicals confront and why they have turned to political action as a means of dealing with those problems.

The Supreme Court's 1962 decision to ban school prayer was one of the first stages of the "invasion." The school prayer decision rankles many evangelicals to this day. Evangelicals often argue that the decision's impact has been immense. The group Intercessors for America passes out fliers tracing America's woes—declining SAT scores, rising incidence of sexually transmitted disease, more violent crime—directly back to the school prayer decision.[45] Such arguments may seem an overblown case of symbolic politics but beneath the symbols lie

Table 2.3
Evangelical Attitudes

(Whites)	Evangelical %	Nonevangelical %	No religious preference %
Say "A religious person" a perfect description of self	35	8	—
Believe in clear standards of good and evil	54	35	23
Women should return to their "traditional role in society" (agree)	40	23	20
Strong supporter of the anti-abortion movement	45	21	14
Strong civil rights supporter	33	38	49
(All races)	Evangelical		Nonevangelical
Oppose legalization of homosexuality	73		46
Sometimes think AIDS a punishment for declining moral standards	61		35

Source: George Gallup, Jr., and Jim Castelli, *The People's Religion* (New York: Macmillan, 1989), chaps. 3 and 6. Gallup and Castelli use a loose doctrinal measure of evangelicalism, including all who say yes to the following question: "Would you describe yourself as a Born-Again Christian, or not?" See page 93.

some very real developments. The values of the evangelical subculture were coming to receive less respect and the government was intervening increasingly in local affairs, making protection of local subcultural values more difficult.

In the case of school prayer, what was at stake was not merely whether students would recite a short prayer on school-day mornings. What was at stake was the extent to which in local school districts throughout the land, religious values would be affirmed in the classroom. In many areas dominated by evangelicals, public school instruction was infused with evangelical values—from prayer and the posting of the Ten Commandments to the affirmation of subcultural family and patriotic beliefs. Describing her own Bible Belt childhood, journalist Carol Flake recounts, "When I was growing up, there was no need in my town for a separate Christian school; there was no chasm between the Christian boosterism I learned at church and the patriotic values I absorbed in civics class or the rugged individualism I cheered at football games."[46] As the Supreme Court came to enforce the separation of church and state, all this was felt to be threatened. The local school might no longer be a subcultural ally.

Nor was the prayer decision the only government threat to the subculture. Evangelical alternatives to public education continually ran afoul of the authorities. Accreditation for private Christian schools was often difficult to come by. Some evangelicals—particularly those in the home-schooling movement—refused to abide by state regulation and ended up in prison. School practices discriminatory to women and minorities have come under increasing scrutiny. A critical issue in the 1970s and early 1980s concerned the IRS's decision to revoke the tax exempt status of Christian institutions that practiced discrimination. The most celebrated case involved Bob Jones University, a fundamentalist institution that banned interracial dating. The Reagan administration attempted to intervene on behalf of the school but backed away from this stance in the face of adverse publicity and pressure from Congress.[47] Controversy has also surrounded the rights of religious clubs within public schools. Congress has addressed the issue with the 1984 Equal Access Act and the 1994 Religious Freedom Restoration Act, but heated debate over the limits of religious expression in the schools continues.

The most far-reaching federal intervention in local affairs during the 1960s and 1970s was its effort on behalf of desegregation. To promote the rights of African Americans, the federal government and courts forced their will upon recalcitrant states and localities. These efforts reshaped American society, particularly in the South. Evangelicals are heavily concentrated in the South and, as noted earlier, their racial attitudes are generally conservative. The civil rights revolution was a challenge to the beliefs of many evangelicals. Even among those who did not directly oppose it, the federal government's aggressive intervention in local affairs served to unsettle habitual subcultural patterns, reenforcing a more general sense of unease with shifting societal trends.[48]

A second Supreme Court decision is seen by evangelicals as an even more critical attack on their subculture than was the school prayer decision; that decision was the abortion ruling, *Roe v. Wade*. Roe did two things. First, it kept states from limiting abortion. Thus, even in areas where evangelicals predominated, they were unable to bring the law into line with subcultural values. Second, the decision greatly increased the visibility of abortion. Prior to the decision, abortion was often talked about in hushed terms, particularly within evangelical circles. After the decision, the issue stood as a public affront to evangelical values. As Kristin Luker describes the impact of Roe, "Abortion was no longer a technical, medical matter controlled by professionals; it was now emphatically a public and moral issue of nationwide concern."[49]

The media joined the government as an agent of invasion. In the 1950s and early 1960s, network fare offered little challenge to evangelical values. Promiscuity, much less homosexuality, was not to be seen. Even husbands and wives slept in separate beds. Today's Christian Broadcasting Network (CBN), promoting itself as "the family channel," uses the shows of this era as its standard fare, as "Christian" alternatives to the rival networks. Along with Pat Robertson's "700 Club," CBN broadcasts a steady stream of shows such as "Flipper," "Gunsmoke," and "Dobie Gillis."[50] As the 1960s wore into the 1970s, what appeared on the screen grew more threatening to evangelical family values. More and more explicit programming appeared on the networks. Cable television, from MTV to the Playboy Channel, provided an even greater challenge.

MTV and Playboy represent two of the most important forces evangelicals have been confronted with over the last two decades: rock and roll and pornography. In the 1950s, Elvis Presley was banned from swiveling his hips on television. Today such antics would be considered incredibly tame. From Elvis to psychedelia, from punk to Madonna, rock music has steadily pushed outward the bounds of the permissible. And as it grew more and more outrageous, rock music was becoming harder and harder to escape, pushing its influence into every nook and cranny of American culture. (Some evangelicals have attempted to turn rock music to Christian ends rather than simply resist it. A burgeoning industry, featuring everything from Christian rap to Christian heavy metal, is testimony to their efforts.) Pornography has also become ubiquitous. Not only is it more common and explicit, court rulings, upholding new interpretations of First Amendment rights, have made local regulation more difficult. Given limits on regulation and new technologies of dissemination, evangelicals have found it hard to wall their subculture off from the influence of pornography.

Increasing governmental regulation and the intrusiveness of the mass media are part of a more general trend toward the nationalization of

American politics and culture. As national culture and politics become more homogenized, maintaining local or regional subcultures becomes more difficult. Just as McDonalds has come to be known throughout the land, so too have the cultural and political styles of Hollywood, Washington, New York, and San Francisco. While residents of the small-town South would once have had vague inklings that decadent, liberal things were going on in these places, now those things confront them daily on their TV screens.

Who Is Invading?

What threatened evangelicals was not simply their inability to isolate themselves but the fact that the forces that were intruding upon them were hostile to their values. Evangelicals had long been at odds with the broader culture; that is why they built up their own subcultural network of institutions. But the gap between evangelical values and those of the broader culture grew markedly greater in the 1960s and 1970s. In the 1950s, evangelicals held to religious doctrines that were felt to be unusual by many. The aversion of some evangelicals to alcohol or dancing may not have found general support. But in their beliefs about family, patriarchy, patriotism, and sexual norms, evangelicals were generally in synch with the broader culture. In the 1960s and 1970s, an array of social movements came directly to threaten their beliefs.

There is no need to recount here the history of the civil rights, student, gay and lesbian, and women's movements. Combined with the sexual "revolution" and the previously mentioned rise of rock music, these movements posed a direct challenge to personal relationships at the heart of the evangelical value system. Relations between White and Black, men and women, gay and straight, were opened for reevaluation. In place of the rigid boundaries and codes of behavior characteristic of evangelicalism, these movements championed flexible roles, egalitarianism, experimentation, and behavior guided by the demands of human fulfillment rather than those of biblical strictures.

These movements have proven influential but their success has been uneven. Some segments of the population have shown much more receptivity to their message of moral liberalism than have others. Constructing a measure of moral conservatism—consisting of positions on homosexual relations, abortion, women's role in the home, and school prayer—John Simpson found that the key correlates of moral liberalism are: youth, residence in the nation's twelve largest metropolitan areas, residence in New England or the Pacific states, upper-class status, being secular or Jewish, and, most strikingly, high levels of education.[51] Only 36 percent of those with graduate education are moral conservatives whereas 87 percent of those with less than a high school degree fall into the conservative category. Not surprisingly, Simpson finds that nonmainline (mostly evangelical) Protestants who attend church regularly show extremely low levels of support for moral liberalism.[52] The picture that emerges is consistent with that of a variety of other studies; the moral liberalism promoted by the social movements of the 1960s and 1970s has found its strongest support among well-educated, secular, cosmopolitan elites.[53]

Crucial to evangelicals is the fact that supporters of cultural liberalism are particularly strong precisely in those institutions that are invading their subculture. If moral liberalism is strongest among the most highly educated, it should come as little surprise that evangelicals' positions find limited support in academia, the public-education establishment, or government bureaucracies. Surveys of reporters and television correspondents have shown very low levels of religiosity and high levels of cultural liberalism.[54] Thus evangelicals find that they are both losing control of their local subcultures and losing control to elites particularly hostile to their values.[55]

Evangelical Resurgence, Modernist Vulnerabilities

As evangelicals pondered how to respond to the pressures upon their subculture, a shifting balance of societal forces was opening new political opportunities to them. Throughout the 1960s and 1970s, evangelical denominations were growing steadily, televangelists were expanding their media empires, and their followers were moving slowly up the socioeconomic scale. In 1976, evangelicals saw one of their own—Southern Baptist Jimmy Carter—elected to the presidency. Carter's administration was to prove a disappointment to the conservative evangelicals who would go on to form the Christian Right. Nonetheless, the attention and credibility Carter brought to evangelicals helped them emerge from the societal isolation in which they had languished for so many years.

Not only were evangelicals growing in number, resources, and credibility, their opponents were growing more vulnerable. As students of social movements and social revolutions have often noted, success can depend as much on the breakdown of the opposition as on the extent of one's own strength.[56] In the 1950s and early 1960s, evangelicals faced a self-confident and generally respected set of academic, media, and governmental elites. A frontal assault upon them from a set of "backward" evangelicals would have had a hard time gaining credibility. Furthermore, if the best and the brightest seemed to be effective, if they seemed to know what they were doing in the public realms of government and economics, many evangelicals were content to confine their religious life to the private realm. But the 1960s and the years since have dealt a series of blows to America's secular elites. From failure in Vietnam to rioting in the streets, Watergate, stagnant economic performance, and the Iranian hostage crisis, events built upon each other to undermine confidence. If the "best and the brightest" did not know what they were doing, perhaps evangelical religious values *did* have a place in the public realm.

Implications

Evangelicals have been constrained but not eliminated by the forces of modernity; in recent years their subculture has been invaded. What do these facts mean for our understanding of the political activities of the Christian Right? The possibilities and limitations of the movement cannot be derived entirely from the social forces affecting its constituency. Shifting structures of political opportunities, alliance formation, and external organizers, as we shall see in upcoming chapters, all have played key roles in determining the fate of the Christian Right. Nonetheless, the forces of modernity and subcultural invasion have shaped the movement in critical ways.

Subcultural Defense

The Christian Right has been mobilized in defense of an embattled subculture and, in particular, in defense of those institutions that pass this culture on to the next generation. Asked what held his constituency together, Gary Bauer, head of the Family Research Council, replied:

> The only common denominator I can see in all that is that there is a child connection. Whether you are talking about abortion or childcare or the influence of pornography or these issues about what's on the TV screen during prime time, what tends to motivate most of our folks is a fear that their children are being peeled away, seduced by the popular culture, or that what they are trying to do at home is being undermined either intentionally or unintentionally by the government and the culture at large.[57]

Given the constituency's fear that popular culture and government agencies will "peel away" their children, the Christian Right's issue selection becomes more understandable. If the goal is to pass subcultural values on to the next generation, the key institutions for performing this task are the schools, the media, the church, and the family. Not surprisingly, it is with these institutions that the movement has been most centrally concerned.

Christian Right activists have fought against the teaching of evolution, the removal of prayer from the public schools, offensive textbooks, and sex education. Secular humanist forces in education (particularly the National Education Association) were a prime villain in Pat Robertson's campaign rhetoric, as they have been throughout Christian Right propaganda. Losing faith in the public schools, evangelicals have established a growing network of Christian schools as alternatives. Defense of the rights of these schools has been a key aspect of movement activism.[58]

The national media, transmitting messages likely to undermine subcultural values, have been an object of attack from the movement's beginning. As the media have brought the reality of cultural pluralism ever more insistently into their homes, Christian Right activists have boycotted shows, called for stricter regulation of sexually explicit materials, and lamented the lack of positive depictions of their values and lifestyles. As with the schools, they have developed their own Christian alternative: a massive array of television networks, radio stations, bookstores, and publishing houses. Defense of the rights of these institutions, particularly of Christian broadcasters, has been of key concern to the movement.[59]

Given the American tradition of the separation of church and state, the position of the local church has been relatively secure from state intervention. Nonetheless, movement activists remain alert to challenges to church privileges. Potential legal challenges to church tax statuses are often invoked in depictions of the secular humanist menace. More important has been Christian Right activism within churches, particularly within the massive Southern Baptist Convention. Over the last two decades, conservative forces have managed to seize leadership positions and gradually extend their control throughout denominational institutions. Closely allied with the Christian Right, these conservative leaders aim to tightly control the doctrines and values promoted by the denomination.[60]

Finally, there is the family. No institution is more important to the Christian Right's agenda. Movement rhetoric emphasizes the defense of "family values." Pat Robertson's cable network is known as the "family" channel; the dominant force in Christian radio is James Dobson's "Focus on the Family" show. The centrality of the family to movement politics is closely linked to its role as a transmitter of threatened values in a hostile modern world.[61] As evangelical religious values lose their sway outside the private realm, evangelical parents can no longer expect their values to be reenforced in the schools, in the media, and in politics. Indeed they can safely expect their children to be exposed to quite different values in these realms. Thus, the evangelical family assumes ever more importance as a bulwark against the outside world.

The Christian Right's battle on behalf of the "family" aims to reenforce its values within families and to shore up the position of evangelical families in the transmission of those values. The movement favors tax breaks and changes in welfare regulations to support families that stay together. It strongly opposes attempts to limit parental authority and defends hierarchical relations between children and parents. The movement is particularly worried about the assumption of family functions by the state, the market, or the media. Thus, Christian Right leaders rail against government attempts to regulate parental home schooling or the use of corporal punishment. They worry that mothers working outside the home will rely increasingly on secular childcare. Therefore they promote incentives to support mothers who stay at home and to allow daycare credits to be used in church-based care centers.[62] In their attacks upon feminism, Christian Right spokespersons often attack feminist women for adopting the competitive, market-oriented values of men.[63] They argue that the family should be a realm of nurturance isolated from the competition of the market, a private realm in which women promote values threatened in the world outside.

Thus far I have argued that the Christian Right is primarily concerned with intergenerational value transmission and the educational, media, church, and family structures necessary for that transmission. However, two important qualifications to this characterization should be noted.

One qualification concerns "family values." Thus far the family has been presented solely as means for the transmission of evangelical values. Its value as a means of transmission is critical to understanding why "the family" has assumed such a central role in Christian Right ideology. But the vision of the family promulgated by the movement is also an end in itself—one of the values meant to be transmitted to the next generation. The movement's attraction to patriarchy, heterosexuality, and marriage-based norms of sexual behavior are strongly rooted in evangelical (and much of the broader American) culture. A particular vision of the family has become closely intertwined with evangelical religious doctrine. I do not mean to imply that this vision would easily be jettisoned should a more efficient means of transmitting religious doctrines be found.

A second qualification concerns abortion. Abortion is the movement's first issue priority. *Roe v. Wade* was a catalyst spurring many evangelicals to political action.[64] Yet abortion does not fit neatly into the transmission of the values schema provided above. Abortion politics **are** closely linked to the politics of motherhood and family.[65] Opposition to the right to abortion is found to be closely tied to the affirmation of distinct social roles for men and women, opposition to contemporary feminism, and opposition to sex outside of marriage.[66] Thus, the abortion issue can be seen in part as a battle to uphold "traditional family values," to uphold a model of the family capable of resisting secular pressures and transmitting evangelical values to the next generation. Certainly abortion and family issues often blur into one another in the rhetoric of the Christian Right. Nonetheless, it must be admitted that the abortion issue also has a logic of its own. Christian Right activists believe abortion is murder and this inspires its own brand of passionate commitment. The logic of the abortion controversy ties it to issues such as euthanasia as well as to "the family."[67]

The Christian Right's abiding concern with the defense of subcultural values is critical to an understanding of the movement's political role and, in particular, its relations with the Republican party. This concern provides clear limitations upon leadership maneuverability. Many attempts have been made to mobilize the Christian Right constituency on behalf of free market economics, the gold standard, and anticommunist crusades. These efforts have produced limited results. Campaigns stressing anticommunist themes have had the greatest success, but the issue is obviously less compelling than it used to be.[68] Any Christian Right leader or organization that tries to move away from a primary focus upon family issues is in serious danger of undermining constituency support. My interviews with local Christian Right activists left little doubt that it was social issue concerns, issues of subcultural defense, that fired their enthusiasm.

These social issue concerns are not those of the Republican party as a whole; defense of subcultural family values underlies the movement's differences with other elements of the party. Surveys taken during Pat Robertson's presidential campaign provided vivid illustration of this point. Sharp differences divided activists supporting Robertson and other elements of the GOP. While differences on foreign policy and domestic economic policy were modest, strong differences existed on domestic "social issues." Not only were the Robertson supporters distinctly more conservative on these issues, social issues were of much greater salience to the Robertsonites. When questioned as to the most important issue facing the nation, the vast majority of Robertson's supporters named a social issue. Few supporters of rival candidates did so.[69] These differences continue to play a critical role in shaping the Christian Right/Republican party relationship.

Rationality

If the Christian Right's political agenda can be understood as an effort to bolster the institutions that protect an embattled subculture, then the movement looks far more "rational" than status politics theorists would give it credit for. What does it mean to claim that the Christian Right is "rational"? This claim is not meant as an endorsement of the ends the movement pursues nor of the means by which it pursues them. I argee that examples of moralism or conspiratorial thinking can be found in the movement. My claim is much more modest: the political activity of the Christian Right can best be understood as a set of measures reasonably calculated to support a way of life and a set of values threatened by the trends of contemporary American society. To find that a movement is acting reasonably to promote the values it holds dear should not be an earth-shattering discovery, yet it goes directly against the status politics model's emphasis on the "paranoid style" of status-based movements.

The "rationality" of the movement can be traced back to the fact that the movement is about, by and large, what it *says* it is about: "family" and—above all—religious values. Too many commentators continue to discount the power of religion and cultural concerns in American politics. If religious and cultural claims are really based in economic or status concerns, then one need not take them seriously on their own terms. Yet, as observation of world politics in the last few decades clearly demonstrates, religion is not yet spent as a social force. Analysts ignore it at their peril.

My analysis of the relationship between evangelicals and modernity suggests one reason to view the movement as more rational than do many observers. If evangelicals can adapt to and survive in the modern world, perhaps their efforts to preserve their values and way of life are not doomed. Viewing the Christian Right as a practical response to real divisions within the American social structure leads to a very different picture of the movement than does viewing it as an outburst of displaced frustration against the inevitable course of modernity. The movement appears more stably rooted in the fabric of American society; it also can be seen to have more in common with "normal" interest-based politics. This being the case, the movement's possibilities for operating within the political mainstream and its possibilities for alliance are enhanced.

Movement rationality is to be seen as well in the movement's relatively accurate understanding of the social forces with which it is contending. If evangelical children watch network television and go to public schools and universities, they are likely to be exposed to values at odds with those of their parents. There is a real threat that children will react positively to those values and be "peeled away" from parental values. Supporting evangelical churches and families, building their own broadcasting and school systems, is a strategy likely to enhance the viability of evangelical values.

Even the "secular humanist menace," so often cited as the prime example of the movement's conspiratorial mindset, can be seen as a relatively accurate understanding of the situation faced by the movement. The forces of modernity, described earlier in this chapter, are generally secular and humanist. Movements promoting moral liberalism have been intruding upon their subculture. Laments about the dangers of secular humanism tend to target institutions and ideologies that really do threaten evangelical values. As I read movement literature, listened to its broadcasts, attended its conferences, and interviewed its participants, I was often struck by the similarities between the analyses made in movement ideology and academic theories of social change in the postindustrial (or postmodern) era.

This is not to say that movement discourse concerning "secular humanism" is entirely accurate. It reduces complex social forces to the plottings of small organized bands of humanists. It is overblown and simplistic, depicting the world in crude dichotomies of good and evil.[70] In some cases, it draws upon the nasty tradition of anti-Semitic conspiracy theories.[71] Nonetheless, the discourse is not simply a reflection of displaced status anxieties; it is focusing attention on quite real threats to movement values. To the extent that the movement does engage in conspiratorial thinking, its roots lie not in displaced status anxieties but in the heritage of fundamentalist Christianity. To those who inherit a religious tradition that sees world events in terms of a titanic struggle between God and Satan, it should be no surprise that black and white, conspiratorial thinking comes easily.

Evangelical Dilemmas in the Promotion of Cultural Conservatism

The forces that have invaded the evangelical subculture have proven troubling to many nonevangelicals as well. Opposition to feminism, abortion, and gay and lesbian rights is widespread. So too is unease over the spread of pornography, permissive norms of sexual behavior, and the more explicit fare now offered on television. In a troubling world, religion and the family are seen by many Americans as vital bastions of stable values. Thus, a politics of "cultural conservatism"— promoting a return to "traditional family values"—might have real potential.

The Christian Right would appear well placed to lead a culturally conservative coalition. Evangelicals are a large constituency. And they are well organized. From the local church to the fundraising empires of the televangelists, evangelicals have in place institutional structures with impressive potential for political use. Conservative cultural norms and visions of the family are closely intertwined with evangelical religious doctrines. The force of religious belief is thus likely to give additional impetus to this constituency's activism on behalf of a culturally conservative agenda.

Unfortunately for the Christian Right, its sources of strength are also its prime sources of weakness. The religious constituency, organization, and doctrines that fuel movement activism are also what undermine its ability to build alliances with others who share its views. The strict religious doctrines that promote evangelical growth in the private realm prove a liability in the public world of politics. While devotion to biblical inerrancy and millennial prophecy may help anchor a stable system of meaning for troubled individuals, they are unlikely to prove acceptable in public discourse. A political candidate who bases her positions on biblical authority, prophetic predictions, or direct revelation will have a hard time finding acceptance. Furthermore, being strict about one's religious doctrines involves, among other things, intolerance for deviation. Thus, despite common political interests, cooperation between charismatics, Pentecostalists, neoevangelicals, and fundamentalists (not to mention conservative Catholics, Jews, and secularists) is often difficult to achieve. While the Christian Right is motivated to act on behalf of a culturally conservative agenda, it is not well suited to put together a broad culturally conservative coalition.

The problem is not only one of doctrine, it is one of organization. Much of the Christian Right's strength lies in the religiously based organizational resources it can draw on. The movement has tapped into church networks, broadcast its message through the religious media, and drawn on the credibility of established evangelical leaders. Built upon religious organization and enthusiasm, the Christian Right can not easily drop religious aspects of its appeals.

The Christian Right confronts a difficult dilemma: to gain public acceptability, build alliances, and effectively promote its political agenda, it needs to downplay divisive religious doctrine and express its case in more secular terms, in terms likely to find favor in the public realm of politics.[72] Yet such a strategy is likely to undermine the religious enthusiasm and organization upon which the movement and its leaders have built their fortunes. No easy solution to this dilemma has been found. Religious messages can be reformulated to gain broader appeal, movement leaders can broadcast different messages to internal and external audiences, but, as we shall see in later chapters, neither strategy is without its pitfalls.

Chapter 3

The Party Setting

To understand a relationship one must know something about both sides of it. Chapters 1 and 2 focused on the origins and motivations of the Christian Right. We now need some background on the Republican party side of the relationship. As the evangelical constituency was getting ready for political activism, the American party system was undergoing profound changes. This chapter describes the most important of those changes and, using the categories of "exit," "voice," and "loyalty" developed by Albert Hirschman, analyzes their impact on the Christian Right.

Party Change

In the 1960s, 1970s, and 1980s, "party reform" was the subject of seemingly endless scholarly and popular debate.[1] The debate was heated because something very important was believed to be at stake: control of the nation's major political parties, particularly control over their presidential nominations. Much of the debate addressed the question of how party reform affected social movement access to party decision making, a question of obvious relevance to the case of the Christian Right. However, the debate focused almost entirely on the Democratic party and the social movements active within it.

This focus made some sense. The 1968 Democratic convention was a debacle. Anti–Vietnam War activists within the convention hall felt they had been cheated by a presidential nominating system biased in favor of party regulars and their candidate, Hubert Humphrey. Outside the convention hall, protesters engaged in bloody clashes with the Chicago police. The public relations disaster of the convention, combined with a long-term weakening of the position of the regular party organizations that controlled it, helped provide the opening for reform. The Democrats' McGovern-Fraser commission, set up to re-write the party's nominating rules for 1972, produced a profound alteration in party affairs. While crucial reforms started in the Demo-cratic party, the impact of the McGovern-Fraser commission was felt in the Republican party as well. Furthermore, additional changes, such as new campaign finance laws and the growing importance of televi-sion, directly affected both parties.

The reshaping óf the nominating system altered the political ter-rain that the Christian Right was to eventually enter. The changes both opened up opportunities for, and created obstacles to, Christian Right influence. Before getting to those opportunities and obstacles, we need to examine the changes that created them. Four changes are crucial to our story: the proliferation of primaries, the opening up of presiden-tial caucuses, campaign finance reform, and the ever growing role of television.

The system the McGovern-Fraser commission set out to reform included primaries, but their role in the nominating process was a sec-ondary one. Hubert Humphrey, for example, had won the 1968 Dem-ocratic nomination without contesting a single primary. The majority of delegates were chosen in caucuses of varying degrees of openness. Often these caucuses were open only to party officials, poorly publi-cized, and/or held well before the year of the election. In practice this meant that state party organizations dominated the caucuses and controlled large blocs of delegates on the convention floor. Obtaining the party's nomination required extensive negotiations to win the sup-port of these delegations.

The intent of the McGovern-Fraser commission was not to encour-age a proliferation of primaries.[2] The commission gave states an op-tion. They could select delegates by means of a primary or they could use a reformed caucus system, one that was well publicized, held in the year of the election, and open to all party members. However, faced with the option of a caucus regulated by new and complex na-tional rules, a caucus that might prove difficult for party officials to control, states opted for primaries. As largely Democratically controlled state legislatures enacted laws establishing state primaries, they gen-erally put in place a similar set of rules for the Republicans. The McGovern-Fraser commission and the participatory reform ethos of the era fueled a dramatic increase in the number of primaries (table 3.1). Between the 1968 and 1972 conventions, the number of primaries nearly doubled. By 1972, 67 percent of the delegates to the Demo-cratic National Convention were chosen in primaries, as were 59 per-cent of the Republican delegates. By 1992 the numbers were up to 66 percent for the Democrats and 84 percent for the Republicans.[3] The upshot of these changes was a rapid shift from a nomination system dominated by state party organizations to one dominated by the acquisition of delegates in primary elections. Up through 1968, primaries were a useful means for candidates to win a few delegates and provide a demonstration of their popular appeal for state party leaders; after 1968, success in primaries was the key to nomination.

Caucuses have become much less common in the postreform period, but they still play a role in the nomination process. In 1988, the 23 percent of Republican delegates chosen in caucuses loomed large in Pat Robertson's presidential nomination strategy. In 1992, 16 per-

Table 3.1
Number of Primaries

	Party	
Year	Democratic	Republican
1968	14	13
1972	23	22
1976	29	28
1988	32	34
1992	35	38
1996	34	41

Source: Figures for 1968–1992 are from William G. Mayer, "Caucuses: How They Work, What Difference They Make," in *In Pursuit of the White House,* ed. William G. Mayer (Chatham: Chatham House, 1996), 119, 122. Figures for 1996 are from "1996 Presidential Primary and Caucus Calendar," *Congressional Quarterly Weekly Report* 54, no. 2 (January 13, 1996): 98–99. States with mixed caucus/primary systems are not counted as primary states.

cent of Republican delegates and between 13 percent and 18 percent of Democratic delegates were chosen in caucuses.[4] It is important to remember, however, that prereform and the postreform caucuses differed greatly, especially in the Democratic party. The McGovern-Fraser commission set strict national guidelines regulating caucus procedures to make certain that caucuses were open to the participation of all Democrats. Republican practice is more mixed. The GOP did not follow the Democrats in adopting strict central regulation of nominating procedures. While some states, such as Iowa, feature open, well-attended caucuses, other states, such as Arizona and Montana, limit participation to elected precinct committeemen and committeewomen.[5] Republican rules also allow greater flexibility to choose amongst proportional or winner-take-all delegate selection systems. Lack of strict central regulation means that various factions have an incentive to take over state party organizations in an attempt to rewrite or reinterpret the rules to help their favored candidate. (This fact will become significant in chapter 5 as we deal with the struggles surrounding Pat Robertson's presidential campaign.)

A crucial fact to remember about caucuses is that, attempts to open them up notwithstanding, turnout is very low. Participating in a caucus requires significantly more time and dedication than voting in a primary. William Mayer calculated primary and caucus turnout as a percentage of overall party voters. Primary turnout is low; in 1988 average Republican primary turnout was 19 percent. Turnout at caucuses, however, was abysmally low; only 3 percent of party voters, on average, turned out for Republican caucuses that year. Figures for the Democrats in 1988 and 1992 showed even larger gaps between primary and caucus turnout.[6] Low caucus turnout means that a relatively small group of dedicated, well-organized activists have opportunities for success not available in the higher turnout environment of a primary.

Changes in campaign finance laws have also played a critical role in altering the nature of party politics. In response to rapidly escalating campaign expenditures and especially to financial abuses uncovered in the Watergate scandal, Congress passed the 1974 Federal Election Campaign Act (FECA), a sweeping revision of campaign finance rules. FECA set overall and state-by-state spending limits for candidates. (Pat Robertson's campaign would bump up against the overall spending limit in 1988.) In addition, FECA limited individual contributions to a candidate to $1,000 per election; PACs could contribute no more than $5,000. No longer could a few "fat cats" be counted on to bankroll a campaign. The spending limits forced candidates to build a broader base of financial support. FECA's rules governing federal matching funds provided further encouragement. To qualify for matching funds in a presidential nominating contest, a candidate must raise $5,000 in at least twenty states utilizing donations of $250 or less. After this is achieved, the candidate qualifies for federal matching of the first $250 of each donation he or she receives.[7] The effect of FECA is to compel candidates to build a large network of small donors. As constructing such a network is a difficult and time-consuming effort, candidates are encouraged to start campaigns early. The pressure to start early has been augmented by the increased "front-loading" of the primary season. It is no longer feasible to expect an early caucus or primary victory to generate the donations needed to fuel one's campaign in later states; the contests simply come too fast.

A final contributor to the new campaign environment has been the growing role of television. In a manner more immediate and compelling than those of newspapers or radio, television offers candidates an opportunity to reach into living rooms and connect directly to voters.

The complexities of network—and now cable—television's impact upon presidential politics have been dealt with elsewhere.[8] Here I simply want to make a few basic points. First, candidates who have mastered the medium are at an advantage. Pat Robertson provides a case in point, although, as we shall see in chapter 5, his years of media experience had not always taught him the right lessons. Second, television has combined with the rise of the primary to displace state and local party organizations. It encourages us to think that we know candidates as individuals and it allows candidates to appeal directly to us without the intermediation of party organizations. Third, television, radio, and the print media have bathed the nominating process in an incredible glare of publicity. Whereas deals were once made behind closed doors, bargaining and coalition formation are now much more open. This can create problems for the Christian Right; in the glare of media scrutiny, the movement's public credibility problems are magnified.

Changes in primaries, caucuses, campaign finance, and the role of television have enhanced the influence of some actors in the nominating process and undermined the influence of others. The debate that swirled around Democratic party reform was generally based on the assumption that the new system undermined the influence of local party organizations and increased the influence of civil rights, antiwar, and feminist activists. The 1972 nomination of the candidate supported by these activists, McGovern-Fraser commission cochair George McGovern, added credence to this assumption. Reform defenders hailed this opening of the party system to previously excluded groups and the movements that represented them.[9] Critics charged that reform promoted the nomination of unelectable "outsider" candidates who would have difficulty governing if they were, in fact, elected.[10] Other observers questioned the significance of the McGovern-Fraser reforms and stressed the long-term nature of changes in the nominating systems.[11]

What opportunities and obstacles does the new party system provide for the Christian Right? To answer this question we will need to pay particular attention to the resources possessed by the movement, to differences between the Democratic and Republican parties, and to the various ways in which parties can be influenced. To distinguish between different methods of influencing parties, I will draw on Albert Hirschman's distinction between "exit," "voice," and "loyalty."

Exit, Voice, and Party Loyalty

Albert O. Hirschman's *Exit, Voice, and Loyalty* analyzes the complex interplay between two mechanisms designed to counteract organizational decline: exit and voice. These concepts are developed from economic theories of the business firm but, as he makes clear, can be applied to a wide variety of organizations, including political parties. Hirschman's categories provide a helpful tool for the analysis of relationships between the Christian Right and the Republican party. As succeeding chapters will show, the Christian Right's constituency has moved from influence derived primarily from a threat of "exit" to influence based on the exercise of "voice" within the GOP. Furthermore, the norms of "loyalty" operative within the party work to constrain the Christian Right's options. The changes discussed in the previous section have affected exit and voice. How have they been affected and, more basic, what do these two terms mean?

Exit

Hirschman describes "exit" this way: "Some customers stop buying the firm's products or some members leave the organization: this is the *exit option*. As a result, revenues drop, membership declines and management is impelled to search for ways and means to correct for whatever faults led to exit."[12] This seems fairly clear for the business organization, but how does it apply to political parties?[13] At first glance, the parallel appears straightforward. Citizens dissatisfied with the party's "product" stop voting for its candidates and volunteering to work for party organizations. "Management" must respond to provide a more satisfactory product. However, serious complications arise in the case of American political parties.

There are a number of different forms of exit. In a two-party system, voters can exit from a major party by defecting to the opposing major party, by supporting a minor party, or by dropping out of politics altogether. Each of these three options is a form of exit, but they are likely to arise under very different sets of conditions. The causes of exit to a radical third party will quite likely differ from those that drive centrist voters into the arms of the opposing major party or that cause alienated citizens to drop out of the political system altogether. As the causes of exit differ, so too must the response taken by "management" to stem that exit. Over the last twenty years, as the Christian Right has become more closely tied to the Republican party, each of these three exit modes has become a less feasible option. More about this comes later.

Distinctions also need to be made concerning who exits. Hirschman deals with exit entirely in terms of the choices of voters.[14] Limiting study to the exit of voters does simplify analysis but it seems inconsistent with his definition of exit in the firm. If exit occurs when "some customers stop buying the firm's product *or some members leave the organization*," it would seem that the withdrawal of volunteers from party organizations should be covered as well.[15] Republican leaders have had to worry that a "product" insufficiently attractive to the Christian Right would result in the exit of significant organizational resources from the party's campaign efforts. Church and ministry networks may not be mobilized in support of party candidates and positions, voter registration drives may not occur, a valuable pool of volunteers for party work may dry up.

Voice

As Hirschman admits, voice is a much "messier" concept than exit. He says, "The firm's customers or the organization's members express their dissatisfaction directly to management or to some other authority to which management is subordinate or through general protest addressed to anyone who cares to listen: this is the *voice option*."[16] Whereas a customer can either exit or not exit, the voicing of dissatisfaction can vary greatly in form and intensity. The messiness of voice is very much in evidence in the case of political parties. But Hirschman has little to say concerning exactly what this voice consists of.[17] So, as it applies to political parties in this study, "voice" will refer to the following activities, undertaken by individuals or by organizations: (1) influencing the selection of party candidates by voting in primaries, attending caucus meetings, or working within the campaign organizations of candidates seeking nomination; (2) influencing formal party organizations by taking part in their activities or by seizing control of them; (3) influencing the actions of the party's elected officials through lobbying, letter writing, or protest actions.

Some of these forms of voice, (voting in primaries, for example) look very similar to exit activities (such as voting in general elections). The key distinction is that voice is aimed at changing the party's "product"—its candidates and its policies—while exit consists of abandoning that product when it proves unacceptable. Thus, voice and exit are often closely related in practice. The threat of exit can be used to amplify the power of voice. Voicing complaints may be a prelude to exit. Some strategies, such as temporary boycotts of the party, may combine elements of both exit and voice.[18] Nonetheless, the distinction between exit and voice is an important one. Voicing complaints *within* a party requires different resources for success and leads to different outcomes than does the picking and choosing *between* parties embodied in exit. As the Christian Right has come to rely more heavily upon voice within the Republican party, it has exercised new powers but, along with them, has had to face a new set of dilemmas.

Exit, Voice, and Party Change

The party changes discussed in the first part of this chapter affected the exercise of exit and voice in a variety of ways relevant to the Christian Right. One important change involves the nature of the party "management" that responds to the exercise of exit and/or voice. Self-starting presidential candidates have gained at the expense of established party organizations.[19] Therefore, the chapters that follow will focus heavily on Christian Right relations with GOP presidential candidates and presidents. Recently gained Christian Right control of many local party organizations, while by no means unimportant, means significantly less than it would have in times past.

As management has been reshaped, the resources required to influence it by means of voice have changed. Having a voice in the presidential nominating process now depends less on the ability to gain the favor of party leaders and more on the possession of resources necessary to prevail in primaries and caucuses. The impact of these changes on the Christian Right is mixed.

In many ways party changes have worked to enhance the Christian Right's potential for voice. As established local party leaders lost their hold over the nomination, openings arose for outsiders. Especially in the Christian Right's early stages, the movement met with limited sympathy from local party leaders. While they generally wanted the movement's support, they were hesitant to give the newcomers a significant voice in party decision making. They certainly did not want Pat Robertson as their party's standard-bearer. The reformed party environment did not guarantee Christian Right influence or Pat Robertson's nomination; however, it did give the movement greater opportunities to bypass resistant party establishments and appeal directly to primary and caucus electorates.

The Christian Right is well provided with many of the resources critical to success in primaries and caucuses. This should not be surprising. Historically, evangelists have faced many of the same challenges that confront contemporary political candidates. Independent evangelists, operating outside denominational control—and support—had to develop highly sophisticated fundraising and message disseminating organizations in order to survive. Over the last century, evangelical organizations have pioneered many of the techniques now used by political candidates. These religiously based organizations can prove politically useful. Church networks built up for religious purposes provide a preexisting, well-organized base for campaigns to tap into.[20] Sermons to local church audiences, evangelical publications, television and radio ministries, all can provide valuable assistance in disseminating a political message. Few human institutions have generated as much volunteer effort as religion.

Drawing on religious enthusiasm, the Christian Right has mobilized a formidable grassroots organization that has repeatedly shown its ability to pack caucus and party meetings, staff phone banks, and distribute campaign literature. At the moment, the Christian Coalition's million plus member grassroots organization is the envy of both friend and foe. While the Christian Right is not a dominant factor in Republican party finance, contemporary party change has enhanced the value of its financial resources.[21] Campaign finance reform has made large pools of small contributors a necessity in any serious campaign for a major party nomination; evangelical religious organizations have the mailing lists, fundraising experience, and media skills needed to generate such contributions. If these fundraising capabilities can be transferred to the political realm—as they were to some extent in the Robertson campaign—Christian Right voice is further enhanced.

The contemporary presidential nominating system also presents serious problems for the Christian Right. Money, volunteers, and organization may prove sufficient to dominate a low-turnout caucus; they are helpful, but not sufficient, in primaries where turnout is far higher. Victory in primaries requires a level of popular support the movement has difficulty obtaining. Christian Right figures such as Pat Robertson evoke very negative responses from the general public.[22] Of course, lack of public support is a problem in most conceivable nominating systems. Established party leaders were never anxious to pick nominees or back causes that the public hated. Thus, the *fact* that lack of support hurts the Christian Right's strength within political parties is not due to changes in nominating procedures. What the new procedures have done, however, is affect the *manner* in which lack of support hurts the movement.

One problem for the Christian Right is the impact of the current nominating system on coalition building. Candidates at various levels perceived to be from the Christian Right have had difficulty winning. Pat Robertson provides a case in point at the presidential level.[23] Nonmovement candidates who include the Christian Right as a part of their coalition have had greater success. Ronald Reagan and George Bush are examples. The task of coalition building, however, has been made more difficult by party changes. Primaries—and to a lesser extent caucuses—take place in an unprecedented glare of media attention. Candidates must broadcast their message to a wide audience of potential primary voters or caucus-goers. Successful coalitions with the Christian Right can be formed in such an environment, as the experience of 1980, 1984, and 1988 showed, but the process is difficult. It becomes even more difficult as the Christian Right demands a greater, and more visible, role in those coalitions.

Some of the difficulties of coalition formation go back to dilemmas discussed in chapters 1 and 2. The problem faced by the Christian Right is that the messages necessary to mobilize movement resources, to evoke enthusiasm, donations, and volunteer effort from its core constituency, are likely to alienate the voters beyond that core.[24] Or, to put this in the language of earlier chapters, the values of the evangelical subculture are not well received when given a public airing outside that subculture. Coming up with a message that will play well both inside and outside the evangelical subculture is not easy. And, given the very public nature of the contemporary nominating process, it is difficult for the movement to successfully broadcast different messages to the two audiences. Pat Robertson's presidential campaign and the Christian Coalition have both had to deal with this dilemma.[25]

A final problem the new nominating system presents for the Christian Right is the flip side of one of its advantages: the diminution of the role of local party establishments. This diminution provided an opening for the movement to promote candidates opposed by those establishments. In the late 1980s and the 1990s, however, the Christian Right began to win control of state and local Republican parties. With control of an estimated eighteen state Republican parties and influence in thirteen more, the Christian Right now has much greater influence at the local organizational level than it does in caucuses and primaries.[26] Unfortunately for the movement, this influence means significantly less than it would have under the old nominating system.

Critics of Democratic party reform often argued that the new nominating system—and especially primaries—would undermine moderate, patronage-oriented party "regulars" and increase the role of issue-oriented activists ("purists"). The issue-oriented activists of the Christian Right have much in common with the "purists" they described. Why then have they done better at the state and local organizational level than in primaries? First, the Christian Right's grassroots organization is very well suited for the task of mobilizing people to pack local party meetings. Second, the Republican party has not centrally regulated delegate selection procedures. This means that control of state parties can prove a valuable tool as the supporters of various candidates attempt to adjust the rules in their favor. Thus, especially during the Robertson campaign, Christian Right activists have had an incentive to get involved in party affairs. Finally, critics of party reform based their predictions on the existence of strong regular party organizations driven heavily by patronage concerns. An organization interested in the spoils of victory should, theoretically, be more interested in victory than ideological purity. However, patronage-based party organizations have been in a state of decline for many decades. As patronage has dwindled as an incentive for involvement in local party affairs, ideological incentives have grown in importance. Thus the moderate, pragmatic candidates favored by reform critics now may fare better among primary electorates than at the party organizational level.

Overall, we see that the new nominating system is a mixed blessing for the Christian Right. It changes the nature of the party management that responds to exit or voice. It opened up opportunities for voice, allowing the movement to bypass the opposition of established party elites and make use of its formidable organizational resources. However, the Christian Right is better suited to prevail in low-turnout caucuses than in primaries. The publicity of the current system makes coalition formation difficult and, it turns out, the initial opposition of local party organizations may have been easier to overcome than the opposition of primary electorates.

Before proceeding further, we need to examine Hirschman's third category, "loyalty." Republican norms of loyalty have played an important role in the Christian Right's exercise of exit and voice.

Loyalty

For Hirschman, loyalty serves a different function than exit or voice. While exit and voice are mechanisms by which customers faced with products of low quality can create pressure for improvement, loyalty works to help determine the balance struck between exit and voice. Hirschman argues that those loyal to an organization or firm are, because of their attachment to it, reluctant to exercise the option of exit. As loyalty raises the cost of exit, customers are more likely to stay put and utilize voice.[27]

The concept of loyalty, as used by Hirschman, needs modification for two reasons. First, its definition is suspiciously close to the phenomenon it is purported to explain. If loyalty is defined as a reluctance to exit, to then use loyalty as an explanation for a lack of exit is dangerously circular. Second, Hirschman's definition of "loyalty" is too abstract to encompass the very real attachments that affect behavior toward American political parties.[28]

For the purposes of this study, therefore, I offer a reformulation of Hirschman's concept of loyalty. To develop my theory of loyalty, I draw upon Jo Freeman's work on American party "cultures."[29] Concerned with delineating the characteristics that separate the Democratic and Republican parties, Freeman argues that their authority structures are strikingly different. In the Democratic party, she claims, power flows upward. Constituency groups are seen as the building blocks of the party. Particularistic group loyalties and group appeals are an accepted aspect of party life. In this pluralistic party, group leaders are expected to vocally press their claims, even if this involves challenging party leaders. In the Republican party, Freeman argues, power flows from the leadership downward. Influence is based not on the constituency you represent, but on the leader you have supported. When that leader wins, you win. Those who back losers retain much less influence than their counterparts in the Democratic party. Group loyalties and appeals are viewed with suspicion; primary allegiance is owed to the party at large. The Republican party, she says, is held together by a high degree of social homogeneity and by the conviction that its vision is applicable to all Americans, regardless of their group characteristics.

Republican party culture thus involves a distinct set of norms of loyalty, profoundly affecting the likelihood and nature of Christian Right exit and voice. Suspicion of group attachments inhibits voice that takes the form of group demands. It also tends to discourage threats of group exit.[30] Either of these strategies is likely to lead to charges that those engaging in them are "disloyal," that they are not "true Republicans." These charges are particularly potent when utilized against the Christian Right. If the glue that holds the party together is social homogeneity, Christian Right activists stand out from other party activists in their socioeconomic backgrounds and, particularly, in their religious beliefs. Pentecostalists and Episcopalians do not mix easily.[31] Furthermore, as a relatively new constituency within the Republican party's electoral coalition, Christian Right activists often lack a proven track record of party service. Many of the Republican activists I interviewed felt that the Christian Right was being presumptuous, demanding influence without putting in the necessary years toiling on the party's behalf.

If direct assertion of group demands runs counter to party norms, other forms of voice are available. Faithful party service can help establish legitimacy. Group ties can be downplayed as party ties are highlighted. Then, as Freeman's description of party culture indicates, the best means for a Republican party out group to effectively utilize its "voice" is to back a factional leader able to win and willing to grant them access. When Reagan was at last able to win nomination, his longtime supporters were rewarded for their efforts. More liberal Republicans converted quickly or found themselves left out in the cold.

To sum up, "loyalty," as I use it, is a context-specific category; it operates differently in America's two major parties. Republican loyalty norms do not preclude the direct assertion of group demands. However, they do tilt the playing field to favor strategies of achieving voice by demonstrating party loyalty and backing winning factional leaders. Whereas Jesse Jackson and feminist leaders could make appeals on behalf of African Americans and women and gain legitimacy in the Democratic party to the extent they were seen as representatives of those groups, such a strategy in the GOP would invite charges that one was not a "true" Republican.[32] The Christian Right activists mobilized into the party by the Robertson campaign and those active today in the Christian Coalition have worked hard to establish their status as "true" Republicans. After his bid for the nomination failed, Robertson fell in line behind George Bush. In 1992, despite ideological affinities with challenger Pat Buchanan, Robertson threw his support to Bush again. Christian Coalition executive director Ralph Reed has repeatedly stressed his willingness to moderate his group's demands to accommodate the strategic interests of the party as a whole. After many years of loyal support for the GOP, the coalition has gained legitimacy in the party and with it, perhaps, greater leeway to voice its demands. Nonetheless, the Christian Coalition, with its strategy of gaining influence within the GOP, remains much more restrained than other Christian Right groups in its criticism of party leaders and positions.

The Christian Right on New Party Terrain

Far-reaching changes have altered the American party terrain; exit, voice, and loyalty provide useful categories for understanding the movement/party interactions that take place on that terrain. The distinction between exit and voice helps highlight the shifting strategies employed by the Christian Right in its relations with the Republican party. Chapters 4 through 6 document the shift from a reliance on the threat of exit to the development of capacity to exercise voice within the party. The analysis of party change and voice in this chapter can help us understand the opportunities and obstacles the Christian Right faced as it tried to exercise that voice. Finally, an understanding of the norms of loyalty operative within the Republican party provides further understanding of the constraints that have shaped movement strategy.

With the terrain of party/movement interaction laid out and categorized, it is now time to delve into the history of that interaction.

Chapter 4

From Ambivalence
to Alliance

Time and *Newsweek* magazines proclaimed 1976 the "year of the evangelical," as public attention was focused on the large, and until then largely ignored, evangelical subculture. Evangelicals were prominent in politics as well that year but primarily in the person of "born-again" Democratic presidential candidate Jimmy Carter. Few Americans had heard of Jerry Falwell or Pat Robertson; those familiar with their broadcasts knew them primarily as religious, not political, figures. The partisan allegiances of evangelicals were uncertain. While Jesse Helms made strong appeals to this constituency on behalf of Republican challenger Ronald Reagan, these efforts were overshadowed by Jimmy Carter's very public professions of faith. The equivocal position of evangelicals is well reflected in the stand Pat Robertson took in the 1976 campaign. Publicly, Robertson backed fellow Southern Baptist Jimmy Carter, but he claims to have had doubts as the campaign went along, leading him to make a last-minute decision to vote for Gerald Ford.[1]

Twelve years later, in the 1988 campaign, no such ambiguity existed. Evangelicals had become an established component of the Republican electoral coalition. Jerry Falwell and Pat Robertson had become two of the best known figures in American political life, and their partisanship was clear. No one thought it possible that they would endorse a Democratic presidential candidate. Falwell was ardently courted by, and publicly endorsed, the eventual victor George Bush. Robertson was himself a candidate for the Republican nomination, coming in third in a crowded field of contenders. A featured speaker at the Republican convention, Robertson drew upon Dickens's *A Tale of Two Cities* in his address. He declared, "Our tale of two cities is really a choice between two paths. Two visions of America. Two philosophies of the future." Robertson painted a stark contrast between the Democratic "city"—a liberal nightmare of welfare dependency, higher taxes, ACLU radicalism, and godlessness—and the Republican "city" to be established under the leadership of George Bush—a conservative utopia of self-help, limited government, strong families, and publicly affirmed faith.[2]

The 1992 convention even more firmly established the link between the Christian Right and the Republican party. Movement leaders were prominent throughout the convention, which opened with a fiery invocation by fundamentalist preacher James Kennedy. Jerry Falwell and Pat Robertson were given places of honor, sitting in the presidential and vice-presidential boxes. Robertson spoke again, warning, "When Bill Clinton talks about family values, he is not talking about either families or values. He is talking about a radical plan to destroy the traditional family and transfer its functions to the federal government."[3] Pat Buchanan put forth his famous battle cry, "There is a religious war going on in our country for the soul of America. It is a cultural war, as critical to the kind of nation we will be—as was the Cold War itself."[4]

Sounding a similar theme, Vice President Dan Quayle declared that "the gap between us and our opponents is a cultural divide."[5] Culturally conservative rhetoric came not only from the speakers, but was also to be found in the platform. Christian Right activists played a prominent role in producing a platform markedly more conservative on social issues than the already conservative platforms of the 1980s.[6] As cultural war was declared, the Christian Right and the Republican party were clearly allies. The Democrats were just as clearly the enemy.

How did evangelicals go from being an unorganized constituency of questionable partisanship to produce a well-organized movement clearly aligned with the Republicans? How did their voice within, and potential for exit from, the Republican party change with these developments? Over the last two decades, evangelicals have moved from a position of influence through potential exit to a position where exit is difficult and the exercise of voice has become central to their influence within the Republican party. As America's two major parties have come to divide more clearly on issues of concern to the evangelical constituency, as movements opposed by that constituency have solidified their position within the Democratic party, the threat to defect from the Republicans has become less plausible. Third party options are not viable, and Christian Right organizations have developed ties to the Republican party that would be expensive to break. Over the same period that exit became a less viable option, the movement developed powerful organizational resources, resources that provided at least the potential for the significant exercise of voice within the Republican party. At first, these resources were mobilized primarily under the leadership of New Right and Republican party organizers, figures external to the movement. As time went on, however, the Christian Right developed its own cadre of leaders. Many of the outsiders who assisted in the birth of the movement soon came to be overshadowed by their offspring. As the movement built both its resources and its ties to the Republican party, it began to demand a voice within that party.

My explanation is clearly a simplification of a complex reality. As will be clear from the account that follows, early incarnations of the Christian Right did attempt to exercise voice, and exit remains an important weapon in the movement's arsenal. One strategy has not replaced the other; however, the balance between them has shifted.

This chapter is built upon a further simplification: the assumption that a unified entity (the Christian Right) is attempting through exit or voice to influence a second unified entity (the Republican party). This simplification is a useful one for the development of theory that would avoid drowning in a sea of details, but it must be recognized eventually that it is, in fact, simplification. This chapter, and the chapters that follow, will pay careful attention to the factional differences and organizational rivalries that pervade the movement and the party. The exit and voice options are not equally attractive to all elements of the Christian Right; nor are all elements of the party equally susceptible to movement influence.

Precursors: Crusading against Godless Communism

In the 1950s and 1960s, the most visible attempts to link conservative Protestantism and conservative politics came in the form of anticommunist "crusades" sponsored by Carl McIntire and Billy James Hargis. Many of the themes that would later be developed by the Christian Right are found in their campaigns but important differences exist. Examining these differences can help us understand why the Christian Right has become a broader, more powerful movement than its predecessors.

Carl McIntire: Fundamentalist

Carl McIntire played a key role as both a religious and political forerunner of the Christian Right. In the 1930s, he was a leader of a fundamentalist group that split from the Presbyterian Church, or more precisely, McIntire broke from a group that had previously split with the main body of Presbyterians. McIntire was adamant in his insistence on doctrinal purity and on the need to separate oneself from the impure. He created the American Council of Christian Churches (ACCC) in 1941 in order to combat the ecumenical alliance of mainline Protestants, the Federal Council of Churches (FCC).[7] Designed to unite separatist fundamentalists and contest the FCC's claim to represent all Protestants, the ACCC has been marked by schism and controversy. After all, getting separatists to unite is no easy task. Many religiously conservative Protestants could not abide McIntire's combative personality or his doctrinal rigidity. In 1942, more moderate forces created the National Association of Evangelicals. The NAE hoped to carry its message to the broader culture rather than isolating itself from it. Unlike McIntire's group, the NAE was willing to accept as members individuals who retained membership in denominations affiliated with the liberal FCC and—of even greater importance—was willing to accept Pentecostalists and charismatics.

McIntire and the ACCC launched blistering attacks against the Federal Council of Churches, communism, and, as it became clear that it would not follow McIntire's lead, the National Association of Evangelicals. Through the mid-1950s these attacks were disseminated primarily by means of the ACCC publication *Christian Beacon*, which, by the late 1960s, had reached a circulation of approximately eighty-four thousand. In 1958, McIntire moved into broadcasting, syndicating a radio show that eventually found airtime on over six hundred stations. While McIntire's message found listeners, he was never able to gain the credibility or support garnered by later Christian Right figures.[8]

McIntire's limited appeal was due in large part to the religious exclusivity of his message. Rooted in the culture of separatist fundamentalism, McIntire expressed that culture's tendencies toward schism, a tendency manifested in the creation of innumerable independent fundamentalist churches. The primary target of McIntire's wrath was the Federal (after 1950, National) Council of Churches, but Catholics also faced attack. In their study, *The Radical Right*, Benjamin R. Epstein and Arnold Forster declare: "In addition to his obvious hatred for 'modern' Protestantism, Rev. Carl McIntire harbors little good will for the Roman Catholic Church. He has a record of anti-Catholicism and of association with anti-Catholic bigots."[9] McIntire's ill-tempered assaults undermined his credibility with the mainstream media and with the general public. Few Catholics or mainstream Protestants were likely to find his messages palatable.

Even more problematic were McIntire's stormy relations with those who could be considered his natural allies, the charismatics and moderate evangelicals who formed the National Association of Evangelicals. Many NAE members shared McIntire's concerns about the liberal course taken by the Protestant denominations of the National Council of Churches; they feared communism and were distressed by social trends inimical to their traditional moral standards. Yet McIntire's religious exclusivity posed a serious roadblock to any attempt at a common front on these issues. Ironically, McIntire's own downfall as leader of the ACCC came when that body's executive committee denounced *him* for violating separatist principles, for sacrificing separation from the religiously impure in his pursuit of political goals.[10]

Religious conflicts haunt the Christian Right to this day. Pat Robertson found it extremely difficult to expand from his charismatic and Pentecostalist base to obtain support from fundamentalists.[11] Falwell's Moral Majority had similar difficulties expanding beyond its base of fundamentalist Baptist churches. Southern Baptist Convention president Bailey Smith's 1980 claim that God does not hear the prayer of Jews raised skepticism concerning the Christian Right's tolerance of religious diversity.[12] Nonetheless, present divisions are not nearly so great as those aroused by McIntire. Unlike McIntire, few Christian Right leaders today are closely associated with denominational controversies.

Whereas McIntire founded the ACCC to do battle with backsliders from the true faith, contemporary televangelists rarely emphasize denominational ties and tend to avoid doctrinal controversies. Presenting basic messages that focus on the viewer's decision to accept Christ, televangelists attempt to appeal to the broadest possible array of viewers (and potential donors). Christian Right figures—Bailey Smith notwithstanding—now stress the *Judeo*-Christian values upon which, they claim, this nation was founded. Cooperation with conservative Catholics such as Phyllis Schlafly has become routine. All this is not to say that religious differences do not cause division within the Christian Right or that prejudice against Jews and Catholics has disappeared. However, these differences and prejudices are no longer emphasized to the degree they once were, which creates the potential for broader political alliances than the Reverend Carl McIntire could ever have hoped to achieve.

Carl McIntire's message suffered from an additional limitation: its central focus upon the threat of internal communist subversion. The limitations of such a message can be seen most clearly in the case of his protégé, the Reverend Billy James Hargis.

Billy James Hargis and the Communist Threat

Hargis's organization, Christian Crusade, founded by the young preacher in 1948, sounded many of the same themes as did McIntire's *Christian Beacon*. In the early 1950s, Hargis and McIntire cooperated on a project attacking the World Council of Churches and on a much-publicized plan to use balloons to float Bibles over the Iron Curtain to the countries of the Eastern Bloc. A product of Ozark Bible College, Hargis shared the fundamentalist perspective of McIntire, particularly McIntire's hostility to liberal Protestantism. Hargis, however, was less closely linked to denominational conflicts. Early in his career, after a dispute with his local church, Hargis vowed never again to associate with any denomination.[13] Christian Crusade was founded as an anticommunist organization not, like the ACCC, as a means of fighting doctrinal battles. The "crusade" was a personal vehicle of Hargis's, not a coalition of fundamentalist denominations. In the 1950s, Hargis did have praise for the well-known anti-Semite Gerald Winrod, but refrained from such associations in the 1960s. Unlike McIntire, Hargis did not attack Catholicism and even included Catholics on the crusade's advisory board.[14] Billy James Hargis was no model of toleration, but his crusade did mark at least a partial move away from McIntire's sectarianism, opening possibilities for a broader movement.

Yet despite the fact that Hargis articulated many of the themes that were to become staples of the Christian Right, his support remained quite limited.[15] This limited appeal may have been due, in part, to the manner in which these themes were expressed. In *Why I Fight for a Christian America*, Hargis decries the social phenomena—pornography, abortion, drugs, sex education, rock music, women's liberation—that are the objects of attack of today's Christian Right. Hargis refers readers to his previous work, *Is the Little Red Schoolhouse the Proper Place to Teach Raw Sex?* and urges them to contribute to his effort to keep sexually explicit programs off network television. He calls for women to take the "God appointed place for their sex" and labels abortion "murder."[16] Like today's movement, Hargis complains of media hostility and government regulation of religious broadcasters. His solution is similar as well: a return of America to its status as a "Christian nation." He cites the biblical verse (2 Chron. 7:14) that has become the standard invocation at all Christian Right events: "If my people, which are called by my name, shall humble themselves and pray, and seek my face, and turn from their wicked ways; then I will hear from Heaven, and will forgive their sins, and will heal their land."[17]

What then separates Hargis's message from that prevalent within today's Christian Right? It is the fact that Hargis, like McIntire, makes internal communist subversion the centerpiece of his analysis. Rock musicians are "Marxist minstrels"; declining moral standards will bring America to the condition of countries behind the Iron Curtain. While fearful of war with the communist powers, Hargis warns that

> of even greater potential danger is the constant and growing threat of Communist takeover from within. When I first began to sound this warning after World War II, most people in this country dismissed it as something that could never happen here. But today there is not just a danger of this happening, but a real possibility that our children or grandchildren will grow up reading Marx instead of the Bible, and singing the *Internationale* instead of *The Star Spangled Banner*.[18]

Communism is, in Hargis's view, the main vehicle by which Satan hopes to undermine America.

Ideological formulations at odds with the facts of the world have shown remarkable tenacity; still, if the contradictions become too glaring, the ideology is likely to run into trouble, particularly if, as was the case with Hargis, the ideology lacks the backing of governmental or economic elites. By the late 1960s, an increasing number of Americans were troubled by threats to traditional moral norms—from rock music, the women's movement, new religious movements, and the increased visibility of gays and lesbians demanding their rights—but arguing that these developments were all part of a communist conspiracy strained credibility. Strident anticommunism had a definite attraction at the height of the Cold War in the 1950s, but as tensions with the Soviet Union eased and as the 1960s demonstrated the very real domestic roots of troubling societal developments, Hargis's message lost much of its appeal.

The contemporary Christian Right is certainly anticommunist, but "secular humanism" has taken center stage, eclipsing internal threats of subversion. Continuities are clear. For Hargis, a key aspect of communism was its rejection of God and its elevation of human beings over God. Nonetheless, the language of "secular humanism" marks a distinct ideological advance over Hargis's formulations. The advantages of the new language are twofold. First, it is not so obviously false as the old. Second, it paves the way for a different and more viable coalition.

A secular humanist threat provides a more plausible rationale to motivate people than does the threat of communist subversion. As demonstrated in chapter 2, many of the trends opposed by the Christian Right are linked to secularism and humanism. Religious strictures concerning sex roles and family life have lost ground to secular arguments based on norms of human fulfillment. Media and educational elites are more likely than the general public to adopt liberal positions on social issues, positions often derived from secular and humanist premises. The secular humanist thesis even bears striking similarities to academic theories of a "new class." The secular humanist argument may not be a sophisticated academic theory, but it does bear enough of a relation to reality to mobilize those concerned about contemporary social trends, provide links between the movement and more intellectual analysis of those trends, and avoid some of the obvious absurdities of Hargis's position.

Certainly, descriptions of the secular humanist menace can take on implausibly conspiratorial forms. For example, Tim LaHaye's *Battle for the Mind* claims a mere 275,000 dedicated humanists control our media, educational system, and government. Tremendous importance is placed on the rather obscure Humanist Manifestos I and II. Even the time-worn conspiracy of the Illuminati is hinted at.[19] The Illuminati, an atheist group allegedly born out of eighteenth-century Freemasonry and linked to Karl Marx, the French and Russian Revolutions, and international financiers, plays a much larger role in Pat Robertson's *New World Order*. Drawing both on secular conspiracy theory and religious prophecy, Robertson sees hidden conspiracies as the real moving forces in world history. The book "shines light on the invisible hand shaping U.S. government policies" declares a back-cover endorsement from the John Birch Society publication *The New American*.[20] The humanist conspiracy theories of LaHaye and Robertson move far from the realm of academic respectability (and basic rules of evidence and logic). The extreme conspiratorial elements of Christian Right thought are both disturbing and worthy of attention. However, it is the more moderate versions of the secular humanist argument that have been the main basis of the movement's appeal and that represent an advance in basic plausibility over the theories of McIntire and Hargis.

A moderate secular humanist argument also provides the basis for a different, and possibly more effective, coalition than did Hargis's stress on an internal communist threat. Hargis's position created possibilities for alliances with nonfundamentalist anticommunists; the John Birch Society, led by Unitarian Robert Welch, provides the most obvious example. But Welch's narrow conspiratorial focus proved implausible to many potential allies. Furthermore, Hargis's anticommunist message was not well suited to mobilize the potential of an evangelical constituency; anticommunism did not tap directly into the religious values that motivated this constituency. In identifying secular humanism as its enemy, the current Christian Right makes a specifically religious appeal to a religious base but makes this appeal in a very general, nondenominational manner. All faiths can potentially rally against secularism.

Emergence of the New Christian Right

Like McIntire and Hargis, today's Christian Right attempts to mobilize a base of religiously conservative Protestants for politically conservative ends. However, the Christian Right does so in a more credible and less sectarian manner. This is due, in part, to the ideological innovation represented by the "secular humanism" thesis—but only in part. McIntire and Hargis could not have mobilized the equivalent of the Christian Right in the 1950s or 1960s simply by espousing the proper rhetoric. The social conditions that would make the new language effective had not yet emerged. For religious disputes to subside in importance, it is necessary not simply to avoid McIntire's divisive rhetoric but also for the religious tensions in the movement constituency to lessen. For the rhetoric of secular humanism to evoke a response, an actual secular humanist menace has to be perceived by substantial segments of the public.

By the early 1970s, the social conditions that would provide the grounds for an effective new rhetoric were in place. Evangelical denominations were growing, interdenominational hostilities were lessening, and the evangelical subculture was finding that it could no longer isolate itself from hostile forces in the broader society. The constituency was poised to produce something that went far beyond the limits reached by Carl McIntire and Billy James Hargis.

The production of that "something" depended on more than a message and threatened constituency: it required *resources*. The late 1970s provided a critical confluence of outside organizers, internal organizational resources, and external aid, promoting the translation of a conservative evangelical constituency into a powerful political movement.[21]

Proud Parent: The New Right

In its infancy, the Christian Right was nurtured by a related—but nonetheless distinct—movement: the New Right. The New Right traced its origins back to the more conservative elements of the 1964 Goldwater campaign. Richard Viguerie's direct mail empire had its origins in that campaign; Viguerie copied, by hand, the names and addresses of over twelve thousand of Goldwater's major contributors. Through the 1960s and 1970s, he pioneered the building of ever larger and more precise contributor lists, as he raised funds for a diverse array of right-wing candidates and causes. Morton Blackwell—Goldwater's youngest convention delegate—went on to work for Viguerie, edit the *New Right Report*, and run training schools for young right-wing activists. Howard Phillips, an early leader in the pro-Goldwater Young Americans for Freedom, went on to cofound the Conservative Caucus. Paul Weyrich began to make his mark in Washington a bit later. In 1973, with the financial backing of beer tycoon Joseph Coors, Weyrich (and Edwin Fuelner) formed the Heritage Foundation, a conservative think tank. Weyrich went on to create the Committee for the Survival of a Free Congress and offshoots such as the Free Congress Research and Education Foundation. Other prominent New Right leaders included Terry Dolan of the National Conservative Political Action Committee (NCPAC), Senator Jesse Helms, and Reed Larson of the anti-union National Right to Work Committee.

By the mid-1970s, the leaders of the New Right had developed a wide-ranging, interlocking network of direct mail operations, political action committees, and lobbying groups. What was "new" about this New Right network? In many ways, it simply marked a new and more effective marketing operation on behalf of the old causes of the Republican party's more conservative wing: militant anticommunism, anti-unionism, and opposition to big government.[22] Like the Goldwater movement, the New Right had its base in the South and the West. Its business support came from Sun Belt entrepreneurs rather than more established corporations.

Several characteristics did tend to differentiate the New Right from more established conservatives and the Republican party. First, the movement's tone was populist, strident, and anti–status quo. The New Right portrayed itself as "blue collar" rather than "blue blood." Attacking "the establishment" in the name of "the people," leaders criticized big business as well as big government and big labor. They showed little respect for educated elites. Not for them were intellectual ruminations on the decline of Western culture or a Burkean defense of existing institutions. The New Right stoked popular anger in an attempt to shake things up. Second, the New Right had an ambivalent attitude toward the Republican party. Leading members developed ties to George Wallace and toyed with the possibility of a third party candidacy in 1976. The party was far less important than single-issue campaigns against bussing, the SALT and Panama Canal treaties, or gun control. Third, the New Right emphasized social conservatism in an effort to win over non-Republican audiences. Attacks upon abortion rights, feminism, and pornography were central features in their appeals. Phyllis Schlafly, a figure closely tied to the New Right, developed an effective movement dedicated to blocking ratification of the Equal Rights Amendment.[23]

As leaders of the New Right surveyed the political landscape in the mid to late 1970s, a large—and largely unmobilized—constituency presented itself: evangelicals. The New Right was in a particularly good position to reach out to this constituency. Evangelicals, as we saw in chapter 2, are distinctly conservative on the social issues—abortion, gay rights, and the ERA—that the New Right had made its own. Furthermore, the New Right's distance from the upper class traditions of the Republican party was useful in its attempt to mobilize the poorer, traditionally Democratic, evangelical constituency. In my interviews with state-level activists, I found that a large social and cultural gap continues to separate conservative evangelicals from those they refer to as "country club Republicans."

Evangelical Institutions: A Valuable Prize

Comprising roughly 20 percent of the U.S. population, the evangelical constituency was an important prize for the New Right to win. In addition to its overall size, it provided a potentially powerful set of organizational resources. As evangelicals defended their threatened subculture, they had developed an impressive array of institutions to promote and protect subcultural values. Television networks, local congregations, denominational hierarchies, alternative school systems, all were dedicated to passing on a threatened set of *religious* values. If they could be used to transmit *political* messages, these institutions could prove to be an invaluable political resource.

Compared to most political organizations, the capacities of evangelical religious institutions are impressive indeed. Their fundraising abilities dwarf those of political parties and candidates. Table 4.1 provides a comparison of the fundraising of a variety of political and religious institutions during the first decade of the Christian Right's organizing efforts. The revenues of the Southern Baptist Convention easily outstripped those of the much touted Republican fundraising apparatus. The revenues of a New Right group such as Weyrich's Free Congress Foundation were, in comparison, a mere drop in the bucket. Of course, Southern Baptist leaders could not simply take $4.2 billion in annual receipts and spend it on political causes. The wishes of local Southern Baptists—and federal election law—prevented such a course of action. But if political organizations could tap into religious networks to raise only a fraction of that sum, it would prove a valuable resource indeed. The 1988 GOP nominating campaign provides an example of this potential. Accustomed to raising $230 million a year at the Christian Broadcasting Network, political newcomer Pat Robertson proved able to raise the $28 million needed to keep pace with the effort of vice president and party favorite George Bush.[24]

In addition to fundraising capacities, evangelical institutions include communications networks reaching millions of viewers, listeners, and readers, grassroots organization (the local congregation), and a highly devoted set of followers. What political organizer would not envy the regular communication to millions of devoted viewers available to the televangelists? What political group can match the fifteen million locally organized members of the Southern Baptist Convention? How many political organizations are as central to the life of their members as are evangelical churches?

While these religious resources were formidable, as late as the 1970s there was serious doubt that they could be transferred to political ends. Suspicion of political activity ran high among evangelicals. Creation of an evangelical subculture had, in part, been an effort to wall themselves off from the corruptions of the world. Entering the political arena involved a foray back into that world of corruption. Premillennialist eschatology emphasized the futility of attempts to reform a doomed world; many evangelicals believed that their job was a strictly religious one: to save as many souls as possible before the end came. Not all these doubts have been overcome. Separatist fundamentalists such as Bob Jones, Jr., continue to denounce political activism and fundamentalists such as Jerry Falwell who engage in it. Nonetheless, a significant segment of the evangelical community and its institutions *have* indeed been mobilized for political ends in the last decade and a half. Several factors have contributed to this mobilization.

Table 4.1
Fundraising—Religious and Political

Group	Annual receipts (in millions)
Southern Baptist Convention	4,292.0 (1987)
Republican Party	298.0 (1984)
Christian Broadcasting Network	230.0 (1986)
Democratic Party	98.0 (1984)
Free Congress Research and Educational Foundation (Weyrich)	2.6 (1986)

Source: On Southern Baptist finances, see Constant Jacquet, ed., *Yearbook of Canadian & American Churches* (Nashville: Abingdon Press, 1989), 256. On party committees, see Larry J. Sabata, *The Party's Just Begun* (Glenview: Scott, Foresman and Company, 1988), 76. The figures on the parties include the National Committee as well as the Senate and House committees. On CBN, see Jeffrey K. Hadden and Anson Shipe, *Televangelism* (New York: Henry Holt, 1988), 254. On the Free Congress Foundation, see Free Congress Research and Educational Foundation, *1986 Annual Report,* 36.

First, the evangelical subculture was finding it harder and harder to isolate itself from troubling societal trends, rendering a separatist, non-political strategy less tenable (see chapter 2 also). Second, religious institutions themselves were seen to be threatened. Evangelical schools and broadcasters faced challenges from federal regulators. Convincing religious institutions to rally on behalf of abstract political principles might be difficult; getting them to organize in defense of their own tax status was much easier. Third, issues close to the perceived religious mission of evangelical institutions were becoming politicized. As social issues such as abortion, pornography, and school prayer increasingly became the subject of political debate, the political mobilization of religious institutions and leaders was facilitated. For evangelical church organizations to lobby on behalf of free market economics involves quite a leap from their religious values; to get them involved in struggles for school prayer and "family values" flowed much more freely from their primary mission. (This third argument is based on the discussion of core evangelical values in chapter 2. In other religious communities—for example, among Latin American liberation theologians—religious and economic themes may be much more closely intertwined.)

From Potential to Political Reality

Yet even with the many factors inclining evangelicals and their religious institutions toward political action, such action remained to be organized. In this task, New Right leaders played a central role. Individual evangelicals had, of course, long participated in a variety of right-wing causes, including those of the New Right. What was new in the mid to late 1970s were the initiatives taken by New Right figures to enlist evangelical leaders and tap into evangelical religious networks. This initiative took some effort. Few of the original New Right leaders were themselves evangelicals. Richard Viguerie and Phyllis Schlafly were Roman Catholics. Paul Weyrich was an Eastern Rite Catholic. Howard Phillips was Jewish.[25] Yet in the late 1970s, they were the catalyst that helped propel the evangelical constituency on its way toward political mobilization.

New Right leaders played a crucial role in bringing together political operatives and religious figures. Paul Weyrich and Howard Phillips helped recruit two critical early Christian Right organizers: Robert Billings and Ed McAteer. In 1976, Billings had won a GOP congressional nomination in Indiana. After losing in the general election, he came to Washington at the urging of Paul Weyrich and founded the National Christian Action Coalition (NCAC) in 1977. Billings's background was with the Christian schools movement and his new organization's primary focus was defeating what Billings termed "an attempt by the IRS to control the private schools." Ed McAteer's background included a quarter century stint as a salesman for Colgate-Palmolive, but in addition he had developed extensive contacts in evangelical circles, particularly among Southern Baptists. Hired as national field director of Howard Phillips's Conservative Caucus in 1978, McAteer's contacts put him "in a prime position to introduce evangelicals to various conservative groups and leaders such as the Heritage Founda-

tion and Richard Viguerie." Paul Weyrich claims that McAteer played
an "indispensable" role, bringing him around to meet most evangelical leaders.[26]

As the Christian Right took off in the last few years of the 1970s,
Billings, McAteer, and the leaders of the New Right were at the center of things. At the early meetings from which the Moral Majority
emerged, Jerry Falwell was joined by Paul Weyrich, Ed McAteer, and
Howard Phillips. Weyrich was actually the one who came up with the
organization's name.[27] Bob Billings was brought aboard soon thereafter and became the new organization's first president. Another key
organization in the early days of the Christian Right—The Religious
Roundtable—emerged from a meeting attended by Weyrich, Phillips,
McAteer, Richard Viguerie, Phyllis Schlafly, and Southern Baptist
Convention president Adrian Rogers. Ed McAteer became president of
the roundtable.

The role played by the New Right leaders in the founding of these
organizations was twofold. First, the New Right leaders had to convince evangelical religious figures to enter the political arena. Richard Viguerie states, "he [Weyrich] and Howard Phillips spent countless
hours with electronic ministers like Jerry Falwell, James Robison, and
Pat Robertson, urging them to get involved in conservative politics."[28]
Convincing them was not always an easy task. Many were afraid that
political involvement would upset their religious followers, possibly
undercutting contributions. In my interview with him, Paul Weyrich
described what he felt was one of the most important meetings he
had had with evangelical leaders. In that 1979 meeting, Weyrich convinced them to chip in for an opinion survey of their followers.[29] That
survey probed attitudes toward political involvement on the part of
their ministers. When the results came in, showing that respondents
would support—and even donate to—political efforts, a major stum-
bling block was overcome. Weyrich says:

> Spontaneously, from there, grew all of the different groups. Following
> that, then Falwell said "O.K., I'm serious. Let's do it." And Robertson
> started taking an interest and James Robison started taking an interest
> and Charles Stanley started to take an interest and James Kennedy started
> to take an interest and on and on. . . . Some of them went formal—i.e.,
> the Moral Majority—others stayed with their ministry but got into these
> [political] topics which they were unwilling to address before.[30]

Second, even after evangelical leaders were convinced that political action was appropriate, New Right leaders still had to instruct them
how to go about it. Experienced New Right activists helped explain

the political ropes to the evangelical neophytes. "In 1980," Weyrich explains, "the religious right's leadership was to some extent subservient; they were so new to politics, they deferred to people like Howard Phillips or myself."[31]

In the years after 1980, as Weyrich freely admits, the dominant position of New Right leaders eroded. As Christian Right figures like Falwell gained political experience, they were determined to make their own decisions. With their access to the grassroots base and to the funding that grew from tapping into the evangelical constituency and its institutions, the Christian Right soon began to outgrow the movement that had helped nurture it in its early years. In the 1980s New Right groups such as the National Conservative Political Action Committee, Viguerie's mail order empire, and Phillips's Conservative Caucus fell on hard times.[32] While Christian Right organizations have come and gone, the level of donations and particularly of grassroots activism have remained far higher than anything the New Right can muster. Again, Paul Weyrich describes the situation nicely: "Today the values oriented conservatives dominate the movement. . . . The Religious Right has always been the ones with the troops. The New Right had some ability to raise money, but it had very little ability to turn out people."[33]

As the 1970s flowed into the 1980s, the Christian Right was developing its independence and its capacities. Movement organizations such as the Moral Majority gained members and national notoriety. Just as important was the politicization of the evangelical subculture. From the programming of Christian television and radio stations to the output of evangelical publishing houses, a coherent socially conservative message was coming to be heard. Together, new organizations and new forms of evangelical political discourse were laying the foundation of a powerful social movement. But a key question remained: how would this movement fit into partisan politics?

No Exit

In the early to mid-1970s, the partisan identity of the evangelical constituency was open to question. Some early organizers struck populist themes, pronouncing a plague on both parties' houses. Yet by the late 1970s and into the 1980s, as the Christian Right organized a segment of this constituency, its members were developing increasingly strong ties to the Republican party. As leaders built a well-organized movement, the options for partisan exit open to them and their organized followers had already diminished.

Analyzing exit, we must distinguish between exit by voters and exit by organized activists. Furthermore, we should know the location exited to, whether to the opposing major party, to a third party, or to political inactivity. In the remainder of this section, I examine the possibilities for exit from the Republican party. Defection to the Democrats became increasingly implausible as time went on, third party options were never viable, and political inactivity grew more expensive. Throughout, I distinguish between incentives affecting the evangelical constituency and those affecting movement organizations and leaders.

In the Beginning . . .

It is now common to consider white evangelical Protestants a Republican constituency. Yet it would be a mistake to overlook their remaining Democratic attachments. Even more of a mistake would be to read their present Republican leanings back into past decades. White evangelicals were a central component of the Democrats' New Deal electoral coalition. Disproportionately southern and of lower socioeconomic status, evangelicals identified overwhelmingly with the Democratic party through the 1960s. It was the mainline Protestant denominations, with their more northern and affluent congregations, that formed the backbone of the Republican coalition, as they had since that party was founded. The turbulent politics of the 1960s strained evangelical ties to the party of Roosevelt but, by the end of that decade, evangelical attachments had not yet shifted to the Republicans.

As white evangelicals were awakening from their political slumber, therefore, the partisan tinge of their mobilization was open to question. As late as 1976, Jimmy Carter could make a credible Democratic appeal for this constituency's support, an appeal that met with quite a bit of success. Yet a Democratic evangelical option was not to be. Over the years, the attachment of the evangelical constituency, and particularly of Christian Right leaders, has grown more and more solidly Republican. The Democratic option has become less and less plausible, undermining any realistic threat of movement defection from the Republican fold.

Let us review briefly the position of evangelicals and the major parties in the 1960s. Evangelical voters identified strongly as Democrats, but their presidential voting patterns were more mixed.[34] Faced with a Catholic Democratic candidate in 1960, a slight majority of evangelical Protestants went for the Republican, Richard Nixon. In 1964, they swung strongly back to Democrat Lyndon Johnson. In 1968,

Hubert Humphrey trailed both Richard Nixon and independent candidate George Wallace among evangelicals. Table 4.2 tells the story: evangelicals identified as Democrats but often defected. In each of these elections, author Paul Lopatto calculated the "expected" vote (based on party identification) for various religious groups; in each case, evangelicals are the religious group that shows the greatest deviation from their "expected" vote and in each case that deviation favors the Republicans.

The unclear partisan allegiance shown by evangelical voters during the 1960s is likely related to the lack of clear differences between the parties on issues that would appeal specifically to an evangelical constituency. If we look back to 1960, the primary division between the parties was economic, pitting Democrats who favored a moderate expansion of the welfare state against Republicans who opposed such an expansion. Each party was internally divided on foreign policy and racial issues.[35] The social issues that would play such a key role in the rise of the Christian Right—school prayer, abortion, gay rights, support for the "traditional" family—were not part of the partisan agenda. (The Equal Rights Amendment had appeared in party platforms but only on the *Republican* side.) Over the next few decades, not only would these issues of concern to the evangelical community

Table 4.2
Evangelical Protestants in the 1960s:
Party Identification and Presidential Vote

Year	Democratic		Republican		Independent	
	I.D.	Vote	I.D.	Vote	I.D.	Vote
1960	62	48	24	52	14	
1964	76	67	15	33	9	
1968	59	22	12	46	29	32*

Source: Paul Lopatto, *Religion and the Presidential Election* (New York: Praeger, 1985), 55, 156, & 157.

Note: The figures on party identification here are for evangelical Protestants of the 36–55 age group. Lopato does not give aggregate figures for all age groups together. The 56 and older category figures are very similar, although Republican allegiance is higher (21 percent) in 1968. The under 36 age group differs significantly in two respects: Republican I.D. increases over the period.

*This figure is for candidate George Wallace.

force their way onto the political agenda, the parties would come to assume very different positions regarding them. To see how this occurred, a review of recent presidential campaigns is illustrative. In the themes stressed—and the platforms adopted—by the two parties, we can trace the process of issue emergence and partisan differentiation.

1964

Racial issues had long been on the political agenda, but partisan divisions on race were unclear; the 1964 presidential election was a crucial one in defining the racial position of the parties. That year saw the passage of a landmark Civil Rights Act, aggressively pushed through Congress by Democratic president Lyndon Johnson. Even more important was the position taken by the GOP standard-bearer Barry Goldwater, one of the few Republican Senators to have opposed the Civil Rights Act. Goldwater did not defend segregation; he based his opposition to the act on a defense of states' rights and limited federal powers.[36] Whatever Goldwater's personal motivations, however, his position was seen as a major shift in the GOP's racial policy. The results were dramatic. The Republican share of the African-American vote collapsed. Whereas Eisenhower and Nixon had carried 40 percent and 33 percent of the African-American vote, respectively in the previous two elections, Goldwater carried less than 10 percent. African Americans have continued to vote overwhelmingly Democratic in the presidential elections since. White southerners, on the other hand, flocked to the GOP. Despite his disastrous showing overall, Goldwater won five Deep South states that had not gone to the Republicans since Reconstruction.[37] In the aftermath of 1964, the positions of party activists on racial issues grew more and more clearly distinct. The mass public as well began to perceive clear differences between the parties on racial issues.[38]

Not only did 1964 serve to define the parties on race, but it greatly accelerated the process of unmooring southern whites from their traditional attachment to the Democratic party. As conservative southern whites left the Democratic party, they were replaced by newly enfranchised African Americans. The electoral base of the Democratic party—including the South—became more consistently moderate to liberal. On the Republican side, an influx of white southerners, combined with decline of the party's northern liberal wing, gave the GOP a more consistently conservative electoral base.[39] In their losing effort, Goldwater Republicans laid the foundation for the eventual triumph of the Republican Right under the leadership of Ronald Reagan.

The impact on evangelicals was threefold. First, evangelicals tend to be conservative on racial issues (see chapter 2) so some found the new Republican position attractive. Second, by cutting the ties that had linked southern whites to the Democrats, the creation of genuine partisan competition in the South—for evangelicals as well as others— was hastened. Third, by contributing to the creation of more uniformly liberal and conservative parties, the events of 1964 helped pave the way for the assumption of clearly differentiated positions on issues of concern to evangelicals.

The year 1964 also saw the first hints of Republican social conservatism to come, with the entrance of the school prayer issue into partisan politics. Responding to recent Supreme Court decisions, the 1964 Republican platform expressed its "support of a Constitutional amendment permitting those individuals and groups that choose to do so to exercise their religion freely in public places, providing religious exercises are not prepared or prescribed by the state."[40]

1972

As 1964 was a turning point for the Republicans, so too was 1972 for the Democrats. A new and quite different set of activists propelled George McGovern to the nomination and helped redefine the party's image. Those who watched the 1972 nomination battle and convention saw the party represented by a very new set of people. Young antiwar activists, sporting countercultural styles of dress and grooming, came to supplant images of Chicago boss Richard Daley and AFL-CIO chief George Meany. Republicans took advantage of these images to label McGovern the candidate of "acid, amnesty, and abortion" (even though McGovern never took an explicit position in favor of any of these things). Such pictures were bound to have an impact upon evangelical audiences.

Image had some basis in reality, as an examination of the Democratic platform of 1972 demonstrates. The social issues that would become the mainstays of the Christian Right finally made their way to prominence in a major party platform and the Democrats placed themselves solidly on the liberal side of these issues. Full sections on the rights of women, family planning, and the right to be different appear where before there had been silence or, at most, fleeting references.[41] The section on the rights of women expressed strong support for the Equal Rights Amendment and went on to urge action to overturn a long list of discriminatory practices. The platform urged that family planning services "necessary to permit individuals to determine and achieve the number and spacing of their children, should be available to all regardless of sex, age, marital status, economic group or ethnic origin."[42] Complaining that "official policy too often forces people into a mold of artificial homogeneity," the platform went beyond the rhetoric of integration to endorse Black pride and the affirmation of multiple cultural identities. Furthermore, in a vague but evocative challenge to evangelical norms, the section on the right to be different declared: "Americans should be free to make their own choice of lifestyles and private habits without being subject to discrimination or prosecution."[43]

McGovern's followers and platform posed a clear challenge to the values of the evangelical subculture: "traditional" family structures, strict norms of sexual behavior, racial conservatism, strident promilitary nationalism. Thus, it should come as no surprise that McGovern did particularly poorly among evangelicals. A mere 20 percent of evangelicals backed McGovern's candidacy, a figure far below his dismal national showing. The year 1972 marked the only election in the period from 1960 to 1980 when evangelicals backed the GOP in greater numbers than their more traditionally Republican mainline Protestant counterparts.[44]

Nor was the impact of the McGovernites a one-shot affair. The new breed of Democrat associated with his campaign, many the products of the great social movements of the 1960s, stayed on in the party, giving it a distinctly more liberal tinge.[45] Moreover, they represented a new breed of liberalism, focusing their attention on social and environmental issues and questioning American militarism. Whereas an older breed of liberalism—focusing on New Deal style social programs—might prove appealing to evangelicals, many of whom were not financially well off, the new liberalism tended to strike directly at evangelical nationalism and norms of personal behavior.

1976

In 1976, neither party defined itself as dramatically as did the Republicans in 1964 or the Democrats in 1972. Jimmy Carter and Gerald Ford ran centrist campaigns; their ideological positions were not clearly delineated. An examination of the 1976 platforms, however, reveals that differences were to be found on social issues of concern to evangelicals. Both parties supported the ERA. But Republican support came only after a heated internal battle in which Reagan supporters nearly succeeded in overturning the party's historic commitment to the amendment.[46] Of particular significance was the entrance of the abortion issue into the partisan arena. In the wake of the 1973 *Roe v. Wade* decision, the parties took cautious but nonetheless opposing positions on the issue: the Republicans for, and the Democrats against, a constitutional amendment to overturn *Roe v. Wade*.[47] Another indication of emerging partisan divisions is a section in the Republican platform entitled "The American Family." Its specific contents are nothing particularly new, but it does mark the emergence of a new rhetoric. Stressing the immense value of families, the inability of government to replace their functions, and the intrusion of government upon the family, this section hints at the rhetoric that has become the mainstay of the Christian Right.[48]

While platform differences were important, "born again" Democrat Jimmy Carter was the biggest story of 1976. Carter's open espousal of his religious beliefs was a source of pride to many evangelicals. As John F. Kennedy's nomination and election signaled to Catholics that they had at last gained acceptance in American society, Carter's campaign represented acceptance to many evangelicals. Carter improved dramatically upon Humphrey's and McGovern's poor showings among evangelicals. This higher level of evangelical support has often been credited with providing Carter his margin of victory in a very close general election. However, Carter by no means commanded the united support of evangelicals. In fact, Paul Lopatto finds the evangelical vote split fifty-fifty between Carter and Ford. While this is a great improvement over the 20 percent garnered by McGovern, it indicates that the GOP's attraction to evangelicals was strong enough to match the pull of group loyalty. Carter managed to slow an evangelical movement to the Republicans, but he would prove unable to stop it.[49]

1980

With the nomination of Ronald Reagan, the GOP assumed the thoroughgoing social conservatism that defines it to this day. The Democrats, infused with the energy of progressive social movement activists, continued their move in the direction of social liberalism.

The parties' 1980 platforms presented a stark contrast. Stands on abortion, cautiously stated in 1976, moved into much clearer opposition. Both sides placed fewer qualifiers before their statements of position. The Republicans reaffirm their support for a constitutional amendment to "restore the protection of the right to life for unborn children." The party goes on record in support of efforts to cut off the use of tax dollars to support abortion and calls for the appointment of judges "who respect traditional family values and the sanctity of innocent human life." The Democratic platform, on the other hand, "recognizes reproductive freedom as a fundamental human right." The Democrats affirm their support for the Supreme Court's abortion rulings and their opposition to "legislative restrictions that deny poor Americans their right to privacy by funding or advocating one or a limited number of reproductive choices only."[50]

In 1980, the Republicans reversed their long-standing support for the Equal Rights Amendment; their platform denounced federal pressures on states that had not ratified the amendment. The Democrats not only reaffirmed their support for the amendment, the party went on to make the issue a very high priority.[51] The platform declared that the party would offer no support to Democratic candidates who opposed the ERA and vowed to hold no party meetings or conventions in states that had not ratified the amendment.

Beyond the ERA, both parties devoted a good deal of space to the conditions and rights of women but, in doing so, their emphases were strikingly different. The Democrats offered sections on women in business and women and the economy. They promised government action to aid women-owned businesses, to assist women's entrance into fields traditionally reserved for men, and to enforce equal pay for jobs of comparable worth. While the Republicans affirmed a vague support for women's economic rights, much greater emphasis was placed on women's role within the family and on the threat to it posed by government interference. The Republicans "applaud our society's increasing awareness of the role of homemakers in the economy" and declared: "The family is the foundation of our social order. . . . But the Democrats have shunted the family aside. They have given its power to the bureaucracy, its jurisdiction to the courts, and its resources to government grantors. For the first time in our history, there is a real concern the family may not survive."

Not only were there disputes over whether the economic rights or the family role of women should be stressed, by 1980 the very definition of "family" had become a point of contention. The Democrats did not ignore the family, but their wording is revealing: "The Democratic Party supports efforts to make federal programs more sensitive to the needs of the family, *in all its diverse forms*" (emphasis mine). The Republicans, needless to say, did not speak of the family's diverse forms; they spoke of one "true" form: "We reaffirm our belief in the traditional role and values of the family in our society. . . . The importance of support of the mother and homemaker in maintaining the values of this country cannot be over-emphasized."[52] The platform endorsed the "traditional" family at several other points; it denounced the Carter administration's White House Conference on Families (it was deemed too feminist) and called for the appointment of judges who would uphold "traditional family values."

Neither the family's "diverse forms" nor its "traditional role and values" were spelled out in any great detail, but these terms clearly evoke quite different images. When these images were combined with the Democrats' focus on the working woman and the Republicans' odes to the homemaker, the contrast between party visions becomes apparent. The contrast was heightened by an explicit Democratic defense of gay and lesbian rights, a first in a major party platform.[53] Gay and lesbian families may have fallen under the "diverse" label; there can be little doubt that the "traditional" label was *not* meant to apply to them.

The contrast between party platforms extended to other issues of concern to evangelicals as well. The Republicans denounced the Carter administration's education policies, alleging that federal bureaucracies were usurping the rightful powers of parents and local school districts. The GOP platform called for an end to IRS harassment of "independent"—often evangelical—schools and supported school prayer.[54] The platforms also staked out clearly differentiated positions on racial and military issues.

National party platforms are not perfect measures. They may be distorted by short-term tactical calculations of the campaign or the idiosyncrasies of a particular candidate. As a reflection of the dominant faction of the presidential wing of the party, they fail to deal with internal party diversity. On social issues, Republican liberals and Democratic conservatives are still to be found. Nonetheless, the sweeping changes recorded in party platforms from 1960 to 1980 (and which have remained in the platforms ever since), cannot be dismissed as accidental. They reflect deep-rooted divisions among party activists and affect the attitudes of the general public toward the two parties.

Party Activists

Divisions on social issues were not limited to the platforms. As opposing social movements gained footholds in the parties—feminists, gays and lesbians, civil rights groups in the Democratic party, anti-abortionists and evangelical groups within the Republican party— the positions of party activists diverged quite sharply. The views of delegates to the 1984 conventions give one an idea of the gap that existed. Of Democratic delegates, 90 percent approved of the ERA;

only 28 percent of the Republican delegates indicated approval. Also among Democratic delegates, 67 percent believed prayer should not be allowed in school; only 14 percent of the Republicans agreed with them. Of Republican delegates, 59% percent believed that abortion should never be permitted or should be permitted only when the mother's life is in danger; only 24 percent of the Democratic delegates agreed.[55]

Group Associations: The Public's Perceptions

Public attitudes toward the parties, and the groups associated with them, reflect the shifts in the platforms and among activists. Miller, Wlezien, and Hildreth examine "feeling thermometers" in which respondents were asked to rate various social groups and the parties on a scale from 1 to 100. Table 4.3 shows their findings. In 1972, the Democratic party was most closely associated with poor people, the middle class, Blacks, Catholics, liberals, and labor unions. In 1984, the party remained linked with unions and liberals in the public mind. But several other groups associated with a new breed of Democratic activists, groups not previously associated with the party, moved to the fore: women's liberationists, civil rights leaders, Black militants, and gays and lesbians. The Republican group associations of 1972 remained in 1984. But newly included questions showed that the party had become closely identified with evangelicals/the Moral Majority and anti-abortionists.[56]

Party Divisions and Exit

On the issues identified as of particular importance to the evangelical subculture in chapter 2—the family, traditional conceptions of sexual behavior and of gender roles, abortion, and, to a lesser extent, racial conservatism and promilitary nationalism—the parties had by 1980 taken clearly opposing positions. Twenty years earlier these had not been issues for partisan contention. Either they were not addressed or divisions did not fall along party lines. Racial issues began to take on a partisan hue in the wake of the 1964 election. Support for a strong military began to divide along party lines in the wake of the Vietnam War. The social issues so central to the Christian Right took time to force their way onto the partisan agenda. The platforms of the 1960s had much to say on defense, the economy, crime, and race; discussion of abortion, sex roles, and the family was notable by its absence. In the 1970s these issues crept into platforms and—from election to election—the space devoted to them expanded. Gradually, the parties

Table 4.3
Groups Most Closely Associated with the Parties

	1972	1984
Democrats	Middle class	Black Militants
	Poor people	Liberals
	Blacks	Women's liberation
	Catholics	Civil rights leaders
	Labor unions	Labor unions
	Liberals	Gays and lesbians*
Republicans	Conservatives	Evangelical/Moral Majority
	The military	Big business
	Middle class	Conservatives
	Big business	The military
		Antiabortionists

Source: Arthur H. Miller, Christopher Wlezien, and Anne Hildreth, "A Reference Group Theory of Partisan Coalitions," *The Journal of Politics* 5, no. 4 (1991): 1134–149.

*Not included on the 1972 survey.

assumed bolder and more distinct stances, the Republicans eventually dropped the ERA, and the Democrats came out explicitly for gay and lesbian and reproductive rights. These shifts went beyond mere platform rhetoric; they reflected the attitudes of party activists and the public's perceptions of what the parties represented.

These partisan differences played a critical role in shaping the situation facing the Christian Right as it emerged in the late 1970s. As the movement developed the self-consciousness and organization necessary to become a player in partisan politics, its party choices were becoming more and more seriously constrained. Exit to the Democrats no longer was a plausible option for movement leaders. As social liberalism and the movements that championed it secured their position within the Democratic party, the chance that that party would prove receptive to—or even avoid offending—socially conservative evangelicals grew more and more remote.

Evangelicals might be attracted to the Democrats on *economic* grounds. The evangelical constituency is not particularly well to do; it might well prove receptive to some sort of economic populism. Yet even if evangelicals could be led to the Democrats on these grounds, leading such a defection from the Republicans is not a plausible option for the Christian Right. Such a defection would necessarily involve downplaying the social issues on which the Democrats and evangelicals disagree. But the movement has been built—in its fundraising, its activism, and its leaders' reputations—on the promotion of a social issue agenda. While Republicans might have some reason to fear an economically based defection to the Democrats on the part of evangelicals, they have little reason to fear that the Christian Right would lead such a defection.

Third Party Exit?

As late as 1980, Richard Viguerie would say of the New Right: "We are Republican, Democratic, and Independent. Our first commitment is to political principles, not political parties. We are mostly middle and working class. We wear a blue as well as a white collar. . . . We live and work on Main Street, not Wall Street. We're more at home on the front porch than in the boardroom."[57] This is not exactly a ringing endorsement of the GOP, a party quite often linked to Wall Street and the boardroom. Many early New Right leaders shared Viguerie's sentiments, denouncing the Republicans in terms almost as harsh as those they aimed at the Democrats. If the Democrats were no longer a plausible option, perhaps the Christian Right could join the New Right in a third party effort. Appeals to an evangelical constituency had been issued before in the course of third party campaigns, most notably in 1968 and in 1976.

George Wallace's independent campaign for president in 1968 stressed law and order and race much more than it did the social issues that were eventually to appeal to the Christian Right. Nonetheless, he did particularly well among white evangelicals. Wallace garnered 32 percent of the evangelical vote putting him well ahead of Democrat Hubert Humphrey (22 percent) and of his total among all voters (13.5 percent).[58]

Wallace's case is well known, but less attention has been paid to third party maneuvering that preceded the 1976 election. As that election approached, many conservative activists were extremely unhappy with the record of Republican President Gerald Ford. Particularly offensive in their eyes was Ford's selection of Nelson Rockefeller, the nemesis of the Republican Right, as his vice president. At the same time, the GOP appeared a particularly weak vehicle; crippled by the impact of Watergate, the party was seen by many to be on its last legs. Under these conditions, a number of conservative activists thought the time was ripe for a new party. In the words of William Rusher, this party was to be "a new vehicle for a particular coalition of existing forces, brought together by their common opposition to the liberals who dominated the Democratic party: the economic and *social conservatives* (emphasis mine)."[59] Rusher and other party organizers felt the Republican party was unwilling—or unable—to reach out to social conservatives. A new party that did so, it was hoped, could tap into a large new pool of conservative voters, in particular the supporters of George Wallace.

Besides Rusher (an editor of *National Review* and a leader of the 1964 Draft Goldwater movement), consideration of a third party effort drew in many prominent figures on the Right, including Phyllis Schlafly, Congressmen John Ashbrook and Robert Bauman, and Senator Jesse Helms.[60] Nonetheless, the effort did not get far. The key to the organizers' strategy was to convince Ronald Reagan to be the new party's standard-bearer. When Reagan decided instead to challenge President Ford for the Republican nomination, the plan lost much of its steam. Rusher, along with New Right leaders Richard Viguerie and Howard Phillips, persisted. Their plan was to utilize the American Independent party (a remnant from George Wallace's 1968 campaign) as their vehicle. They worked to get the party onto the ballot in various states and searched for a candidate. Even after he failed to get the GOP nomination, Ronald Reagan refused to run as the candidate of the new independent party. Other leading conservatives proved unwilling as well. In the end, the third party organizers put forward the relatively unknown Robert Morris (president of the University of Dallas) with Richard Viguerie as his proposed running mate. Even this effort failed. The organizers lacked the strength to control the American Independent party convention; old Wallace activists rejected their candidates and nominated instead the racist ex-governor of Georgia, Lester Maddox. No match for another Georgian governor, Maddox received a mere two-tenths of 1 percent of the vote.[61]

American politics is notoriously hard on third parties. The reasons are well known. Plurality based winner-take-all electoral systems provide little reward to minor party efforts that fall short of outright victory. In many parliamentary systems of government, the millions of votes received by third party candidates George Wallace (1968) and Ross Perot (1992) would have entitled their followers to a sizable bloc of seats in the national legislature. In the American system, Wallace's 13.5 percent and Perot's 19 percent of the vote got them nothing.

Seeing such results, some citizens are loath to "waste" their votes and thereby undermine the fortunes of the major party candidate to whom they feel closer. Beyond such strategic considerations is the sheer force of tradition. The Republicans and Democrats have defined American politics for so long that alternatives have a hard time gaining credibility.

Another critical difficulty for minor parties is the permeable nature of the *major* parties. The party changes described in chapter 3 have only increased that permeability by undermining the gatekeeper functions of party leaders. Anyone can declare themselves a Democrat or Republican, run in primaries or caucuses, and attempt to gain a major party nomination. As David Duke has recently demonstrated, parties have few means by which to rid themselves of unwelcome intruders. Both before and after 1968, George Wallace decided that his cause could better be pursued by running as a candidate for the Democrat party nomination. The third party efforts of William Rusher and friends were undermined, in large part, by the refusal of their favored candidate—Ronald Reagan—to forsake the Republican route to the presidency. Despite his setback in 1976, it is hard to argue that Reagan made an unwise choice.

Given a long history of failure, and the inherent difficulties of third party efforts in the United States, Christian Right leaders are likely to find this exit option unpalatable. Threatened exit to a third party may provide leverage in dealings with the Republicans, but the threat would be a very expensive one to carry through on. For little prospect of third party success, movement leaders would sacrifice their hard-earned ties to the party. There is no guarantee that leaders could convince their constituency to follow them off well-worn major party paths. Given the high value Republican party culture places on loyal party service, defection to a third party—or even threatened defection—is likely to do serious and long-lasting damage to one's position within the party. Members of Christian Right organizations such as Christian Coalition have worked hard to get themselves accepted as "true" Republicans, threats to defect undermine their ongoing efforts to bolster their credibility. (See chapter 6 for further discussion of this issue.)[62]

Republican Pull

Given the unpromising nature of Democratic and third party options, the Christian Right was naturally "pushed" toward an alliance with the Republicans. More than "push" was involved, however. As the

Christian Right emerged onto the national political scene, the Republican party was making active efforts to court it. The party, as discussed earlier, was producing platforms that gave more and more prominence to the social issues dear to the heart of conservative evangelicals. Furthermore, the Republican National Committee and GOP standard-bearer Ronald Reagan were actively wooing evangelical leaders; New Right operatives were not the only political figures circulating among evangelical elites.

In late 1979, Republican National Committee chairman Bill Brock invited over twenty evangelical leaders to RNC headquarters. In a meeting that lasted more than three hours, Brock and other top party officials invited the leaders to state their concerns and asked how the party could be more sensitive to them. Over the years, many similar meetings have taken place with the RNC as well as with the Senate and House Republican Committees.[63] In 1988, describing the approach to his organization taken by the two major parties, Robert Dugan, political director of the National Association of Evangelicals (NAE) stated:

> The NAE has been sought, wooed, approached by the Republican National Committee and by all of the Republican presidential candidates continuously, over more than recent months, going back a long time. On the other hand, The DNC has not approached us at all, nor has any other Democratic presidential candidate sought contact of any sort, at least with us the NAE, with an eye towards understanding the evangelical community perhaps sifting out a few votes here or there. And that goes back a long time. By the way, it is not that we haven't tried. Over the years, for example, before the details were known, we sought year after year to get Senator Gary Hart to speak to our federal seminar of college students and got terrible treatment from his staff which showed zero interest in making a connection with the evangelical community.[64]

In my interview with him, Dugan stressed his continued frustration in his attempts to gain a hearing from the Democrats.[65] Although the NAE has leaned toward the Republicans, particularly in the last few years, it has been more moderate than most of the organizations of the Christian Right; Democratic attention thus was not completely implausible.

As Dugan argues, Republican presidential candidates, as well as party officials, have played a critical role in the courting of the Christian Right. The key figure in this regard was Ronald Reagan. In 1976, Reagan was the man New Right leaders had tried to enlist as the standard-bearer of their contemplated third party effort. Reagan chose to remain in the GOP, to try for its presidential nomination. He came extremely close to defeating President Gerald Ford. In the process, Reagan solidified his position as the champion of the party's right wing. At the convention, his forces helped engineer an anti-abortion plank and very nearly managed to overturn the GOP's long-standing commitment to the Equal Rights Amendment. Reagan was therefore well placed to pick up the support of the Christian Right in 1980. Although some New Right and Christian Right leaders showed an early interest in other candidates, most notably Illinois congressman Philip Crane and former Texas governor John Connally, Reagan was quite acceptable to them, and they enthusiastically jumped on the Reagan bandwagon.

The most dramatic symbol of Reagan's effort to reach out to the Religious Right came in August of 1980. Candidate Reagan attended a "national affairs briefing" sponsored by Ed McAteer's Religious Roundtable. Before a crowd of more than 10,000 conservative Christians, Reagan sounded themes straight out of the Christian Right's own hymn book. He expressed doubts concerning the theory of evolution, denounced "moral neutrality" on the part of government, and traced problems from crime to drug abuse back to a lack of moral teaching in the schools.[66] Making his sympathies clear, Reagan declared: "I know you can't support me, but I want you to know that I endorse you and what you are doing." Jerry Falwell, in keeping with the supposedly nonpartisan nature of the event, told delegates to vote for the "Reagan of their choice."[67] The meeting, coming in the midst of the presidential campaign, generated tremendous media coverage, helping gain national exposure for the fledgling Christian Right movement and for its leaders.

Republican Victory—The Right's Contribution

The 1980 general election produced a stunning victory for Ronald Reagan and for the Republican party in Congress. The New Right and Christian Right had played highly visible roles in that success. McAteer's Religious Roundtable rallied ministers around the country to Reagan's cause. The Roundtable and Moral Majority conducted registration drives. Christian Voice—an organization headed by the Reverend Robert Grant and, in its early years, publicized by Pat Robertson—widely distributed its moral "report cards" rating the voting records of members of Congress. An offshoot of Christian Voice ran anti-Carter ads and sent pro-Reagan materials to ministers around the country.[68] The NCPAC (National Conservative Political Action Committee) ran campaigns against a number of liberal senators. Most of these senators lost, including such well-known figures as Frank Church, Birch Bayh, and George McGovern. The Democrats lost control of the Senate for the first time in decades; talk of realignment filled the air. The New Right and Christian Right rushed to take credit; much of the media played along, giving them an incredible run of publicity. Liberal groups joined in, warning that the radical right was poised to sweep all before it.

Later analysis tended to discount the role played by the New Right and Christian Right in the Republican victories of 1980. The year 1980 was a bad one for Democrats whether or not they were targeted by the Christian Right. Far more important than the efforts of conservative groups was the state of the economy. In 1980 personal income dropped significantly, its worst showing since 1932. In the candidates' debate Ronald Reagan asked voters if they were better off than they were four years ago. The answer was a resounding no and Jimmy Carter—like Herbert Hoover in 1932—was voted decisively out of office, taking many of his fellow party members with him. In 1982, with the economy performing poorly under a Republican president, the Republicans suffered and so too did the success rates of conservative groups. NCPAC targeted nineteen House and twelve Senate races; in each branch only one of their favored candidates was victorious. Negative publicity surrounding NCPAC efforts may actually have helped some of the candidates it opposed. Christian Voice was active in the election but in 1982 was unwilling to admit how many races it had targeted.[69]

In the early 1980s, the Christian Right was establishing itself as a visible—and controversial—presence on the American political scene. It had publicly linked itself to the successful wing of a successful party. However, although its ties to the party were well publicized, its effectiveness on behalf of that party was unclear. Mobilizing evangelical supporters to the Republican cause and conducting registration and voter education drives could no doubt be useful. But publicity surrounding ties to the controversial movement might also prove counterproductive for Republican candidates.

The movement's ability to swing an evangelical constituency to the Republican cause had not been clearly established either. In 1980, Jimmy Carter's support among conservative Protestants fell well below its 1976 level. Lopatto finds that he received 40 percent of their vote as compared to Reagan's 56 percent and John Anderson's 4 percent. (Carter received 50 percent in 1976.) But the swing to the Republicans among conservative Protestants was not unusual; it roughly matched the swing that took place among other groups.[70] Furthermore, the fall was from unusually strong evangelical support for the Democrats in 1976. Conservative Protestant support for the Democratic nominee remained well above the levels of 1968 and 1972.

To the Victor Go the Spoils:
But Are They Enough?

In the Reagan administration's first term in office, the movements that had backed it so prominently were rewarded in a number of ways. Reagan spoke out strongly against abortion and even wrote a book condemning it while in office. Although the administration lacked the votes in Congress (or the Supreme Court) to reverse *Roe v. Wade*, the administration was able to win some further restrictions on federal funding. The Legal Services Administration was prevented from taking legal action to "promote, defend, or protect homosexuality."[71] The White House pushed a school prayer amendment that received the votes of a majority of the Senate (although short of the two-thirds needed to amend the Constitution). The White House and the Christian Right were more successful on an "equal access" bill, reversing court decisions that had restricted the ability of religious groups to operate within the public schools. Even in areas where the movement lost, as with school prayer and abortion, it managed to place issues on the legislative agenda that had received far less attention in previous years.[72]

The movement's rewards went beyond assistance in legislative battles. Movement figures were appointed to positions in the Reagan administration. The New Right's Morton Blackwell was appointed a special assistant to the president for public liaison. Robert Billings, after leaving the Moral Majority to join the Reagan campaign effort, was rewarded with a post in the Department of Education. In a case of great concern to the Christian Right, the Reagan Justice Department backed fundamentalist Bob Jones University in its suit against the IRS (the IRS was attempting to revoke the school's tax-exempt status due to its racially discriminatory practices). Under intense public pressure the Justice Department was forced to back off—a bit—from its original position. In the end, the Supreme Court ruled eight to one against Bob Jones and the administration.[73] Symbolic acts on the part of the administration were designed to reach out to evangelicals as well. Reagan promoted 1983 as "the year of the Bible" and appeared at National Religious Broadcasters conventions.

Relations between the movement and the administration were not perfect, however. The nomination of Sandra Day O'Connor, thought to be "soft" on abortion, was a source of contention. Jerry Falwell and the Moral Majority lobbied hard against her confirmation but their efforts met with little response. While the administration sided with the Christian Right on key social issues, many felt that these issues were not receiving the priority treatment they deserved. Reagan, they argued, was paying lip service to these issues and expending his political capital in other areas, particularly on behalf of his economic agenda. Furthermore, while movement figures had gotten some low-level appointments, Reagan had also reached out to moderate elements of the party in his choice of running mate George Bush and in his selection of top advisors such as James Baker.

The Christian and the New Right responded much differently to this uneven measure of success. Many New Right figures were very critical of the administration. Unhappy with the appointment of moderates, the failure to move fast enough on social issues, and the continued upper class, high finance oriented bent of the Reagan administration, New Right leaders complained vehemently. Published in 1983, Richard Viguerie's *Establishment vs. the People* denounced Ronald Reagan as a backslider declaring, "Alas, like Jimmy Carter, the man he defeated and replaced, Ronald Reagan has turned his back on the populist cause."[74] Viguerie promoted a third party option as an alternative to the Democratic and Republican party "establishments."

Christian Right leaders, the televangelists in particular, were much more hesitant to criticize the president or to talk of exiting the party. When the "Statement of Conservative Leaders" highly critical of the administration was issued in January of 1982, the big names of the New Right could all be found at the end; those of the televangelists were conspicuous by their absence.[75]

Some of these differences may be traced back to questions of style, temperament, or personality, but more than that was involved in the divergent approaches of the two sides. Newer to politics, Christian Right leaders were perhaps more impressed by the symbolic gestures the administration made toward them. After complaining about Jerry Falwell's excessive loyalty to the GOP, Paul Weyrich went on to say: "Most leaders of the religious right behaved the same way as Falwell. They were so happy, after years of isolation, to get invited to state dinners at the White House that many forgot what moved them to get involved in politics in the first place."[76]

Yet one can also interpret the phenomenon Weyrich describes in a somewhat different manner. After "years of isolation," recognition for evangelical leaders and the subculture they represented was an important goal in and of itself. To affirm that evangelicals were no longer a fringe group but had instead been accepted into the halls of power was no small feat. And, of course, photo opportunities with the president were very useful for bolstering the image and credibility of televangelists among their audiences. The audiences were important for a second reason; they were enthusiastic about Reagan. Unlike the New Right leaders, the televangelists had a real constituency whose reactions had to be taken into account. Convincing their audiences that Ronald Reagan had sold out to the conservative cause would not have been easy.[77]

1984: Evangelical Mobilization and Realignment

As the 1984 election approached, the Christian Right rallied enthusiastically behind the president. The American Coalition for Traditional Values (ACTV) was formed as a vehicle to mobilize evangelicals on Reagan's behalf. The main funding came by way of a million dollar grant from a project headed by Republican fundraiser Joe Rodgers. Headed by the Reverend Tim LaHaye, ACTV organization was drawn heavily from the ranks of Christian Voice and the Moral Majority. A network consisting of 350 field directors worked to organize voter registration drives through local churches. While the organization's tax status officially required it to refrain from endorsing candidates, the organization's materials left no doubt where it stood. Among other things, these materials included a "leadership manual" with an introduction by Ronald Reagan. The ACTV's recruiting efforts brought in a quite sizable bloc of voters. Exactly how many is a matter of some dispute; estimates of the number registered vary from a low of 200,000 to a high of three million. The Christian Right's efforts on behalf of the party were rewarded at the 1984 convention. As in 1980, conservative evangelicals obtained a platform very much to their liking. Furthermore, the movement was given prominent billing in the ceremonies themselves. The 1984 convention opened and closed with prayers led by prominent Christian Right figures, the Reverends James Robison and Jerry Falwell, respectively.[78]

The efforts of ACTV and the GOP's courting of evangelicals appeared to pay off in the 1984 election. Reagan garnered an extremely impressive 80 percent of the white evangelical vote.[79] The increase in Reagan support from 1980 to 1984 among this group was well above the national average. Of particular importance were trends in partisanship. Not only were evangelicals voting for the Republican standard-bearer—a trend that could be seen as far back as 1968—they were now coming to *identify* themselves as Republicans. Since 1960, white evangelicals had identified primarily as Democrats, their votes for Republican presidential candidates notwithstanding. In 1980, the Democrats retained a 52 percent to 35 percent edge among this group. But 1984 marked a dramatic reversal; by a 47 percent to 41 percent margin, white evangelicals identified as Republicans. Furthermore, the shift in allegiance was most pronounced among evangelicals who were regular churchgoers, suggesting that the shifts were related to specifically religious cues or to educational and mobilizational efforts undertaken through the churches.[80] The evangelical clergy was shifting even more dramatically than the evangelical public. A survey of Southern Baptist ministers in 1980 found them to identify as Democrats by a 41 percent to 29 percent margin; in 1984, 66 percent identified themselves as Republicans, a mere 26 percent were Democrats.[81]

Shifts in evangelical partisanship, and shifts of such a dramatic nature among the clergy, suggest something beyond the previously common defections at the level of presidential voting. Among one segment of the public, at least, the realignment to the Republicans—searched for but not found in 1980—was now taking place. That the evangelical shift to the Republicans took place *after* the dramatic election of 1980 should not be surprising. In 1980 the Democratic ticket retained the pull of the openly evangelical Jimmy Carter; in 1984 Walter Mondale held no such attraction to evangelicals. Furthermore, newly developed distinctions between the parties are likely to take time to impress themselves on the mind of the general public.[82]

Party differences on issues of concern to an evangelical constituency, as shown earlier in the chapter, emerged slowly and haltingly over a period of decades. To communicate them to the evangelical constituency would require clear stands on the part of party leaders (like Ronald Reagan), cues from community opinion leaders (like the shifting Southern Baptist clergy), and the dissemination of pro-Republican themes in the subcultural media (among the televangelists, Christian radio networks, and evangelical publishing houses). Time lags in group response are most likely to occur in the case of *partisanship*. While evangelicals might quickly conclude that a George McGovern was not for them, for this perception to extend itself to the Democratic party as a whole—and for evangelical individuals to shift deep-seated attachments of partisan identification—was likely to take much longer.

The evangelical shift to the Republicans that occurred in 1984 appears to have been a durable one. From 1982 to 1986, a significant increase in white evangelical support for Republican congressional candidates was also recorded.[83] George Bush—a candidate much less close to evangelicals than Ronald Reagan—managed to garner somewhere between 70 and 80 percent of the white evangelical vote in 1988 and over 60 percent in the three-way race of 1992.[84] The shift to Republican identification continued through 1988. Reviewing National Election Survey data from 1980, 1984, and 1988, Smidt and Kellstedt conclude:

> The shift toward increased Republican identifications within the ranks of evangelicals which transpired during the first term of the Reagan administration continued to be evident during the first presidential election of the post-Reagan era. Thus, the realignment which took place among evangelicals during the early 1980's seems to have solidified. Moreover, this shift appears to have been most evident among younger evangelicals, and, as a result, its effects are likely to be felt for elections to come.[85]

Party Bound

By the mid-1980s, the white evangelical constituency had followed the earlier migration of Christian Right leaders into the Republican fold. Exit to the Democrats or to a Christian Right third party was declining in likelihood. This did not mean that Republicans could entirely discount the risk of evangelical or Christian Right exit. A sharp enough shift in party policies could produce another evangelical realignment. But, assuming some basic gestures were made to this constituency, the threat of exit would not appear to be a powerful one. What, then, could the Christian Right do to make the party take notice of its concerns?

One form of exit, not yet discussed, is plausible under contemporary conditions. That form is exit by withdrawal. Rather than bolting to opposing parties, evangelical activists and voters could simply stay home. Given the useful service provided by organizations such as ACTV and the overwhelming Republican vote among white evangelicals, by the mid-1980s withdrawal was a significant threat. There is some reason to believe that the party suffered from such a withdrawal in 1986. Tim LaHaye, who had headed the ACTV effort in 1984, wanted to launch a similar effort in 1986. The support that had come from Republican party fundraising sources in 1984 was not forthcoming in 1986 and no such effort was launched.[86] The Republican party lost eight Senate seats, many of the losses coming by extremely small margins. Significantly, while white evangelicals voted even more Republican than they had in 1988, their turnout was particularly low. An ABC-Washington Post poll found that white evangelicals made up only 12 percent of the voting public, down from 17 percent in 1984. A. James Reichley concludes that "the decline in voting among evangelicals by itself was probably enough to account for Republican setbacks in the South and possibly in some farm states of the Midwest."[87] Whether an ACTV-style effort would have been enough to bolster evangelical turnout and save Republican seats in the Senate is difficult to determine but the 1986 results indicate that withdrawal—by activists and by evangelical voters—had the potential to do serious damage to the party's fortunes.

Why had the Republicans refused to fund another ACTV? Tim La-Haye says: "They refused because they were afraid of these evangelical Christians who, in some communities, were working to take over the Republican apparatus—which we had nothing to do with. But it was that fear, I think, that caused them to turn down my request."[88] The fear on the part of Republican leaders reflected an important phenomena. By the mid-1980s, Christian Right influence was not entirely reliant upon the utilization of the exit option. The movement was determined to exercise a voice within the party. We now turn to an examination of those attempts at voice.

Chapter 5

Pat Crashes the Party

The trick for the Republicans is to get the support of evangelicals and the Religious Right without being identified with it.

—A. James Reichley

The attitude of most professional politicians toward the evangelical community is: One, they don't understand us. Two, they can't control us. Three, they are not really sure they like us. But four, they *do* want our vote.

—Tim LaHaye

By the mid-1980s, the Christian Right was determined to contribute more than its votes. Whether the Republican establishment was comfortable with this prospect or not, the Christian Right wanted a voice within the party. Party leaders would now have to worry about more than the potential *exit* of Christian conservatives; they would have to deal with them face to face. Republican politicians found themselves challenged in primaries; state parties had to deal with an influx of movement activists. Finally, there was the most visible sign that the Christian Right was no longer content to be a party auxiliary: the 1988 presidential campaign of Marion G. (Pat) Robertson.

Robertson failed, but his campaign is worthy of our extended attention here for two reasons. First, Robertson's specific experiences provide a window onto more general problems the Christian Right encounters as it attempts to exercise its voice within the GOP. Second, although Robertson failed to win the nomination, his campaign had a far-reaching impact on the Christian Right. It mobilized a new, charismatic wave of activists to supplement the largely fundamentalist base of the movement's early years. It helped Robertson supplant Jerry Falwell as the Christian Right's most visible spokesman. It played a key role in the transformation of the Christian Right from a Washington-oriented to a truly grassroots movement.[1] Finally, Robertson's campaign laid the foundation for what has become the Christian Right's most powerful organization, the Christian Coalition.

Robertson's campaign faced three difficult challenges. First, Robertson had to mobilize and unite his base constituency. While it was often assumed that evangelicals and Christian Right leaders would rally to his cause, such assumptions ignored serious divisions that Robertson would have to overcome to win their support. Second, Robertson had to augment the support of his base constituency by obtaining the maximum possible benefit from the organizational resources available to him. For his long shot candidacy to succeed, Robertson would need to skillfully utilize the audience, funding sources, and networks of volunteers that his background gave him access to. Finally, Robertson had to reach out, to attract a measure of support from beyond his evangelical and Christian Right base. Given the general public's suspicions of the evangelical subculture—and of televangelists in particular—this would not be an easy task.

These three challenges—uniting an evangelical base, making the most of organizational resources, and reaching out to build alliances beyond a base constituency—were not unique to the Robertson campaign. In one form or another, they have to be dealt with in all Christian Right endeavors. This chapter is organized around Robertson's response to these challenges, but it illustrates problems faced by the movement as a whole.

The Campaign's Beginning and Its Strategy

American presidential campaigns begin long before the official announcement of candidacy. Pat Robertson's campaign was no exception. According to Robertson, the idea of a presidential bid arose in late 1984. Robertson claims to have resisted a number of suggestions from friends to run for political office. But late in 1984, he prayed about the idea and felt that the Lord was telling him to run:

> As I set aside several days for earnest prayer, I was startled when an impression came into my mind: *You will not want to do this,* [run for president] but *you should do this.*
>
> I didn't really want to accept that. It was easy to rationalize that that suggestion had come through some quirky mental process, through some power of suggestion. But it came back again and again over several weeks.
>
> As I prayed, I went from "This can't be right, Lord" to "Please don't let me be mislead about this." I knew the still voice of the Lord. It

persisted and deepened. Over and over, *You won't want to do this, but . . . .* (Emphasis Robertson's)[2]

Robertson here plays the standard role of the reluctant candidate, lacking personal ambition, who must be drafted to stand for political leadership. The drafting party, however, is anything but standard.

The divine inspiration of Robertson's candidacy was not emphasized in the campaign for obvious reasons. While many of Robertson's core supporters felt their efforts had supernatural backing, this was not a feeling to be broadcast to the general public. Robertson hinted at his divine communications to church audiences; when word of this leaked out it caused a good bit of negative publicity.[3]

While divine communications were kept quiet, there were more public signs of an impending Robertson candidacy by 1985. In March of that year, the *Saturday Evening Post* published a highly laudatory profile of Robertson and speculated on the possibility of a presidential bid. *Conservative Digest* followed suit in August, featuring supportive comments from a wide array of religious and conservative leaders, including extended praise from Paul Weyrich and Richard Viguerie. By the second half of 1985, Robertson was a key figure in speculation concerning the 1988 Republican nomination contest.[4] The campaign had begun, but what was its strategy? How did an evangelist with no political experience expect to make his way to the White House?

Campaign 1988—The Message

Robertson's rhetorical appeals had to strike a fine balance, motivating his core constituency without scaring off outsiders. As mentioned in chapters 1 and 2, appeals that are effective within the evangelical subculture often lack credibility in public realms such as that of politics. In the face of followers motivated by religious concerns and a general public extremely suspicious of his religious background, that balance would not be an easy one to strike. One solution was to run an essentially schizophrenic campaign, with one set of messages broadcast inward and another broadcast outward. To some extent this is what Robertson attempted. His addresses to religious audiences were often quite different than those meant for secular listeners. Unfortunately for the Robertson campaign, the base constituency and the outside world could not be so neatly segregated. Robertson's opponents and the press took an interest in exposing conflicts between messages aimed inward and those aimed outward.[5] When messages aimed primarily at religious audiences found their way to public attention, they often caused Robertson a good deal of embarrassment. Thus he was forced to develop a message with a more general appeal, one that could play to both sets of audiences.

The promotional video distributed by the Robertson campaign provides, perhaps, the best example of that more general appeal. Used to bolster Robertson's image, to recruit and motivate volunteers throughout the nation, the video bore the title *Pat Robertson: Who Is This Man?*.[6] Examining the answer provided by the Robertson campaign in this video is instructive, as much for what is omitted as for what is included.

Who is Pat Robertson? While the video clearly aims to deflect charges that a religious background makes one ineligible for the nation's highest office, Pat Robertson's own religious background is never specifically raised. No mention is made of Robertson's decades at the Christian Broadcasting Network (CBN). Instead, he is presented as the originator of relief and literacy programs, an outsider who knows how to clean up the mess in Washington and get things done.

As with most presidential campaigns, patriotic themes are prominent. The video opens with shots of the Statue of Liberty, flags wave, love of country is professed. But the form of this patriotic appeal reflects the campaign's religious roots. American evangelicals, as we saw in chapters 1 and 2, are torn between a vision of America as a uniquely "Christian" nation and a vision of themselves as a persecuted minority in a decadent land. The Robertson video reflects these divisions. The problem, the video says, is that the American reality that once reflected the first vision, now reflects the second. The goal of the Robertson campaign is presented as returning the nation to its Christian roots. Speaking on Robertson's behalf, actor Dean Jones declares:

> We seem to be on the brink of tossing away the last vestiges of those foundational truths, those foundational spiritual convictions, on which all of the other things that made America great are built. And we have a historic opportunity in this election to bring a man to the White House who can restate and resensitize the nation to those basic truths.[7]

The video's discussion of domestic issues focuses on the family and "traditional morality." What for other candidates would be questions of economics or social planning—the deficit, welfare, drugs, and ineffective schools—are, for Robertson, questions of morality, character, and faith. The solution to these problems thus lies in moral revival and, at least in the case of schools, in prayer. To foster moral regeneration, Robertson calls for a return of powers to families and localities. When calling for change in welfare, childcare, and education programs, Robertson advocates less federal involvement and greater emphasis on family-based solutions.

Finally, the video emphasizes Robertson's conservatism. The candidate declares: "I am a conservative and I'm going to run like a conservative and I have no intention of taking some liberal as vicepresident to balance the ticket." His anticommunist credentials are stressed. Very early in the video we see Robertson in Honduras, listening to peasants telling stories of purported Sandinista atrocities. He visits with, and offers support to, contra soldiers. Then we see a Robertson speech in which he calls for the roll back of communism, denounces the treachery and deceit of the Communist party, claims "we have stood by as millions became slaves to a new Russian Empire," and decries the actions of bankers and industrialists who "prop up communist dictatorships." Later in the video, Robertson defends Oliver North and warns of Soviet threats to Middle East oil and African minerals.[8]

Strategy

The video *Pat Robertson: Who Is This Man?* is not a perfect representation of the campaign's appeals. These varied over time and according to the particular audience being addressed. Nonetheless, this video, designed for national distribution to varied audiences, is consistent with the general themes of the campaign and illustrates the strategic dilemmas it faced.[9] What strategies do the video's themes reveal?

First, the video reveals a definite defensiveness concerning Robertson's religious background. The campaign was well aware that the public was uneasy with the prospect of an openly religious candidacy, an uneasiness that would have to be overcome for Robertson to succeed. Thus Robertson's years at the Christian Broadcasting Network and specific doctrinal bases for his political positions were deemphasized. At the same time, the case was made that the "foundational truths" of the nation have been based in the spiritual convictions of its people and its leaders. Stressing the religious convictions of former American leaders, the campaign hoped to make Robertson's religious ties less threatening.[10] Throughout the campaign, Robertson attempted to turn the tables on his critics. When they argued that he was violating the traditional separation of church and state and promoting religious intolerance, he would reply that it was the exclusion of religion from political life that was a novel development and that intolerance was being shown against the religious. In the later stages of the campaign, Robertson often complained that his opponents were engaged in discriminatory "Christian bashing."

Second, the evocation of America's religious heritage, the framing of domestic issues in moral terms, the emphasis on the importance of the family and the threats it faced, all worked to mobilize the Christian Right base.[11] These themes were familiar to anyone who watched leading televangelists, listened to "Christian" radio stations, or frequented "Christian" bookstores. They fit well with the movement's emphasis on the secular humanist threat to America's Christian heritage, families, and values; they provided a rallying cry to those who felt their religious subculture to be under attack.

Third, while a case is made that America must return to its moral and religious roots, this case is made in very general terms. Reference is made to our "Judeo-Christian heritage," rather than to doctrines specifically evangelical or, in Robertson's case, charismatic. This serves as a rather vague nostalgic appeal to lost American values and greatness. It might also function to unite a wide variety of cultural conservatives who believe in "traditional moral values" but not necessarily in the theological underpinnings often used to justify those values. By framing the campaign's moral appeal in a general and somewhat vague way, Robertson held open the possibility that he could attract followers beyond a Christian Right base.

Fourth, the Robertson campaign was putting forth the traditional rallying cries of the Republican Right. Stressing uncompromising conservatism, decrying the failure of national leaders to stand up to the communist menace, and voicing suspicion of banking and business elites, the Robertson campaign hoped to position itself as the Right's alternative to the more moderate, establishment-oriented brand of Republicanism embodied by George Bush and Robert Dole. (Jack Kemp provided Robertson's main competition for the title of right-wing champion.) The Robertson campaign hoped to put itself forward as the true heir of the ideological movement that had brought Ronald Reagan to power. If movement conservatives could be added to a newly mobilized Christian Right base, Robertson might have the makings of a powerful bloc of support within the party.

In summary, Robertson's message was calculated to redefine the political significance of his religious background, mobilize a Christian Right base in a manner consistent with a more general appeal, and add to that base the support of the Republican Right. The message was well designed but Robertson needed more than a message: he needed an electoral plan.

Electoral Tactics

Going into the campaign, Robertson faced a situation common to Christian Right organizations. His organizational strength was formidable, but his general popularity was limited. At least a portion of the evangelical constituency was strongly committed to him. He had at his disposal more money and well-organized volunteers than did most of his rivals. Robertson's weakness lay in the very negative feelings he evoked in the general public. Thus, his campaign devised a strategy that attempted to take maximum advantage of his organizational strengths while trying to reassure an anxious public. As described by Robertson's campaign manager, R. Marc Nuttle, the strategy involved a three-pronged attack.[12]

First, the campaign focused on caucus states. Roughly a quarter of the delegates to the 1988 GOP convention were chosen in "caucuses" of party members rather than in primary elections. As participation in the caucus process requires a much higher level of commitment than the simple act of voting in a primary, turnout tends to be very low. Discovering when and where local caucus meetings are to occur, taking the initiative to go there, staying for an extended period, and making a public stand in an often conflictual process, all were requirements that weeded out the fainthearted. If Robertson's supporters had the strength of commitment to overcome these obstacles and the organization to help shepherd them through the process, they could prevail over a more numerous but less committed and well-organized opposition. For Robertson to be competitive, he would have to capture a major share of the five hundred-plus delegates chosen in caucus states.

Second, the campaign targeted primary states where delegates were chosen winner-take-all by congressional district (as opposed to proportional or state level winner-take-all systems). If Robertson could focus on and win a plurality in one of these districts, he would capture *all* of its delegates. Given a large field of competitors, a plurality could be obtained with well under 50 percent of the votes. Particularly promising from the Robertson campaign's point of view were districts in which the GOP was traditionally weak. Where there was little in the way of established party structure or base of support for mainstream Republican candidates, Robertson hoped to use his organization and unorthodox (at least for a Republican) base of support to

propel him to victory. Prominent among the districts targeted were
those of the rural South. Strongholds of evangelical denominations,
traditionally Democratic but morally conservative, these districts represented prime opportunities for Robertson.

Third, Robertson had to contest at least a portion of primaries that
did not operate on a winner-take-all by district basis. Even if Robertson won every single delegate in states operating under the first two
systems discussed (an extremely unlikely prospect), he would still be
just short of the majority needed for the nomination. Thus, Robertson
would have to target a number of key primary states in order to gain
the delegates needed for victory. However, success in the first two
categories of states could keep the campaign's requirements in these
states to a minimum.

In addition to attempts to win delegates by doing well in selected
primaries, Robertson's forces might be able to use their organizational prowess to gain delegates even where they lost. In many primary states, the actual delegates who went on to the national convention in New Orleans were selected in caucuses or state conventions.
These delegates were bound by primary results in their first-round
voting but—should the voting at the national convention go beyond a
single ballot—these delegates were free to vote their preferences in
later rounds. In addition to supporting Robertson (or a Robertson ally)
in a multiballot nomination battle, these delegates would be free to
support Robertson positions in votes on the platform or in conflicts
over convention rules.

Campaign manager Nuttle's three-part plan, augmented by the delegate acquisition strategy described in the preceding paragraph, was
designed to make maximal use of organizational resources and an
enthusiastic core of supporters while placing as little dependence as
possible on the general popularity necessary to win primaries. Nonetheless, as acknowledged in the plan itself, Robertson could not rely
entirely on enthusiasm and organization. Two additional factors were
critical if Robertson was to succeed. First, his potential constituency
included groups not usually active in the Republican nominating process. If these groups could be brought into the process on Robertson's
behalf, they could give him a crucial leg up on the competition. Second, public doubts might be overcome through early success. The
momentum generated by early wins could go a long way toward establishing Robertson as a credible candidate in later contests.

Robertson's strategy relied on attracting two groups that did not
usually participate in the Republican nominating process: Democrats
and African Americans. The voting patterns and partisanship of

evangelicals, as we saw in chapter 4, have been shifting in favor of the Republicans in recent decades; nonetheless, there remain a great many socially conservative evangelical Democrats, particularly in the South. Electoral laws played a key role in determining whether their potential support could be utilized by the Robertson campaign. Some states made it much easier than others for Democrats to participate. Whether one had to switch to the Republican party to take part in the nominating process and, if such a switch was necessary, the ease with which one could switch, varied greatly from state to state. As the campaign progressed, reporters began to look for signs of large scale reregistrations as a means of gauging the potential of Robertson's "invisible army."[13]

Robertson's campaign believed that, unlike the other Republican contenders, it had the potential to attract a significant African-American following. What lay behind this belief? First, there was his background at CBN. Surveys have shown that religious television attracts a disproportionately large African-American audience; and the CBN audience had for the previous decade seen Robertson cohost the "700 Club" with African-American ex-marine Ben Kinchlow.[14] Second, there were similarities between Robertson's beliefs and those of many religious African Americans. Predominantly Baptist and Methodist, African-American churches are often quite conservative in their theology. Third, African Americans, liberal on most other issues, are somewhat more conservative than the general public on the "moral" issues— abortion, gay rights, school prayer, and so on—that formed the basis of Robertson's campaign.[15] Robertson's goal was thus to convert his African-American viewers into political supporters, utilizing ties to their churches and appeals based on moral issues.

This effort to woo African-American voters would not be easy. The vast majority of African Americans are Democrats. These voters would have to be convinced to change parties on Robertson's behalf, a particularly difficult choice when Jesse Jackson was competing on the Democratic side. Furthermore, they would have to be convinced to ignore their liberal positions on nonmoral issues and to ally themselves with conservative whites whose record of support for civil rights was generally poor. Robertson's background included not only his partnership with Ben Kinchlow, but it also included the often-invoked political heritage of his father, Senator A. Willis Robertson, a staunch opponent of desegregation and a signer of the infamous Southern Manifesto of 1956. Pat Robertson, like most Christian Right figures, supported South Africa's white government prior to its fall, criticized the African National Congress, and opposed several major civil rights measures.[16]

Since Jimmy Carter's surprise nomination victory of 1976, it has been a commonplace of campaign wisdom that early success and the momentum it provides are critical to victory. Early success provides publicity and, often, a critical influx of money and volunteers. Unlike many candidates, Robertson was not dependent on early victory to provide him with money or volunteers. However, he was dependent on early successes for another reason. Much of the public did not perceive Robertson to be a viable or credible candidate—and the simplest way to establish viability and credibility was to win. Thus, his staff banked on a set of early victories to alter public perceptions of their candidate and convince voters that a vote for Robertson was not a wasted one. The nominating schedule appeared favorable, with a disproportionate number of caucuses scheduled in the early going. (Michigan and Iowa loomed particularly large in the Robertson strategy.) Early caucus victories could establish Robertson as a serious candidate prior to the all-important "Super Tuesday" primaries and caucuses scheduled for 8 March. From success there, perhaps he would be catapulted to the nomination.

Having summarized Robertson's message and electoral strategy, we should now examine his attempts to sell the message and execute the strategy. Could he appeal to his base while reassuring the general public? How much mileage could he get out of fervor and organization? Could he construct effective alliances with movement conservatives, Democrats, and African Americans? Would early success help overcome public skepticism? An examination of Robertson's campaign will provide the answers.

Robertson's Connections:
Evangelicals and the Christian Right

If the first challenge the campaign faced was the mobilization of a Christian Right core constituency, Pat Robertson appeared in many ways to be the ideal man for the job. Robertson was a prominent figure in the world of American evangelicalism and in the conservative political movement that had grown out of that world. But Robertson was to find that uniting evangelicals and the Christian Right behind his campaign would not be easy. American evangelicalism, as we have seen previously, is seriously divided between its fundamentalist, charismatic, Pentecostal, and neoevangelical wings. Furthermore, much of the evangelical community remains suspicious of the aggressively conservative mix of political and religious doctrines promoted by Christian Right figures such as Robertson. Overcoming these suspicions and internal divisions and uniting evangelicals would be a difficult task. Nor would the Christian Right political movement be easy to unite. Personal, political, and religious differences divided its members as well. Added to Robertson's difficulties was the fact that his Republican rivals had not conceded his "base" constituencies to him; they were actively contending for evangelical and Christian Right support.

In analyzing Robertson's effort to win over his base constituencies, the first task is to examine his history with them. To these constituencies, he was not a new figure. They knew Pat Robertson and this profoundly shaped their response to his appeals.

Robertson As Religious Figure

To understand a religiously-based campaign, it is perhaps best to begin with the religious orientation of its leader.[17] Marion G. (Pat) Robertson was born in 1930 to a family better known for its politics than its religion. His father, A. Willis Robertson, was a congressman— and would later be a senator—from Virginia. His parents were Baptists and his mother worked hard to give him a proper religious upbringing. Yet throughout his early years, Robertson's religious beliefs, as he readily admits, were rather superficial. In college at Washington and Lee and later at Yale Law School, Robertson was known as a partier and something of a Casanova. Robertson's first son Tim was born only ten weeks after his marriage, a fact that came out and produced a brief scandal during his campaign. Responding to the scandal on Ted Koppel's "Nightline" program Robertson declared: "I was engaged in wine, women, and song on a number of continents. I have freely acknowledged that over and over again, but I have also acknowledged that I had an experience with Jesus Christ, we call it being 'born again,' that radically changed my life."[18]

Robertson's "radical change" came as something of a surprise to his wife and his parents. He gave up a promising business career, entered a seminary, and was soon ministering to a poor neighborhood in Brooklyn. Several years later, Robertson bought a small television station and the Christian Broadcasting Network (CBN) was on its way.

More on CBN will follow but, for the moment, I want to focus on the nature of Robertson's religious development. While at the Biblical Seminary in New York, Robertson fell in with an intense group of fellow students seeking a deeper spiritual experience. By 1959, Robertson claims to have experienced the gifts of the Holy Spirit and to have spoken in tongues. In the late 1950s and early 1960s, he associated with many of the leading figures of the emerging charismatic movement. By the 1970s, Robertson was one of the leading figures of that amorphous but rapidly growing movement.[19] In keeping with his charismatic beliefs, Robertson's television programs featured purported faith healings and numerous accounts of miraculous occurrences; his books bore titles such as *Beyond Reason: How Miracles Can Change Your Life.*[20]

Particularly important in Robertson's theological development was a discovery chronicled in his work *The Secret Kingdom*. Meditating on Jesus' claim that "the kingdom of heaven is at hand," Robertson came, in the mid-1970s, to the conclusion that this was not just an announcement of an imminent second coming but that this "secret" kingdom could be entered by believers today. Robertson went on to lay out the eight laws that he believes govern the operation of God's kingdom in this world. The doctrines expounded in *The Secret Kingdom* brought Robertson from an emphasis on salvation and healing to a more this-worldly orientation that fit well with his turn to greater political involvement in the 1970s and 1980s.[21]

Robertson's charismatic background made him a familiar figure to a large religious constituency, a more upscale and socially diverse constituency than the fundamentalists mobilized by leaders such as Jerry Falwell.[22] Much of this constituency remained unmobilized at the outset of Robertson's campaign. Familiarity with the constituency and close ties to its leaders greatly aided Robertson in his attempts to mobilize it. Many of the local activists I interviewed described the Robertson campaign as a second wave of Christian Right activism, a charismatic and Pentecostal addition to the prior political mobilization of fundamentalists; and survey data back their descriptions.[23] Once mobilized, the charismatic movement's strong grassroots organizations might prove a particularly valuable resource for a political campaign.

While Robertson's primary religious identification is as a charismatic, he also has ties to the Southern Baptists and the neoevangelical community. His parents were Baptists, and in the early 1960s Robertson was ordained as a minister in a local Southern Baptist church. His job there helped support his family as Robertson struggled to get his television ministry going. Once CBN was more successful, Robertson gave up his job at the church. Although he still attended services on occasion, Robertson's institutional ties to the church grew steadily weaker. As a prelude to his presidential campaign, Robertson officially resigned his ordination as a Southern Baptist minister. Yet, as his official ties to the church grew weaker, Robertson was building close personal ties to the national leaders of the Southern Baptist Convention (SBC). Closely allied to the political forces of the Christian Right, these leaders were part of a movement to wrest control of the denomination from theologically and politically more moderate forces. In the 1980s, they succeeded, gaining firm control of the denomination's national organization. Robertson's friendship with conservative SBC presidents, such as Adrian Rogers, Charles Stanley, and Jimmy Draper, gave him a potential inroad into the nation's largest Protestant denomination and its millions of members.

Robertson also had close ties to many leading neoevangelicals. Billy Graham appeared on his show and spoke at the dedication of his new broadcast center. Robertson had particularly close ties to Bill Bright, head of the neoevangelical Campus Crusade for Christ. The two became the cosponsors of the first Washington For Jesus rally in 1980.[24] Robertson's ties to neoevangelical leaders should not come as a surprise. Compared to their fundamentalist brethren, neoevangelicals have been relatively open to, and accepting of, Pentecostalists and charismatics. Since its founding, the National Association of Evangelicals has accepted Pentecostal denominations as members.

At first glance, Robertson would appear to have had an excellent prospect of uniting the religiously diverse forces of evangelicalism around himself. His charismatic roots tied him to a large, and largely unmobilized, charismatic and Pentecostalist constituency. Yet at the same time, Robertson maintained close connections with neoevangelicals and with fundamentalist forces within the nation's largest Protestant denomination, the Southern Baptist Convention. Robertson's theology also appeared to lay the foundation for a broad-based appeal. While his belief in the gifts of the Holy Spirit would prove troubling to fundamentalists and some neoevangelicals, the rest of his beliefs were in line with those of most conservative neoevangelicals and fundamentalists.[25] In his role as a televangelist, Robertson attempted to appeal to as broad an audience as possible. Doctrinal controversies within the evangelical community were not emphasized. Instead, Robertson attempted to mobilize the largest possible coalition to combat secular humanism (and, of course, to contribute to CBN).

Robertson may well have been the Christian Right leader best able to bridge the movement's religious divisions; nonetheless, serious barriers had to be overcome to achieve unity. The most significant of these problems was the continuing rift between fundamentalists on one side and charismatics and Pentecostalists on the other. It is important to note that the Southern Baptist church that ordained Robertson in the early 1960s was part of that denomination's theologically and politically more moderate wing. Fundamentalist conservatives within the denomination were not receptive to his charismatic heresy. While Robertson was able to forge a political alliance with fundamentalist leaders of the SBC, he found it difficult to overcome the suspicion of charismatics that marked the fundamentalist constituency within—and outside of—the SBC. If the dispute between fundamentalists and neoevangelicals centers on their willingness to associate with those who deviate from the true faith, charismatics and Pentecostalists—along with mainline Protestants—have been prime "deviants" at the heart of the dispute. On the whole, Robertson's relations with leading fundamentalists have been much less close than his relations with neoevangelicals. Jerry Falwell and Robertson have never been on good terms. Falwell came out quite early for Robertson's opponent, George Bush.

Robertson as Christian Right Leader

As Pat Robertson contemplated a run for the presidency, he brought to his potential campaign a mixed record of involvement in Christian Right causes. From the beginning, Robertson had been a major figure in the movement. His position at CBN gave him great visibility and he was not hesitant to use it to promote his conservative political views. But Robertson remained somewhat removed from many of the interlocking networks of Christian Right leaders. As the campaign commenced, he would have a difficult time rallying these leaders to his cause.

Despite his political heritage, Pat Robertson shunned political involvement during CBN's first decade. While Robertson would occasionally discuss political issues on the air, his ministry was his primary focus. In 1966, A. Willis Robertson was in a difficult battle to keep his Senate seat. Pat Robertson felt the Lord did not want him to divert energy from his ministry to help his father. The Senator lost narrowly, with his son doing little to help him.[26] As with so many other evangelicals, it was not until the 1970s that Robertson's political concerns emerged. In 1974, upset by the content of the Watergate tapes, Robertson went on the air asking Richard Nixon to "repent his sins." His political commentary grew more and more frequent. He sponsored a special telecast entitled "It's Time to Pray America."

Particularly important in his political development was the candidacy of Jimmy Carter. Robertson actively supported Carter's nomination bid.[27] While Jimmy Carter soon proved to be a disappointment to Robertson and other conservative evangelicals, his very public professions of faith encouraged and helped legitimize evangelical political involvement. In the wake of Carter's election, Robertson began sending political commentary to his viewers in the form of a newsletter entitled *Pat Robertson's Perspective*.[28]

As the Christian Right was being organized in the late 1970s, Pat Robertson, with his sizable audience and outspoken political views, was a natural candidate for a leadership role. As New Right leaders reached out to help organize the evangelical constituency, the most visible organizational expression of the emerging movement was the Moral Majority. Paul Weyrich, Richard Viguerie, Howard Phillips, Robert Billings, and Ed McAteer assembled a board of conservative religious figures to lead the new organization. Robertson was not invited. The reasons for this are not entirely clear but are likely linked to Robertson's charismatic beliefs. Paul Weyrich claims:

> There was a decision—for precisely what reason I don't know—not to involve Robertson in the original Moral Majority, which struck me as odd because the first editor, for example, of the Moral Majority Report was a Catholic. So to me it seemed, particularly at that time—things have changed a lot in the last decade—the notion of having a Catholic editor, it seemed to me, was much more dangerous than having someone who was charismatic but at least evangelistically speaking was within the same framework.[29]

Ed McAteer claims that a Falwell aide—who had previously worked for, and had a falling out with, Robertson—was dead set against his involvement.[30] Whatever the exact reason, Robertson was not invited, the Moral Majority—its Catholic editor notwithstanding—ended up being dominated by fundamentalists, both on its board and in its local organizations.[31] In the Christian Right's early years, fundamentalist Jerry Falwell, not the charismatic Robertson, became the movement's most visible spokesman.

Charismatics and Pentecostals were more instrumental in the 1980 "Washington for Jesus" rally. Robertson joined with John Gimenez, Bill Bright (head of Campus Crusade for Christ), and Demos Shakarian (head of the Full Gospel Businessmen's Fellowship International—FGBMFI) in an effort that brought between 200,000 and 500,000 people to the Mall in Washington.[32] There, in what was supposedly a nonpolitical event, they listened to a variety of speakers and prayed for the nation. Robertson views the rally as a pivotal event, a turning point for the nation. In *America's Dates with Destiny*, he declares: "April 29, 1980 was the beginning of a spiritual revolution. And I joined with the 500 thousand other people in the Mall and the millions watching on television in praying that one day this same spiritual revolution would sweep the nation."[33] The secular media did not give much attention to the event but many who attended continue to attach great importance to it. A second "Washington for Jesus" rally was held in 1988.

Robertson was also involved in one of the early Christian Right's more visible organizations, Religious Roundtable. Headed by Ed McAteer, the roundtable brought together leading televangelists with conservative businessmen, military leaders, and political figures.[34] Founded in 1979, with Pat Robertson as a prominent member of its board, the roundtable's most notable achievement was the National Affairs Briefing of 1980 with an attendance of fifteen thosand and a very well-publicized appearance by candidate Ronald Reagan. Yet by that time, Robertson was backing away from the roundtable and, in Paul Weyrich's words, "took some shots at it."[35] McAteer says he received a 1981 resignation letter from Robertson in which the televangelist declared, "Your objective is to change America through political means. Mine is through spiritual means."[36] This action was part of a general pullback from Christian Right organizations in the early 1980s. In the words of Robertson biographer David Harrell: "Then in 1980, at the peak of the efforts to get the religious Right launched, Robertson backed off, severing all formal connections with the new organizations. In the early 1980s observers of the religious Right tended to ignore Robertson. Robertson's retreat surprised many of his peers and supporters."[37] This apparent retreat was highlighted in 1982 when he ceased publication of *Pat Robertson's Perspective*.

Yet, as Harrell later points out, while Robertson was withdrawing from Christian Right organizations he was not necessarily backing away from political involvement. As Robertson cut his ties with the organizations of others, he began to develop political structures of his own: the Freedom Council and the National Legal Foundation (an evangelical counter to the ACLU). The "700 Club" continued to feature political commentary and guests.[38] Robertson maintained close personal ties to New Right leaders such as Paul Weyrich and New Right organizations such as the secretive, but influential, Council on National Policy.[39]

Campaigning for the Base: The Wooing of Christian Right Leaders and the Evangelical Constituency

As the campaign began, Robertson hoped to unite evangelicals and Christian Right leaders behind his presidential effort. He would have to overcome religious divisions and suspicion of televangelists. Furthermore, he had to convince evangelicals and Christian Right leaders that he was a proper choice for the position of president of the United States. Many who expressed admiration for Robertson as a religious leader doubted that he had the political experience necessary to be a successful president.

Robertson's quest for evangelical support commenced on a hopeful note. Evangelist Rex Humbard and Christian Right leader Beverly LaHaye appeared on stage with him as he made an announcement of semicandidacy in 1986. (At this time, Robertson announced that he was looking for the signatures of three million Americans requesting him to run.) Soon thereafter Robertson won the endorsements of Oral Roberts and Jimmy Swaggart, both of whom had previously shied away from political involvement.[40] Early endorsements reflected Robertson's base of support among Pentecostalist and charismatic televangelists. More difficult for Robertson, however, would be the task of gaining the support of noncharismatic religious figures and the political leadership of the Christian Right.

The Religious Right's best known figure, Jerry Falwell, had endorsed Vice President George Bush in 1985. Speculation varies as to Falwell's motivations. Dinesh D'Souza suggests that the endorsement was part of a broader effort to gain mainstream respectability for himself and his followers. Hadden and Shupe see Falwell's early announcement of support as an attempt to discourage the impending candidacy of Robertson. Falwell explained his choice by describing the vice president as a close personal friend, arguing that Bush had been moving to the right since 1980, and pointing out Bush's extensive political experience. Falwell qualified his support for Bush a bit after Robertson entered the race, but he remained in the vice president's camp throughout the campaign. While generally polite towards Robertson's bid, Falwell at times let slip comments that indicated a certain coolness toward his fellow televangelist's campaign. Summing up Robertson's qualifications, Falwell at one point simply stated: "He's probably the best trained television personality running for president."[41]

Other Christian Right figures proved equally difficult for the Robertson campaign to win over. Beverly LaHaye had appeared on the stage with Robertson as he announced a possible candidacy in 1986. Yet in late 1987, Beverly and her husband Tim came out in support of one of Robertson's rivals, Jack Kemp.[42] The couple had been prominent in the Christian Right from the movement's beginning. Pastor Tim LaHaye was author of numerous books popular within the movement, most notably of works warning of the threat posed by "secular humanism." One of the founders of the Moral Majority, Tim LaHaye went on to lead the American Coalition for Traditional Values (ACTV), which carried on a massive mobilization drive to involve conservative Christians in the 1984 elections. His wife, Beverly, founded the Concerned Women for America in 1979. The CWA grew rapidly, eventually claiming half a million members. This number is almost certainly overstated, but by any account CWA is one of the largest and most successful grassroots organizations of the Christian Right.[43] What lay behind the LaHayes' decision for Kemp?[44] Both expressed admiration for Robertson but expressed doubts about his viability as a candidate. Beverly LaHaye justified their ultimate decision in these words: "Tim and I have known Jack Kemp for many years . . . and we felt he had a history and a track record that was very strong. So we then, after a lot of prayer and consideration, decided—even though we loved Pat Robertson—we wanted to support someone who we thought could get the nomination."[45]

Falwell and the LaHayes were not the only Christian Right leaders who failed to rally to Robertson's cause. Robert Grant, chairman of Christian Voice, and Gary Jarmin, a leading figure at Christian Voice and ACTV, both supported Kemp.[46] Ed McAteer, founder and head of the Religious Roundtable, endorsed George Bush. Robert Billings—who served as the first executive director of the Moral Majority, went on to work as "evangelical coordinator" for Reagan's 1980 election campaign, and later took a position at Reagan's Department of Education—worked in 1988 to garner evangelical support for Senator Bob Dole.[47]

Robertson's failure to mobilize Christian Right leaders can be traced to a number of causes. Like the LaHayes, McAteer and Jarmin cited doubts about Robertson's electability in explaining why they had not supported him, with particular emphasis on the difficulties of getting the public to accept a preacher as a presidential candidate.[48] (Interestingly, there were also several comments that indicated that their followers were troubled by the presidential candidate's renunciation of his ordination and perceived rejection of his own call to the ministry.) Electability is a particularly important consideration for leaders of Christian Right political organizations. Backing a loser—particularly when that loser is involved in nasty disputes with the rest of the party—can undermine their credibility and access. Whereas televangelists Oral Roberts and Jimmy Swaggart had little political capital to lose by supporting Robertson, political leaders had to consider the effect of their stance on their future ability to push their agenda. Furthermore, while most televangelists, including Swaggart and Roberts, were charismatics or Pentecostalists, the majority of Christian Right political leaders was not. It is not easy to determine the degree to which religious differences hindered endorsement of Robertson, but it is quite possible they played a role.

The Competition

There are a number of reasons, as we have seen, why Christian Right leaders might not support Robertson, but it is also important to look at the reasons for them to support his Republican rivals. Robertson was not alone in appealing to an evangelical base; Jack Kemp, Bob Dole, and George Bush were all active in their pursuit of evangelical backing.

Kemp

Given his long-standing position as a standard-bearer of the GOP's right wing and his advocacy of the social issue causes dear to the heart of the movement, Jack Kemp should have been in a strong position to pick up Christian Right support. Kemp did gain the support of figures such as Robert Grant, Gary Jarmin, and the LaHayes. From my observations at the 1988 National Religious Broadcasters convention, it seemed clear that Kemp was, other than Robertson, the only candidate to elicit much enthusiastic support from attendees.[49] Nonetheless, Kemp's campaign never seemed to live up to its potential with evangelicals. Christian Right activists at the local, state, and national levels expressed disappointment at Kemp's perceived refusal to play to an evangelical base. Kemp's effort to reach out to nontraditional Republican constituencies such as labor and African Americans did little to excite this base. While his emphasis on monetary issues (the gold standard in particular) helped attract some New Right elements to his campaign, it did not resonate with activists motivated by social issue concerns. In Beverly LaHaye's words:

I think Jack made a mistake . . . he could speak so wisely on the
budget and the economy but when it came to the basic values that
support the family, he was void of speaking out on that—in the early
days, he finally began to develop that as his campaign went on—but
people didn't hear him saying the things that they were concerned
about.[50]

Dole

Senator Robert Dole had fewer existing ties to conservative evangelicals on which to draw. While generally conservative, he was known
more as a Washington insider than as a champion of the conservative
movement. Pursuit of evangelicals as a group was not a central
part of Dole's campaign, but he did make some efforts to overcome
suspicions and attract support. Robert Billings was recruited to do evangelical outreach. Equally important for Dole was the outreach per-
formed by his openly evangelical wife Elizabeth; many activists I
spoke to were quite impressed by her, some referring to her as Dole's
"secret weapon." Finally, Dole's campaign at several points came to
the defense of Robertson's supporters in their combat with pro-Bush
state party hierarchies. Calling on the party to welcome the influx of
new activists, Dole hoped to forge a common front against George
Bush and, perhaps, to gain the backing of Robertson supporters if the
nomination was not decided prior to the national convention.[51]

Bush

Despite his moderate roots and his past support of abortion rights,
George Bush actively pursued evangelical votes. The most visible
success of these efforts came with the early endorsement he received
from Jerry Falwell—but this was just the tip of the iceberg. The Bush
campaign developed and executed a far-reaching plan to win over
evangelical leaders and voters. An examination of internal Bush campaign documents gives an idea of the scope of these efforts. A complex scheme listing evangelical leaders was developed, rating their
importance based on audience, budget, likelihood of political involvement, influence in key campaign states, and so on. Then, "Beginning
in 1985, the Vice President began a series of meetings with evangelical leaders. These were followed up with a consistent correspondence
from the Vice President's religious liaison and, at times, telephone calls
and personal notes from the Vice President."[52]

The document goes on to list a long series of trips to meet with
southern evangelicals, White House receptions for them, and Bush
speeches at events such as the NRB convention. It concludes that

"between 1985 and 1988, the Vice President was photographed with almost 1000 evangelical leaders of influence."[53]

The Bush campaign did not base its entire evangelical strategy on personal meetings and photo sessions. Recognizing that the evangelical "Super Churches" might provide an organizational base for Robertson, the Bush campaign identified the 215 largest southern churches. A Bush supporter was located in each church, and this allowed the campaign "to monitor the Robertson operation and, if need be, to effectively neutralize these giant congregations."[54] In preparation for Super Tuesday, the Bush campaign publicized endorsements from key evangelical leaders, distributed a video aimed at evangelicals in which the vice president discussed his own faith, and sent out mailings targeted to evangelical audiences.

While the Bush campaign was making an attempt to woo an evangelical audience, its strategy was not to confront Robertson directly.[55] In fact, the early thinking within the Bush campaign was that a strong Robertson showing would help its candidate. Whereas Robertson was not considered a serious threat to win the nomination, Jack Kemp was, in the words of one Bush staffer, "a giant" and was, in fact, considered a more serious threat than was Bob Dole. The Bush campaign was therefore happy to see Robertson siphon off some of Kemp's right-wing and evangelical support. As the campaign wore on, strategy shifted. First, it became clear that Kemp was much less of a threat than originally anticipated. Second, the Bush staff began to suspect that Robertson was *not*, in fact, drawing his support from a pool of potential Kemp supporters, but instead from newly mobilized evangelicals whose second choice was George Bush. To defeat the challenge represented by Bob Dole, the campaign decided to move more aggressively to win these evangelicals over to their candidate. Thus, "by the time Iowa hit, a change of policy was official. Lee Atwater ordered the Vice President's evangelical team to haul out its arsenal in the south."[56]

Issues

As Robertson tried to mobilize supporters around social issue concerns, one of his most serious difficulties arose from the fact that his Republican opponents agreed with him. Dole, Kemp, and Bush all opposed abortion. All favored prayer in the schools and opposed the Equal Rights Amendment. Certainly there were questions as to how vigorously each candidate would pursue a social issues agenda. An attentive observer of the campaign would no doubt have been able to infer that a social issues agenda would be a higher priority for a President Robertson than it would be for a President Dole. From the standpoint of the Christian Right, some candidates had questionable pasts: Dole originally voted for the ERA and Bush was pro-choice prior to joining the Reagan ticket in 1980. Nonetheless, issue differences were not large, a fact that became apparent in candidate debates. In the words of Robertson's campaign manager R. Marc Nuttle:

> It is important to note—and I am not sure the press wrote about it—that the Republican candidates agreed on every single solitary issue. . . . The only discernable difference between the candidates during the debates was that George Bush was for the INF treaty and the other candidates were leery of it. Ultimately the candidates all came around to the INF [Intermediate Range Nuclear Forces] treaty and Robertson was no different.[57]

Agreement among the candidates undermined Robertson's appeal. If he had been running as a social conservative in a field of liberals, Robertson might have appealed to a broad array of culturally conservative voters. But in a field of candidates with similar views, Robertson was distinguished primarily by his fervor, his religious background, and his lack of political experience. And these were the attributes the campaign was trying to downplay in its attempt to establish Robertson's credibility beyond his religious base. Robertson's appeal to that religious base was impaired as well. Evangelicals would have to be convinced why they should not vote for more experienced figures with similar views.

Robertson could not assume evangelical support for his candidacy. His Republican rivals conducted vigorous efforts to reach out to evangelical voters, appealing to them with issue positions not far removed from his own. Religious divisions, doubts about his electability, and organizational interests kept many evangelical voters and Christian Right leaders out of Robertson's camp. As for rank and file evangelicals, we shall see in the campaign postmortem where they eventually came down.

Having listed the many challenges facing the Robertson campaign, I do not mean to imply that Robertson lacked a sizable following recruited from an evangelical base. Robertson's appeal inspired many evangelicals, particularly Pentecostals and charismatics, to labor enthusiastically on his behalf. Tens of thousands of volunteers turned out to pack straw polls, party meetings, and caucuses. The question that remained open was whether Robertson's appeal would translate into the millions of evangelical supporters necessary to prevail in primaries across the nation.

The Resources Available . . . and Their Utilization

Robertson evoked tremendous enthusiasm in a core group of evangelical supporters, but this enthusiasm was not the only factor behind his strength at the grassroots level. Robertson's background gave him access to a unique set of organizational resources. These resources allowed him to build upon evangelical enthusiasm and create a grassroots organization capable of vying with that of the sitting vice president, George Bush. Bush built his effort on the support of party leaders and party organizations across the country. Robertson had no such access to existing Republican party structures; his organization was built up on a very different foundation. To understand what that foundation was, it is necessary to examine Robertson's background as a religious broadcaster.

CBN Resources

The Christian Broadcasting Network (CBN) had its beginnings in 1961 with a single run-down UHF station in Tidewater, Virginia. In the following three decades, it expanded to become a nationwide operation, pioneering many of the techniques and appeals now common to the electronic church. Pat Robertson was the network's founder and remains a dominant figure there.

As party leaders have lost their gatekeeper role in the nominating process, candidates' independent campaign organizations have assumed greater and greater importance. At CBN, Robertson had developed a complex organizational structure with striking similarities to those of independent political candidates. As with candidate organizations, the key was fundraising. The Christian Broadcasting Network maintained a donor list of over 900,000 names and was sophisticated in the use of television and direct mail appeals to solicit funds from that list.[58] In 1986, CBN raised $230 million, much of it in the form of small donations from viewers.[59] This $230 million was roughly eight times the maximum that federal election law allows a candidate to spend in a nominating campaign. The CBN's appeal was highly personalized, closely identified with the charismatic presence of its founder and star, Pat Robertson. If the CBN fundraising apparatus, based on donors with strong loyalties to Robertson, could be mobilized to support his *political* endeavors, Robertson's campaign would have a significant advantage over its opponents. But could CBN's resources be so utilized?

Legal restrictions limited the direct use of CBN's organization, but the Robertson campaign was able to work creatively within—and by some accounts exceed—these restrictions to make significant political use of ostensively nonpolitical resources. The CBN donor list was rented to the Robertson campaign, which utilized it on several occasions. Prior to the official start of the campaign, CBN footed the bill for a number of activities that could be reasonably construed as laying the groundwork for Robertson's efforts: flying Robertson to several key states, financing preliminary polling efforts, and making large charitable contributions to distressed farmers in Iowa. Consultants and direct mail operatives who would later help run Robertson's campaign were hired first by CBN or affiliate organizations.[60]

The most significant, and most controversial, use of CBN resources involved an affiliate organization, the Freedom Council. Formed by Robertson in 1981 to promote political education and involvement on the part of evangelical Christians throughout the country, its budget increased dramatically in 1985. One of its major projects in that and the succeeding year was to mobilize evangelicals to get involved in the Michigan Republican caucuses, the first round of which got under way in 1986. The Freedom Council claimed to be a nonpartisan grass-roots organization, but in practice it looked like an arm of the Robertson presidential effort. The vast majority of precinct delegates mobilized by the council supported Robertson. The council's leaders were closely tied to Robertson and many went on to work directly for Robertson's official campaign organization. The Freedom Council's actions were controversial because direct support for a candidate would violate the organization's restrictive tax status. The Freedom Council's close financial ties to CBN were equally problematic. In a one-year period, CBN donated $4.6 million to the council. Yet CBN's tax status prevented it from giving to organizations like the Freedom Council unless it could assure that none of the money was being used for political purposes. Press scrutiny and attendant negative publicity led to the disbanding of the Freedom Council in late 1986, but not before it had performed valuable service on Robertson's behalf.[61]

For the moment, the key point to remember about the Freedom Council and other campaign uses of CBN resources is that they gave Robertson a critical advantage in the nominating process. For a candidate who lacked support from established party leaders and traditional party donors, Robertson was able to draw on quite substantial financial and organizational resources, resources that were available to him very early in the nominating process. Only George Bush, with his extensive ties to party leaders and contributors, was able to match Robertson's fundraising and organizational efforts.

Resources Utilized

Off to an Early Start

The early stages of Robertson's campaign focused on the mobilization of the monetary, volunteer, and organizational resources needed to lay the base for a viable candidacy. Unlike George Bush or Robert Dole, Robertson was not a well-known figure outside his own evangelical constituency. To the extent he was known, he was known as a televangelist, a reputation he wanted to move beyond. Thus, an early and prolonged organizational effort was necessary to introduce and redefine the candidate. Several other factors favored extensive early organization.

First was the fact that Robertson had the capacity to mobilize early. Robertson was not as dependent as other candidates upon the excitement of the campaign season to mobilize his supporters. To the extent that Robertson could draw upon his television audience, preexisting church networks, and the Freedom Council, he had at his disposal a premobilized base of intensely committed and enthusiastic volunteers.

The second reason for early organization lay in the unusual Republican caucus procedures in the state of Michigan. The Michigan process began more than two years prior to the nomination. On 27 May 1986, thousands of candidates filed to run in precinct delegate elections to be held in August of that year. The delegates elected then chose delegates to higher level conventions, culminating in the January 1988 state meeting that would elect delegates to the Republican National Convention. A presidential candidate hoping to be competitive in Michigan therefore needed to mobilize thousands of supporters at an extremely early date. By the time the rest of the nation had begun to focus on the presidential race, it was already too late to have much of an impact in Michigan.

A third reason to organize early lay in the nature of Republican party rules. Unlike the Democrats, the Republicans have little national regulation of their delegate selection process. State parties, therefore, become more important as arbiters of the rules. Control of the state party becomes a valuable asset in the struggle between competing presidential factions. In Michigan, for example, Robertson's supporters used control of the state party to rule 1,200 elected officials (mostly Bush supporters) ineligible to participate in the state convention. Bush supporters used their control of local party organizations to redraw district boundaries in ways that favored the vice president.[62] Similar uses of party organizations were to be found throughout the country. In order for Robertsonites to gain control of party organizations, early grassroots mobilization was critical, particularly given George Bush's strong ties to preexisting local party organizations.

Michigan: The Early Years

The incentives were for Robertson to mobilize early and this he did. Prior to its disbandment in late 1986, the Freedom Council was the key early organizational expression of Robertson's presidential campaign and Michigan was the centerpiece of the Freedom Council's efforts. Michigan would send seventy-seven delegates to the Republican convention and thus was a valuable prize for any campaign. A Robertson victory might also give a critical psychological boost to the campaign. While the initial selection of precinct delegates took place in 1986, the final selection of national convention delegates was to take place in January of 1988. If Robertson could post a victory in a major state at that time, just prior to decisive contests in Iowa, New Hampshire, and the southern Super Tuesday primaries, he could go a long way toward dispelling doubts about his candidacy, establishing momentum, and undermining the widespread impression that he was not a viable candidate. A victory in Michigan would be particularly impressive given George Bush's perceived strength there. Michigan had been one of Bush's best states in 1980. The state party leadership was squarely behind Bush and, it was believed, should easily be able to control the nominating process.

By early 1985, the Freedom Council had targeted Michigan as one of three "model" states in which to test the possibilities of grassroots Christian activism. (The other two states were North Carolina and Florida.) What had been a largely dormant state organization gained new life. In June of 1985, at a Republican party banquet attended by Pat Robertson, state party chair Spencer Abraham announced how Michigan's delegate selection process would work for 1988, a process that emphasized volunteer activism. This announcement had a definite effect on the Freedom Council. In the words of James Muffet, a district Freedom Council organizer, "Michigan was already a target state but when that [the nature of the selection process] became known it became even more important . . . and the dollars started flowing at that point." By the end of 1986, the Freedom Council had spent approximately $400,000 in the state.[63]

This money went to support a very effective grassroots effort aimed at getting conservative Christians active in the political system. More specifically, the focus was on getting them to file nominating petitions to run for the position of precinct delegate. Filing required the support of at least fifteen registered voters; and petitions had to be completed by 27 May 1986. Thus a massive organizational effort was needed years prior to the main events of the nominating campaign. The Freedom Council organized primarily through church networks—particularly in Pentecostal and charismatic Catholic churches but also with some success in fundamentalist Baptist circles. Organizers went into churches to convince members that political activity on their part was called for. If reservations concerning the legitimacy of political action could be overcome, the difficult task of teaching volunteers the rules, teaching them how to become active, still remained. Most of the volunteers—and many of the Freedom Council organizers—were political novices, with no background in party politics. As late as 1985, the woman who was to eventually run Robertson's state campaign "didn't even know what a delegate was."[64]

Despite the difficulties inherent in organizing a constituency unaccustomed to party activism, the Freedom Council made a strong showing, motivating thousands of volunteers to run as precinct delegates. Technically, the Freedom Council was not affiliated with any campaign. Thus, it claimed that the delegates it mobilized might vote for anyone. To promote an appearance of distance from Robertson, the council even made a small monetary contribution to the Kemp campaign.[65] Nonetheless, the vast majority of delegates recruited by the Freedom Council were supporters of Robertson. These delegates were the key that allowed Robertson to compete against a sitting vice president who enjoyed overwhelming support from state party activists. When the dust cleared, Robertson supporters claimed to have filed more candidates for the over nine thousand precincts than any of the other campaigns. After the 5 August 1986 Republican primary in which these candidates competed, Robertson supporters made similar claims. These claims were initially difficult to verify. Gaining a handle on the actual sympathies of thousands of delegates who were not required to publicly declare their preferences was a daunting task. Early news reports had Bush, as expected, well ahead. But as the months wore on, the conventional wisdom shifted; it became clear that Robertson had made a very strong showing.[66] He and Bush had won roughly equal numbers of precinct delegates (somewhat over 40 percent each is the estimate I was most often given) with Jack Kemp's much smaller constituency holding the pivotal balance of power between the two sides. (The other Republican candidates did not make a serious effort to contest Michigan.)[67]

By early 1987, Robertson's prospects looked very good. An alliance had been struck with Kemp supporters. This apparently gave the Robertson-Kemp coalition a majority sufficient to control the process that would lead to the selection of national convention delegates. (The precinct delegates chosen in August of 1986 were to participate in county caucuses that chose delegates to a state convention that then picked the national delegates.) Furthermore, grassroots organization allowed the Robertson-Kemp forces to pull off an unexpected coup. They gained a control of the state Republican committee in February of 1987, which allowed them to appoint sympathetic party officers and to decide rules controversies in ways that favored their side. Overall, the situation looked promising for Robertson—but nothing was certain. Complex and confusing rules governing the selection of delegates to the various levels, shifting alliances and intrigues, and legal challenges left a situation that could only be described as chaotic. In the words of one observer, it was "a system of selecting convention delegates that is all but incomprehensible even to those who designed it." Another simply declared: "This system is a mystery and a mastery of obfuscation."[68]

The Quest for Three Million

Another of Robertson's early organizing efforts was a bit easier to comprehend. On 17 September 1986, Pat Robertson made a declaration of semicandidacy. Speaking from Philadelphia's Independence Hall on the 199th anniversary of the passage of the Constitution, Robertson addressed an audience of nearly 200,000 gathered there and at video hookups in halls throughout the nation. He concluded his address by declaring: "If by September 17th, 1987, one year from today, three million registered voters have signed petitions telling me that they will pray—that they will work—that they will give toward my election, then I will run as a candidate for the nomination of the Republican Party for the office of President of the United States of America."[69]

For the next year, the gathering of signatures was the central organizational focus of the Robertson campaign. The petitions were useful tools for a number of reasons. They allowed Robertson to play the classic role of the reluctant candidate brought into public life by the demands of the people rather than his own ambition. Should Robertson get the three million signatures, it would help start his official campaign off with an appearance of widespread support, an appearance that could help dispel doubts as to whether he was a "serious" candidate. In addition, Robertson's "semicandidacy" allowed him the advantages of campaign organizing without officially declaring his candidacy. This meant that he could stay on the air at CBN promoting his causes and himself to a national audience, without the difficulty of demands for equal time that would come with an official candidacy. (Robertson did give up his position as host of the "700 Club" but he continued to make special appearances as a guest commentator and as a fundraiser.)

Beyond the boost that the petition drive might provide to his image, it served critical organizational functions. As Robertson's Philadelphia speech indicated, the potential candidate was not just asking for signatures; he was requesting prayer, work, and donations. If Robertson could build a volunteer and donor base of just a fraction of the three million petition signers, he would possess an extremely potent organization. Signing up supporters tied in neatly with the building of a grassroots campaign structure. Petition signers provided a valuable list to call upon for contributions, labor to staff phone banks and prepare mailings, and bodies to generate turnout for party meetings and campaign events. A number of outside observers lauded the petition drive as a stroke of organizational genius.[70] But would the scheme's promise pay off?

After stories that the petition drive was behind schedule, raising the extremely embarrassing possibility that the campaign would fail to meet its pre-announced goal, Robertson supporters put on a frenzied final push and—at least by their own count—came up with 3.3 million signatures by their September 1987 deadline.[71] The effectiveness of the signature campaign is hard to measure exactly. List creation did coincide with the development of a grassroots organization that proved quite formidable in contests that required an intense well-organized following, allowing Robertson to win straw polls, pack local party meetings, and score strongly in caucus states. It seems plausible that the petition drive helped foster these efforts. Furthermore, Robertson's early grassroots organization helped him raise large sums of money—and to raise those sums early. As of 30 September 1987, Robertson had raised over $10 million, approximately equivalent to the sum raised by George Bush and far outdistancing all other Republican candidates. By the end of the campaign, Robertson had raised $20.6 million on his own, augmented by $9.7 million in federal matching funds. Robertson relied on small contributors to a much greater extent than his rivals. I have no data on the percentage of these funds that could be attributed to the petition drive; the September 1986 speech-fundraiser at which Robertson announced the petition drive did raise $3 million for his campaign.[72]

There are reasons, however, to question the effectiveness of the petition drive. My interviews with staff members of the Robertson campaign yielded quite mixed opinions on the value of the lists. While great effort went into eliciting the names, some staffers claimed only limited use was made of them.[73] The doubts of two of them are reflected in the following discussion:

> A: We all assumed that if you are going to lay it all on the line and run for president, and you have the names of three million people who love you, who you know you can call on, you go to them . . . but *no*.
> B: Marlene [Elwell—Midwest director] is the only one I know who used that list. We won the Iowa straw poll in September 1987 because Marlene contacted all the Iowans who had signed petitions and got them there. But other than that I didn't get the impression in any state I was in that the people even knew who the petition signers were.[74]

A serious problem that Robertson faced was linked to the petition and grassroots fundraising efforts. They were expensive. The fundraiser that opened the petition drive raised $3 million but barely covered costs.[75] Getting the names themselves was costly in terms of time, labor, and money. The money was a particular problem given that presidential nominating campaigns operate with a strict overall spending limit. Thus, money spent on the petitions cut into the total that could be spent on other aspects of the campaign. In Robertson's words:

> Once my announcement [of semicandidacy] was made I was working under the auspices of "Americans for Robertson", a Federal Election Committee, "Testing the Waters" organization. All the money spent during those 12 months—$10 million in all—counted against my total federal spending limit of $30 million—and when I needed money for television in 1988 it just wasn't there.[76]

Straw Polls and State Parties
The list of three millions' problems notwithstanding, by late 1987 it looked as if Robertson's grassroots organization might pay handsome rewards. Michigan looked securely in Robertson's corner and in straw polls across the country Robertson was scoring impressive wins. He surprised campaign watchers by winning the 12 September 1987 "Cavalcade of Stars" straw poll in Iowa. Bush forces were ready at Florida's state party convention devising a system that reserved nearly half of the votes for state party officials. Nonetheless, Robertson scored strongly, winning 36 percent of the vote overall and a clear majority of the "unreserved" votes.[77] Finally, Robertson ran away with the Virginia straw poll in early December.

These events were essentially beauty contests, tests to see how many supporters could be organized and convinced to make the contribution to the party needed to get a vote. They did generate some attention for Robertson. Furthermore, they reflected the grassroots organization that was doing more substantial work for Robertson across the country. In primary states where the actual selection of delegates took place in caucuses, states such as Georgia, North Carolina, and Oklahoma, Robertson and Bush backers were engaged in fierce struggles for control. In many other states, Robertson's supporters were taking over local, and even state, party committees. In the process, they demonstrated significant Robertson strength—and fueled a great deal of animosity between Robertson backers and party establishments loyal to George Bush.

Reaching beyond the Base, Dealing with Suspicions

Pat Robertson needed more than organization and mobilized evangelicals. He needed to reach beyond an evangelical constituency to attract a broader base of support. Yet this would have to be accomplished in the face of widespread suspicion: suspicion of Robertson, of televangelists in general, and of many of the religious doctrines Robertson espoused. Robertson's task was made even more difficult when a series of ill-timed and highly publicized scandals struck his fellow televangelists. In the words of one Robertson activist, these scandals made the campaign's task "like pulling a dumptruck through a mudhole."[78] To understand the nature of the problems with which the campaign had to deal and its attempts to overcome them, it is necessary to turn, once again, to Robertson's background.

Televangelist

Robertson's primary problem was closely related to the strengths described in earlier sections of this chapter—for the twenty-five years prior to his campaign, he had been a television evangelist. While this had endeared him to a large evangelical audience and provided him with valuable organizational resources, it also, in the eyes of many Americans, was not the sort of background that qualified one to be president. In part, this reflected a belief that a presidential candidate needed prior experience in political office. But the problem was deeper than this, for Robertson's being a televangelist involved more than just a *lack* of political experience; it was seen by many as a strong mark against him. From the fictional Elmer Gantry to the very real exploits of Jim and Tammy Bakker, evangelists have acquired a shady reputation, on par perhaps with the much maligned used-car salesman. The problem this presented was described in the following manner by Robertson's communications director Constance Snapp: "People think he's a hustler on TV trying to steal some old lady's money. But when they see him and hear him they will understand he's something else."[79]

Robertson tried hard to convince the public that he was indeed "something else." When he decided to make his bid for the presidency, Robertson attempted to distance himself from his background as a "TV preacher." He resigned his ordination as a Southern Baptist minister and objected strenuously when members of the press would refer to him as "Reverend" Robertson. His campaign literature described him as a "Christian businessman" managing an extensive international enterprise. Emphasis was placed on his educational background (he is a graduate of Yale Law School) and on his family's political heritage (his father was a U.S. senator from Virginia). When his experience at CBN was brought up, the focus was upon less directly religious affiliate organizations, on his literacy program and on CBN's charitable arm, "Operation Blessing."[80] Despite these efforts Robertson had a difficult time escaping the "televangelist" label.

Dangerous Doctrines?

All candidates aspiring to the presidency must deal with basic questions concerning their faith but, given Robertson's background and the religious fervor of his followers, the examination he received was particularly intense. Many found his doctrines threatening and were afraid that he wanted to impose them upon the rest of the nation. Robertson had to address their concerns without offending supporters who were backing him precisely because they shared his religious beliefs and wanted those beliefs to shape public policy.

Over the years, Robertson had been involved in several doctrinal controversies within the evangelical community. In the 1970s, Robertson was drawn into a heated dispute over an authoritarian form of charismatic religious organization known as "shepherding."[81] Robertson has also been involved in controversies surrounding the advocacy of what has come to be called "prosperity theology."[82] In arguing that the believer can have access to the "secret kingdom" and understand its laws, Robertson often stresses the very material benefits this can bring the believer. In Robertson's accounts, those who master the principles of the kingdom are repeatedly on the receiving end of financial "miracles." These miracles are particularly frequent among those who donate generously to religious organizations such as CBN. (See, for example, the three stories in *Beyond Reason*'s seventh chapter, "God's Marvelous System of Money Management."[83]) While prosperity theology may appeal to some viewers, it is very controversial, helping to undermine the reputation of TV preachers with the general public and creating divisions among evangelicals. (Fundamentalists have been especially critical of the "heresy" of prosperity theology.[84])

Controversies over shepherding and prosperity theology may have done some harm to Robertson's reputation with the general public but, for the most part, these controversies stayed within the evangelical community. Other controversies were much more damaging. Three issues were particularly troubling.

The first issue concerned Robertson's alleged access to the Almighty. Many presidents have made public the fact that they resorted to prayer when they faced difficult decisions. What was troubling about Robertson was not simply the fact of prayer but the very specific nature of divine communications he claimed. For Robertson had at various points in his past claimed to have received "words of God," telling him to do things ranging from the starting of CBN to pulling out of the stock market. During the campaign, Robertson told religious audiences that God had ordered him to run and suggested that divine aid was behind a strong caucus showing. Once the campaign was over, Robertson was more forthright concerning divine communications and his campaign. In *The Plan*, Robertson goes into great detail about God's plans for his campaign and divine intervention that aided his effort at key points.[85]

A second issue raised further questions: Robertson's belief in miracles. His book *Beyond Reason* was subtitled "How Miracles Can Change Your Life" and contained story after miraculous story: cures from blindness and cancer, people saved from death in air wrecks, an orange grove saved from a killer frost, and hurricanes diverted. On the "700 Club," Robertson would often receive "words of knowledge," telling him that a listener's problem was being solved that very moment. During Robertson's presidential campaign, the most prominent coverage of Robertson's belief in miracles concerned his claim to have diverted a hurricane away from the CBN network facilities in Virginia Beach.[86] Footage of Robertson rebuking the hurricane in the name of the Lord received wide play and fueled public doubts.

A third problem stemmed from Robertson's belief in what has be-

come known as "Armageddon theology." Within the evangelical community, speculation concerning biblical prophecies of the "endtime"
are quite popular. The reception of Hal Lindsey's book *The Late Great
Planet Earth* provides strong evidence of this popularity; it sold eighteen million copies in the 1970s, outselling all other books—except
the Bible—for that decade.[87] Works such as Lindsey's weave recent
events into their interpretation of prophecy. The founding of the state
of Israel is seen as the fulfillment of biblical predictions, indicating
that the endtime is near. The events preceding the coming endtime
are held to include an attack upon Israel by a power from the North
(often interpreted as the Soviet Union), the rise of a league of states
lead by the Antichrist, and a cataclysmic series of battles (possibly
nuclear), plagues, and other calamities in which much of the earth's
population will perish. Finally comes the triumphant return of Jesus
Christ. The exact sequence and nature of these events is a subject of
great debate in evangelical circles.

More important than questions concerning the timing of the rapture, however, is the troubling implication of prophetic views in a man
aspiring to the presidency. In the late 1970s, Robertson made claims
implying that the end was near, that depression and a Middle East
war would strike in the early 1980s.[88] In *The Secret Kingdom*, he speculated that the Soviet Union was the power that would attack Israel
from the North (referred to as "Magog" in the Bible) and that the
European Economic Community was the league of nations that would
be led by the Antichrist. Robertson claimed that biblical passages might
foreshadow nuclear war and that new computer technology may allow
the fulfillment of the prophecy that all people shall be forced to bear
the mark of "the beast" (the Antichrist).[89]

Direct communications with God, belief in miracles, Armageddon
theology, all led to questions concerning Robertson's fitness for office. What if Robertson thought he received divine instructions on
issues of public policy? What was one to make of a man who thought
he healed the sick and diverted hurricanes—was he to be trusted in
control of the nuclear button? What if Robertson interpreted international crises in the light of biblical prophecies that implied that Middle East war was foretold as the will of God?[90] While some suspicion
of Robertson's doctrines might be dismissed as prejudice against evangelicals, his record raised very real questions about his potential behavior in the nation's most important office. For those doubtful of his
communications with God or his interpretation of biblical prophecy, a
Robertson presidency might be disturbingly unpredictable.

Church and State

A final doctrinally related problem Robertson had to overcome in his quest for public support was a widespread belief that he was violating the legitimate separation of church and state. This issue is a complex one. The proper "line" between church and state functions has been a point of controversy throughout American history. Much of Robertson's campaign was based on an argument that the current exclusion of religion from the public sphere is inconsistent with the Constitution and with American traditions. And to some extent the public agreed with him. For example, opinion polling has generally found strong support for reversing the Supreme Court's rulings on school prayer.[91]

Nonetheless, several aspects of Robertson's campaign raised particular concern on the church-state front. His religious background and lack of political experience was one problem. Another came from the Christian Right activists who had gone before him. In their zeal, they often portrayed their position as the only "Christian" or "moral" position on the issues, implying little tolerance for dissenting views. Robertson inherited the antipathy they had generated. Several events during the campaign deepened doubts. After Robertson's strong showing in the Michigan caucuses, the Freedom Council put out a letter declaring that "the Christians had won." In an early campaign speech, Robertson implied that Christians were more patriotic than other Americans, leading Secretary of Education William Bennett to publicly denounce his views.[92]

To Overcome Doubts

Robertson would have to overcome doubts about his background as a televangelist, his religious doctrines, and his views on church-state issues if he were to reach beyond his evangelical base to attract a broader following. Before he could convince the public to take a look at his issue positions, he would have to convince them that he was not a dangerous religious fanatic.

His strategy for doing so was discussed in the opening section of this chapter but could be profitably reviewed here. One strategy was to downplay his background as a religious broadcaster, stressing more secular accomplishments and qualifications. Once that was done, Robertson could move to redefine the religious issue. This involved presenting a relatively inclusive depiction of America's "Judeo-Christian" heritage, stressing the alleged historical links between American faith,

morality, and national vitality. Robertson's campaign argued that it was
the recent *secularizing* of the public sphere, not his religious emphasis, that was a new and un-American development. In responding to
criticism of his religious views, Robertson attempted to turn the tables on his accusers, accusing them of prejudice toward evangelicals,
of "Christian bashing." Such was Robertson's strategy—but did he have
the skills necessary to sell his argument to the general public?

Media Skills

In preparation for a presidential campaign, many candidates turn to
consultants to instruct them in the difficult art of presenting themselves before the camera. This was an art that Pat Robertson had over
twenty-five years of daily practice to master. The image he projected
to his "700 Club" audience was—at least compared to rival televangelists—well suited to a political candidate. The format of the "700
Club" did not feature Pat Robertson "preaching." He did not stride
across the stage shouting and quoting Scripture like Jimmy Swaggart.
Robertson sat calmly in his chair and played the role of the talk-show
host/resident expert, interviewing prominent religious and political figures and answering questions posed by his cohost Ben Kinchlow. This
background helped Robertson develop a reasonable and affable on-
screen persona that surprised many who had not seen him prior to his
political campaign. Like Ronald Reagan before him, Robertson's years
in front of the camera had honed the candidate's ability as a commu-
nicator.

While the media skills honed at CBN were similar to those required
of a presidential candidate, they were not identical. Herein lay a problem. Several of the "lessons" that Robertson learned at CBN did not
serve him well on the campaign trail. At CBN, Robertson was used to
being on the air for long periods of time, speaking spontaneously to
an adoring evangelical audience. In a presidential campaign, spontaneous, off-the-cuff remarks are extremely dangerous. A hostile press
corps awaits to pounce on candidate "misstatements." Statements that
were commonplace and acceptable to CBN's evangelical viewers were
likely to alarm a more secular press corps and the audiences it reported to. Robertson's freewheeling style, developed in front of a supportive evangelical audience, was to repeatedly get the candidate into
serious trouble.

The Campaign for General Support

Aiming to overcome doubts, Robertson took his skills and message
on the road. No longer host of the "700 Club," Robertson was mak-

ing appearances in Iowa and New Hampshire. Events appeared to be going according to plan; but in the spring of 1987, the course of events was to deal a serious blow to Robertson's efforts. Given that one of Robertson's most important tasks was to redefine his image—to downplay his televangelist past and project an image in keeping with a more broadly based appeal—few developments could have been more damaging than the events that occurred in March of 1987.

Oral Roberts declared that if viewers did not donate $8 million to his ministry, God would "call him home." The secular media had a field day with Roberts's implication that God was a terrorist, willing to hold a hostage for ransom. While Roberts's ratings had long been slipping, he was one of the founding fathers of the electronic church and a leading figure in the charismatic movement. In 1986, in the wake of Robertson's announcement of semicandidacy, he had given Robertson a ringing public endorsement. At the time, this statement of support had seemed like a major coup for the Robertson campaign. Now it threatened to tarnish Robertson with the ridicule that Roberts was receiving. But the Roberts affair was a minor one compared to what was to happen later in the month.

The first hint of a problem at PTL ("Praise the Lord" or "People that Love") ministries came when Tammy Faye Bakker checked into a clinic for drug rehabilitation. That news was soon eclipsed by an ever-widening scandal involving her husband Jim Bakker. The story started with the revelation of an extramarital sexual encounter and reports that hush money had been paid to silence the woman involved. Then the story exploded in a sea of charges and countercharges. Bakker alleged that evangelist Jimmy Swaggart was masterminding a plot to defame him and seize control of PTL's assets. Leading televangelists leaped into the fray on both sides.[93] Bakker temporarily resigned and left his ministry in the hands of Jerry Falwell. Before long, however, the Bakkers were feuding with Falwell, alleging that Falwell was out to get his hands on their media empire. As the struggle for control of PTL continued, further revelations of sexual adventures and financial misconduct kept pouring forth. It soon became clear that the Bakkers had been defrauding their supporters on a massive scale. Making deceptive fundraising appeals and diverting large sums of ministry money to finance their own lavish lifestyles, the Bakkers had committed offenses that would eventually land Jim in federal prison. For our purposes, however, the details of the scandal are less important than their effect on the Republican nominating campaign.

Robertson tried hard to distance himself from the fray but he could not escape its consequences. The problem was not simply the exist-

ence of scandal but the fact that it engulfed so many of televangelism's leading figures and that it garnered so much media attention.
The ongoing media circus made televangelists the laughingstock of
much of America, reenforcing Elmer Gantry stereotypes, and doing
serious damage to reputations and finances. Polls conducted by the
Los Angeles Times revealed a sharp drop from 1986 approval ratings
for most leading televangelists. Robertson's ratings fell from slightly
favorable to 3 to 2 negative. The Gallup Poll, measuring support in
1980 and then again after the scandals of 1987, found similar declines.
Gallup also reported massive increases in the percentage of the population that believed television preachers were "not trustworthy with
money," "dishonest," and "insincere." Given these perceptions, it is
not surprising that the scandal also undermined fundraising efforts. As
revenues dropped sharply, religious broadcasters—including Robertson's
CBN—were forced to lay off employees.[94]

The PTL scandal put Robertson's campaign in a difficult position.
Instead of projecting the themes he had planned to emphasize, Robertson was forced to spend much of his time on the defensive, trying
to ally public suspicions. His campaign staff redoubled its efforts to
promote him as a "Christian businessman" rather than a television
preacher.[95] The task they faced in convincing the public to embrace
their candidate, never an easy one, had become significantly more
difficult. The PTL affair had reenforced outsiders' fears of the religious subculture whose cause Robertson was championing. It had increased distrust of televangelists among evangelicals as well.[96]

Attempts to move the focus of the campaign away from religious
questions were especially difficult given the similarity of the Republican candidates' issue positions. Robertson's rivals, as discussed earlier, were not far from him on most key issues. In the absence of issue
conflicts, the media naturally focused on the candidates' backgrounds
and personalities and, in Robertson's case, this led invariably back to
the religious roots of his candidacy. Clashes at the state and local level
also helped to make Robertson's attempts at redefinition difficult.
Battles between the backers of Robertson and Bush garnered quite a
bit of media attention and it was hard to ignore the fact that Robertson's troops were motivated by religious concerns.

Opinion Polls

In the Fall of 1987, opinion polls were offering little solace to
candidate Robertson. The long effort to redefine Robertson and broaden
his appeal seemed to be having little impact. In a January 1987 CBS
News/Washington Post Poll, he had been the choice of only 5 percent
of registered Republicans. He was the choice of 7 percent in Novem-

ber. This did put Robertson in third place but he was far behind Bob
Dole (20 percent) and George Bush (48 percent). Jack Kemp (5 percent) and Al Haig (4 percent) were close behind him. The main bright
spot was the South where Robertson was the choice of 13 percent of
registered Republicans.

Robertson *had* become a fairly well-known figure. From May to
November of 1987, the percentage of Republicans claiming that they
"hadn't heard enough" about Robertson to form an opinion dropped
from 42 to 20. Unlike Jack Kemp or Pete du Pont, he was making an
impression.[97] Unfortunately for Robertson, greater knowledge was not
translating into greater support. In May, 14 percent of registered Republicans had a favorable impression of Robertson, 29 percent had an
unfavorable impression. In November, 13 percent responded favorable
and a startling 50 percent responded unfavorable. His 50 percent unfavorable rating contrasted with Bush's 12 percent and Dole's 11 percent. An October/November Harris Poll found similar antipathy toward
Robertson; 51 percent of Republicans polled felt that they "could not
vote for" Robertson if he were nominated for president. Only 13 percent felt that way about Kemp, 8 percent about Bush, and 6 percent
about Dole.[98]

Going into election season Robertson had a difficult assignment.
Unlike Kemp or du Pont, his task was not to win over voters who did
not know him; Robertson had to gain support among a public that
had already formed quite negative opinions of him.

Misstatements

Robertson's effort to reverse those negative opinions were undermined by several of his own statements. These were, for the most part,
misguided statements concerning secular issues. Nonetheless, they
worked to reenforce doubts that had been fueled by religious concerns,
again raising the question of whether Pat Robertson had the background or the qualities of judgment necessary in a presidential candidate. Even more damaging was the fact that many of the statements
came during one of the most critical periods of Robertson's campaign,
the weeks leading up to the decisive Super Tuesday contests. Robertson had just made a strong showing, defeating George Bush in the
Iowa caucuses. His campaign was garnering new attention and credibility. Then Robertson made a series of costly blunders.

Used to speaking off-the-cuff at CBN, harried as he embarked on
an increasingly frantic schedule of campaign events, Robertson made
a series of troublesome misstatements. He announced that there were
Russian missiles in Cuba. He claimed that CBN had given the United
States government information on the whereabouts of American hos-

tages in Lebanon, information that the U.S. government had failed to act upon. Provocative claims like these naturally led to scrutiny from the media and Robertson could produce little evidence to substantiate either claim. Instead of focusing on Robertson's attempts to move beyond his evangelical base and broaden his appeal, the media focused on the misstatements, linking them back to the controversial statements of his televangelist past. Robertson's relations with journalists, never good, turned even more sour.[99]

At this crucial moment, as Robertson was struggling to shed his identification with televangelism, scandal struck again. Jimmy Swaggart, America's top-rated televangelist and an early supporter of Robertson's presidential bid, admitted to a long-standing addiction to pornography and to seeing a prostitute. This obviously was not good news for the Robertson campaign but the candidate managed to compound the problem. In an off-the-cuff remark, Robertson suggested that the Bush campaign was behind the disclosure of the Swaggart scandal, leaking the news in order to discredit Robertson. Again, there was nothing to substantiate the charges and Robertson's credibility suffered a further blow.

What led Robertson to make a series of damaging statements at such a critical juncture in his campaign? Robertson's history at CBN may well have taught him the wrong lessons about public speaking. Spontaneity in front of a loyal evangelical audience is one thing, but in front of the press corps in a presidential campaign it is bound to lead to trouble. Tired of hearing the same stump speeches over and over again, reporters are ready to pounce upon anything out of the ordinary. Robertson was by no means the first presidential candidate to find this out. Robertson himself blamed his gaffes on overwork and overexposure: "My mistakes went up geometrically in relation to the measure of my jet lag and fatigue and the number of press conferences I permitted. It was not by accident that George Bush stopped having press conferences during the general election campaign. He cut his chances for press goofs in half."[100]

It is important to point out, however, that Robertson had been making misguided or ill-advised statements throughout his campaign. Robertson at various points questioned the patriotism of non-Christians, expressed hope that "the wonderful process of the mortality tables" would take care of Supreme Court liberals, and attacked Nancy Reagan the day she entered the hospital for breast cancer surgery. Robertson claimed that he had prayed with Oliver North about his mission to Tehran to negotiate about the hostages. North, in sworn testimony to the Iran/Contra committee, denied he had ever had such a conversation. In "What I Will Do As President," an audiotape distributed by the campaign, Robertson makes the wildly inaccurate statement that 100,000 federal employees serve at the pleasure of the president. (Robertson vows to fire most of them.) Finally, Robertson's resumé contained a number of questionable claims that had to be scaled back when he was publicly challenged. Given this history of questionable statements, Robertson's misguided utterances leading up to Super Tuesday become a bit more comprehensible.[101]

It is difficult to determine exactly how much damage Robertson's misstatements did to his campaign. Campaign manager R. Marc Nuttle argues that, in the wake of his Iowa showing, Robertson was bringing his negatives poll ratings down and beginning to establish credibility. In an interview with author Allen Hertzke, Nuttle claimed that Robertson "had gotten the negatives down from 45 percent to 32 percent with the general population, and down to 15 to 20 percent with our [evangelical] base."[102] Nuttle described what came next in this manner: "Jim and Tammy Faye and Oral Roberts had happened within fourteen months. People were wary, but took a let's see attitude. Then, at a time when Robertson's credibility was in question, we had about four funny facts and Swaggart and we lost twenty points in negatives overnight."[103]

Robertson had had extreme difficulty scoring well in primaries prior to his "funny facts;" therefore one should not assume he was poised for victory had he avoided troubling statements. Nonetheless, it is hard to believe that his statements—well publicized in the press— did not cut at least somewhat into his vote totals.

Robertson's efforts to reach beyond an evangelical base met with very limited success. From the beginning he faced deep suspicions concerning his religious background and doctrines. As his campaign endeavored to overcome these suspicions, its efforts were undermined by a series of well-publicized scandals among his fellow televangelists. Robertson found it difficult to move attention away from his religious background and onto his issue positions, particularly given the similarity of his positions to those of his Republican rivals. Robertson's failure to broaden his base was reflected in low levels of support going into the primary season. Perhaps, as his campaign strategists had hoped, early electoral success could be translated into greater credibility and support for Robertson's candidacy. Unfortunately, at just the moment this plan showed some prospects for success, Robertson undermined his effort with a series of damaging misstatements.

Caucus and Primary Results

Having reviewed Robertson's appeals to his base, the deployment of his organizational resources, and his troubled attempts to establish credibility beyond his base, it is time to examine the results of his efforts.

Michigan

The story begins in Michigan, the state that played such a key role in Robertson's strategy. By the fall of 1987, this key aspect of his strategy was coming unraveled. The dramatic early victory Robertson had counted on in Michigan was slipping away from him. With a Kemp-Robertson alliance in place and in control of the state party, what went wrong? The Kemp-Robertson forces had scored an apparent coup when the state committee they controlled ruled in September of 1987 that 1,200 GOP nominees to state and local offices were not eligible to take part in county conventions that would choose representatives to the state convention. But this apparent victory was reversed on 4 December when the Bush campaign won a court order requiring that the 1,200 nominees, predominantly Bush supporters, be allowed to participate.[104]

A further problem stemmed from the fact that, while Bush and Kemp supporters had taken charge of the state party committee in February of 1987, the majority of county party organizations remained in the hands of Bush supporters. The precinct delegates who would elect representatives to the 1988 state convention were already in place, but the manner by which counties would be districted in those elections was open to interpretation. Bush controlled county party organizations engaged in gerrymanders (or, in the words of a Bush official, "extremely creative apportionment plans") that redrew district boundary lines within the counties.[105] This, combined with the court's ruling on the 1,200 nominees, raised the possibility that the Bush forces might be able to gain a majority at the state convention even in the face of an intact Robertson-Kemp alliance.

Unfortunately for Robertson, this alliance did not remain intact. The first serious crack came in early December. Kemp's Michigan chairman, state senator Richard Posthumus, and several other high-ranking campaign officials defected and allied themselves with the Bush forces. The defectors were driven by several considerations. One of the most important was their long-standing ties to the state party leaders, the vast majority of whom had sided with Bush. The battle in

Michigan had been raging for nearly two years, creating extremely bitter feelings between the warring sides. The battle threatened to cut Kemp leaders off from their associates in the party, old friends who might be critical to their own political futures, friends with whom they had much more in common than with the newly mobilized evangelicals in the Robertson campaign.[106] Another critical factor was the treatment they believed they were receiving from the Robertson campaign. Pat Robertson at one point made an ill-advised boast that he would win forty-four of Michigan's seventy-seven delegates.[107] Given that Bush would almost certainly win at least eighteen, this would leave very few for Kemp. The defectors mistrusted the Robertson forces and felt they were going to be given the short end of the deal. They argued that Kemp could get a better deal in alliance with Bush.

The national Kemp campaign disavowed the defectors at first but as the county conventions met in early January, things were looking steadily worse for the Robertson-Kemp alliance. Marked by walkouts of protesting Robertson supporters, the county conventions were tumultuous affairs. Bush looked to have won the majority of them. Soon thereafter the national Kemp campaign struck a deal with Bush. Bush and Kemp controlled the official state convention where thirty-seven Bush, thirty-two Kemp, and eight Robertson delegates were elected to go to the Republican National Convention. But this was not the only state convention. Robertson supporters and remaining Kemp allies walked out and held their own "rump" convention, seating many of the dissident factions from the county conventions. The rump convention selected forty-three Robertson, twenty-one Kemp, and thirteen Bush delegates.[108]

What was to have been a rousing victory to lead Robertson's forces into the Iowa caucuses had instead turned into a confusing mess. Two rival slates were claiming their right to go to the Republican National Convention in New Orleans. Bush was generally perceived to be the winner but, as the recriminations flew, it was not clear that anyone's campaign had received a decisive boost. Robertson's forces across the country vowed to avenge the "corrupt bargain" that had denied them victory in Michigan.[109] They were to get their revenge in Iowa.

Iowa

Looking at the polls, there was little reason to expect Robertson to score well in the 8 February Iowa precinct caucuses. In early January, the Gallup Poll found Robertson running fourth in the state, supported by only 6 percent of registered Republicans. An 18 January *Des Moines Register* poll showed 11 percent of expected caucusgoers supporting him, versus 41 percent for Bob Dole, 26 percent for George Bush, and 8 percent for Jack Kemp. While the poll results did not look promising, there were reasons to expect Robertson to exceed poll predictions. Robertson's appeal to Democrats indicated the possibility of a base of support not being measured in polls of registered Republicans. Furthermore, Robertson was extremely well organized, building his campaign on the list of forty thousand Iowans who had signed petitions asking him to run. By contrast, the Bush campaign was working from a list of twelve thousand supporters, Kemp from a list of two thousand. The church-based network built by the Robertson forces could help school volunteers in the complexities of the caucus process and escort them to caucus sites. Robertson's supporters appeared very strongly motivated. If turnout was low, it was the Robertson forces that were particularly likely to make the effort to participate in the caucus process. At a National Religious Broadcasters Convention several weeks before the caucus, I saw Robertson supporters half jokingly pray for snow on caucus day. Robertson's potential to score well in caucus settings was underscored just days before the Iowa contest, as he overwhelmed Bush's supporters in the Hawaii caucuses, winning over 80 percent of the vote.[110]

All these factors led observers to expect a strong showing by Robertson's "invisible" army. But no one knew *how* strong. Dole was widely expected to win; the real battle was for second place. While there was speculation that Robertson could finish second, the idea that an evangelist without political experience could defeat the campaign's frontrunner, a sitting vice president, had not really sunk in to the public consciousness. Thus Iowa's results created quite a stir. A total of 108,838 people turned out at Republican caucuses meeting throughout the state. Dole, as expected, came in first with the support of 37.3 percent of the caucusgoers. The surprise was Robertson's second place showing. With the support of 24.6 percent of caucus attendees, Robertson easily bested George Bush who garnered a mere 18.6 percent of the vote. Kemp finished fourth with 11.1 percent.[111]

As one of the campaign's key early tests, Iowa received an inordinate quantity of national media coverage. In the aftermath of the caucuses, national attention was thus focused on Robertson and his "humiliation" of George Bush.[112] Robertson's effort was suddenly being taken seriously. The results provided a tremendous psychological boost to Robertson backers across the nation. In my interviews, Robertson supporters—ignoring the actual showing of Bob Dole—would almost invariably refer to their candidate's Iowa "victory."

New Hampshire

The next contest was New Hampshire. Here Robertson faced a tougher challenge. The state lacked a conservative evangelical constituency. Robertson's "700 Club" was not even broadcast in the state. In the words of his campaign manager, he had "no name recognition" and "no base to go to."[113] While New Hampshire had few evangelicals, it had many Republicans. A Robertson insurgency would have to either overwhelm them or win them over. Finally, and perhaps most important, New Hampshire was a primary rather than a caucus. In a primary, where turnout would be higher, fervor and organization would matter less; widespread appeal would matter more.

Yet despite these weaknesses, Robertson did not bypass the state. With expectations raised after his strong Iowa showing, it was hard to sit New Hampshire out, and Robertson made a number of well-publicized appearances in the state. Perhaps he could surpass expectations again. Aiming for at least a third-place finish, Robertson was hoping that Dole would come in first, dealing a devastating blow to Bush. Then, perhaps, Robertson would be in position to pick up support from a faltering Bush throughout the South.[114] But it was not to be. In the 16 February primary, Bush recovered from his defeat in Iowa, winning 37.6 percent of the vote to Dole's 28.4 percent. Instead of finishing third, Robertson came in an embarrassing fifth. His 9.4 percent of the vote placed him behind both Jack Kemp and Pierre du Pont. The hopes that had been so recently raised in Iowa began to fade.

Despite his New Hampshire setback, Robertson managed to make some strong showings in the next few weeks. He won the 18 February Nevada caucuses, finished a strong second in the 23 February Minnesota caucus, and easily won the Alaska caucuses held at the end of the month.[115] These states provided further evidence of the value of Robertson's organization in a caucus setting. On 23 February, he managed to make one of his strongest showings in a primary, finishing second with just under 20 percent of the vote in South Dakota.[116] While these showings by no means established Robertson as a frontrunner, they did indicate that he might be a force at the convention, perhaps holding the balance of power if Dole and Bush proved to be evenly matched. Furthermore, the campaign was about to head to the South, to the stronghold of evangelicalism and, presumably, to more favorable terrain for Pat Robertson.

South Carolina

In the period leading up to Super Tuesday, Robertson made several of his most damaging "misstatements" and also may have hurt his prospects by means of an ill-conceived challenge to George Bush. Trying to reinvigorate his troops after the dismal showing in New Hampshire, Robertson declared: "Today we played in George Bush's backyard. Now we are going to the South which is my backyard. I throw down the gauntlet to George Bush in South Carolina."[117]

Scheduled for 5 March, the South Carolina primary could establish critical momentum just three days prior to Super Tuesday. It was a southern state, a state with a very large evangelical population, where one might expect Robertson to do well. Why was "throwing down the gauntlet" a mistake? First, against the standard lessons of the "expectations game" it set a very high standard for Robertson. Once one lays down the gauntlet, victory—not just a respectable showing—is what is expected. Second, South Carolina was a Bush stronghold. The governor, Carroll Campbell, was leading a well-oiled Bush organization masterminded by South Carolina native Lee Atwater. *Bush's* strategy was to emphasize South Carolina and Robertson was playing into it. Once again, Robertson's spontaneous remarks were undermining the strategy worked out by his own campaign team. In the words of one Robertson advisor, "Pat was not the best candidate I've ever worked with for taking advice from the staff he was paying."[118]

Robertson's organization was no match for Bush's in South Carolina. Nor could he match Bush's expenditures. The expense of the petition drive was catching up with the campaign. As South Carolina and Super Tuesday were coming up, funds were running short. Only a limited advertising campaign was possible. Given the "gauntlet" laid down by Robertson, the South Carolina results were extremely disappointing. Bush received 48.5 percent of the vote to Robertson's 19.1 percent. Bob Dole, with 20.6 percent of the vote relegated Robertson to third place.[119] Bush, not Robertson, had received the boost for the upcoming Super Tuesday.

Super Tuesday

Super Tuesday's results effectively decided the nominating campaign. Bush won all sixteen of primaries contested that day, most by decisive margins. Robertson ran second in Louisiana and Texas, third behind Bush and Dole in thirteen other primaries, and fourth, behind Bush, Dole, and Kemp, in Massachusetts. Robertson's strongest primary state was Oklahoma, where he received 21.1 percent of the vote. In no other state did he break the 20 percent barrier. In all southern states except North Carolina (9.8 percent) Robertson scored in the teens. In the northern states of Massachusetts, Rhode Island, and

Maryland, Robertson polled well under 10 percent of the vote. Overall, Robertson received 13 percent of the votes cast on Super Tuesday, Bush 57 percent, Dole 24 percent, and Kemp 5 percent.

Yet in keeping with earlier experiences of caucus success, Robertson won the lone caucus scheduled for Super Tuesday—Washington state. While consistently defeated in the Bible Belt, Robertson managed a strong plurality in Washington, gaining the backing of 39 percent of caucus attendees at the precinct level. (This compares to Dole's 26 percent and Bush's 24 percent.) The Robertson forces were able to maintain control of subsequent county conventions and the state convention; their state eventually sent the largest number of Robertson delegates to the national convention in New Orleans. The Robertson victory in Washington illustrates the crucial difference between caucuses and primaries for a candidate with an enthusiastic and well-organized core of supporters but limited popularity with the general public.[120]

Post–Super Tuesday

In the aftermath of Super Tuesday, the Robertson effort continued. But the campaign was being conducted at a much lower level. Money was short and the final outcome was no longer in doubt. The campaign moved to northern and western primaries where Robertson could not expect showings as strong as in caucuses or in southern primaries. He received under 10 percent of the vote in all remaining states, his strongest showing being his 9.1 percent of the vote in Pennsylvania.[121]

On 16 May, Robertson officially suspended his campaign. That day he returned as host of the Christian Broadcasting Network's "700 Club." The scandals of Robertson's fellow televangelists, and his own absence from the network so closely identified with him, had led to a serious fiscal crisis at CBN. Robertson turned his attention from the presidential campaign to reviving the fortunes of his troubled ministry.

In his first few days back on the air, Robertson discussed his presidential effort. He was bitter about the treatment he had received during the campaign, commenting that "running for president makes spontaneity impossible" and complaining about "the incredible antipathy to evangelical Christians in the media, academia, government, and the judiciary."[122] Watching Robertson speak, one could see that he had not particularly enjoyed the campaign experience. Nonetheless, he thought that his efforts might well prove to have been worthwhile.

The key to that, he argued, would be determined by the fate of those he had mobilized to become involved in the political process. Robertson had indeed mobilized many conservative Christian activists, activists who would play a key role in Republican party politics across the country.

Sources of Support

At the close of the campaign, Robertson had fallen far short of his objective—the GOP nomination—but he had managed to finish third in a crowded field, beating out candidates (Representative Jack Kemp, Delaware governor Pierre du Pont, and former NATO chief Alexander Haig) with much longer political resumés. He finished with slightly over a million votes. Where did he get those votes? What were the sources of his support? A brief review of the results can help put Robertson's campaign in perspective.

When and Where

Robertson's campaign was strongest in its early stages. As table 5.1 illustrates, he won 15 percent of the vote in pre–Super Tuesday primaries, 13 percent on Super Tuesday, and only 6 percent thereafter. The falloff from the first to the second period may well be related to the public blunders of the Robertson campaign as it approached Super Tuesday. These blunders aside, one might have expected Robertson to be stronger in the primarily southern Super Tuesday contests than in the predominantly northern ones that preceded them. Another possible factor is money. Robertson spent a lot of money in the early stages of the process; this left him with limited resources to combat Bush across the seventeen states contested on Super Tuesday. After Super Tuesday, Robertson had few resources and the nomination was no longer being seriously contested. In several late primaries, he was not even on the ballot. His weak post–Super Tuesday showing should therefore come as no surprise.

The regional basis of Robertson support was not unexpected. As table 5.2 illustrates, Robertson fared best in southern primaries, where he could draw support from a large evangelical population. (Some caution should be used in reading table 5.2, however. The primaries in different regions were held at different points in the process. Southern primaries came relatively early when Robertson was still strong. The western primaries were bunched toward the tail end of the process.)

Table 5.1
Percentage of Primary Vote by Time Period

	Candidate			
Time period	Bush	Dole	Robertson	Kemp
Pre–Super Tuesday	39	31	15	10
Super Tuesday	57	24	13	5
Post–Super Tuesday	78	15	6	1
Total	68	19	9	3

Source: "1988 Republican Primary Results and 1988 First Round Caucus Results," *Congressional Quarterly* 46, no. 3 (1988): 2254–255.

Table 5.2
Percentage of Primary Vote by Region

	Candidate			
Region	Bush	Dole	Robertson	Kemp
East	72	17	7	1
Midwest	67	23	8	2
South	58	21	14	5
West	81	13	5	0
Total	68	19	9	3

Source: "1988 Republican Primary Results and 1988 First Round Caucus Results," *Congressional Quarterly* 46, no. 3 (1988): 2254–255.

Much more striking than regional or temporal variation in Robertson's fortunes was the contrast between primary and caucus results. The results given in tables 5.1 and 5.2 are for primary states only. As we have seen, Robertson ran far more strongly in caucuses. Table 5.3 illustrates the disparity between primary and caucus results. This disparity is even more striking if we consider two results not included in table 5.3, the strong Robertson showings in the caucus states of Nevada and Michigan. In Nevada, Robertson lost the straw vote in the first-round caucus meetings but won a majority of the delegates in the final round. (Robertson delegates were instructed to vote "uncommitted" in the first round in order to hide their true strength.) In Michigan, an accurate count of first-round caucus results is not available but informal estimates gave Robertson roughly 40 percent of total support at this level, putting him about even with George Bush. Overall, Pat Robertson managed to win four caucus states (Nevada, Alaska, Washington, and Hawaii) and finish a strong second in several others.

Table 5.3
Robertson's Strongest Showings

	Position	% of Vote
In Caucus States		
Hawaii	1st	81.3
Alaska	1st	46.8
Washington	1st	39.0
Minnesota	2nd	28.2
Iowa	2nd	24.6
In Primary States		
Oklahoma	3d	21.1
S. Dakota	2nd	19.6
S. Carolina	3d	19.1
Arkansas	3d	18.9
Louisiana	2nd	18.2

Source: "1988 Republican Primary Results and 1988 First Round Caucus Results," Congressional Quarterly 46, no. 3 (1988): 2254–255.

In contrast to his strength in caucus states, Robertson averaged only 9 percent of the vote in primary states. In no primary state did Robertson even come close to winning. Oklahoma was his strongest primary state, yet he pulled only 21.1 percent of the vote and finished a distant third behind George Bush and Robert Dole.

Table 5.4, focusing on the number of delegates won by Robertson, paints a similar picture. The vast majority of Robertson's delegates were won in caucus states despite the fact that primaries chose a preponderance of the delegates.

Who?

Who supported Robertson's candidacy? Was he able to break beyond a core of evangelical support to gain acceptance from the general public? There is little evidence that Robertson broke beyond an evangelical base. Corwin Smidt and Lyman Kellstedt utilized the National Election Study (NES) Super Tuesday survey and divided white respondents into evangelical and nonevangelical categories. They found that 28.4 percent of evangelicals voted for Robertson, 43.2 percent for Bush. Among nonevangelicals, 0.0 percent voted for Robertson; not one of the 133 white nonevangelicals in the study voted for Robertson. The national NES primary survey finds 17.9 percent of white evangelicals voting for Robertson versus only 3.8 percent of nonevan-

Table 5.4
Robertson's Delegates

Total	128
Won in caucuses	106
Won in primaries	22
Percentage of total delegates won overall	
(128 of 2,277)	5.7
In caucus states	20.1
In primary states	1.2

Source: Calculated from a 12 August 1988 Americans For Robertson press release.

gelicals. These numbers provide a solid indication that Robertson made little headway outside an evangelical base; within that base, the results are mixed. Robertson ran strongly, particularly in the South, but he by no means had this base to himself.

What distinguished pro-Robertson evangelicals from other evangelicals? Clyde Wilcox took the same Super Tuesday data used by Smidt and Kellstedt and analyzed divisions within the evangelical community. What he found was striking. Of the members of Pentecostal denominations, 43 percent rated Robertson more highly than his Republican rivals; 0 percent of the members of fundamentalist denominations did so. Going into Super Tuesday, many observers thought that the enormous Southern Baptist Convention (SBC) would prove a fertile recruiting ground for Robertson. Robertson had been ordained as a Southern Baptist minister and he had the backing of a number of prominent denominational leaders. Nonetheless, only 8 percent of Southern Baptists rated Robertson above his Republican rivals.[123] Wilcox's findings confirm an argument made throughout this book: intra-evangelical religious differences matter. Fundamentalists and Southern Baptists simply did not view Robertson the way that Pentecostalists did.[124]

While the Super Tuesday survey had questions concerning the respondent's denomination, it did not have questions designed to identify charismatics (who may be members of a wide variety of denominations). Other data suggest, however, that charismatics were a significant component of Robertson's base. Smidt and Penning's study of delegates to the Michigan Republican Convention found that 57.3 percent of the Robertson supporters claimed to be "charismatic" (versus a mere 2.7 percent of Bush supporters). James Guth and John Green conducted an extensive series of analyses based on surveys of contributors to Republican political action committees affiliated with various presidential hopefuls. They discovered that 69 percent of Robertson's contributors are willing to label themselves "charismatic" (compared to 2 percent of the contributors to other Republican candidates). Many of those answering "charismatic" in the surveys mentioned above may well be what I have defined as Pentecostals. Nonetheless, it seems plausible that many charismatics rallied to Robertson's cause and that his was a very heavily charismatic/Pentecostalist campaign.[125]

Overall, Robertson's success was limited. His best showings came in caucuses, where organization and fervor, rather than widespread popular support, were the keys to victory. His support, as could be expected, was strongest in the South. Very few nonevangelicals were persuaded to support his effort. Among evangelicals results were mixed. Robertson obtained backing but this group by no means voted as a bloc. Data on voters, activists, and contributors paint a picture of a disproportionately Pentecostalist/charismatic campaign.

On to November—Robertson and His Followers through the General Election

As Robertson's campaign wound down in the spring of 1988, a key question remained: would the ex-candidate and his followers rally to the cause of George Bush? For this to happen, powerful animosities would have to be overcome. The rhetoric of the campaign had become extremely heated; harsh words exchanged during the nomination battles lingered on. Robertsonites remembered that Bush's brother Neil had referred to them as "cockroaches" issuing "from the baseboards of the Bible Belt." Robertson had responded with some very pointed attacks of his own.[126]

These statements notwithstanding, the most lasting anger had developed not between the national campaigns but rather at the state and local levels. Here the insurgent Robertson forces and pro-Bush party establishments confronted each other face-to-face. And in many cases they decided that they did not particularly like each other. Harsh words exchanged during the nomination battles lingered. Bush backers felt that newly mobilized Robertsonites were demanding influence without paying their dues in the party, that the Robertsonites were single-minded zealots who would lead the party to ruin. Robertson backers felt the party establishment was manipulating the rules against them and that the Bush forces were engaged in "Christian bashing." Equally important, very real local positions were still being contested. Neither side would lightly give up their claims to party posts. Nor, as the selection process dragged on, were they willing to give up their chance to go to the national convention.[127]

Despite lingering battles at the state level, Bush-Robertson relations were, for the most part, harmonious. The two met to patch up their differences in late April; Robertson struck a generally conciliatory tone, urging his supporters to turn their attention to attacking the Democrats. Bush began a widespread process of hiring on Robertson leaders for his campaign, starting with Robertson campaign director R. Marc Nuttle. Other top Robertson officials such as Midwest director Marlene Elwell and Robert Pinsky were hired on as well. Similar incorporation took place at the state level. In the words of one Robertson state director: "They hired everyone, all the Robertson consultants, which was a very shrewd move. No one was on the outside to criticize. Everyone was part of the Bush campaign." Incorporation did not always work smoothly but, on the whole, the efforts at conciliation were impressive given previous levels of conflict.[128]

Heading into the convention, the two main issues that remained of concern to the Robertson forces were the platform and Bush's vice presidential choice. The influence of Robertson forces on these two fronts is difficult to gauge, but in both cases they ended up with results that were to their liking.

Robertson and other conservatives had a distinct advantage in their attempts to influence the platform. That advantage was the 1984 platform. Ronald Reagan had run on a very conservative platform that year. George Bush, trying to run as Reagan's heir, would have a difficult time renouncing that platform. Thus conservatives mounted public pressure to "preserve" the Reagan platform.[129] Robertson joined in their efforts. Bush forces showed little desire to craft a more liberal document and, during platform hearings prior to the convention, attempts by GOP moderates such as Connecticut's Lowell Weicker to amend the platform were easily voted down.

Robertson's supporters had little to complain about in the final draft. The text was consistently conservative, particularly on issues of concern to the Christian Right. The document came out in favor of school prayer, the pledge of allegiance, access to school facilities by religious groups, a childcare plan that would not inhibit care by religious organizations, stricter regulations to control pornography, and the tax-exempt status of churches. Finally, and most important for the Christian Right, the platform takes a strong stand against abortion, supporting a human life amendment and calling for legislation to extend Fourteenth Amendment rights to fetuses. Furthermore, it opposes the provision of public funds to finance abortion or to finance any groups that "advocate or support abortion." It reaffirms "support for the appointment of judges at all levels of the judiciary who respect traditional family values and the sanctity of innocent human life."[130]

Robertson backers did not actively lobby for Dan Quayle. Prior to the convention Robertson had expressed support for Bob Dole. Dole's wife Elizabeth was also high on Robertson's list. Angry at what he perceived as Jack Kemp's double cross in Michigan, Robertson told his delegates that he did *not* want Kemp on the ticket. Robertson's personal preferences notwithstanding, the final choice was George Bush's. Robertson's, his supporters', and other conservatives' main means of influencing the selection process was by threatening to make trouble if the ultimate choice was offensive to them.[131]

The Robertson supporters I talked to were most worried about the prospect that Bush would choose a pro-choice candidate such as Illinois governor Jim Thompson, Wyoming senator Alan Simpson, or New Jersey governor Tom Kean. It is hard to gauge what would have happened had Bush picked a more moderate, pro-choice running mate. Robertson delegates I spoke with gave conflicting accounts as to whether some sort of walkout would have occurred. How heavily threats of trouble from the Right influenced Bush's choice is also difficult to determine. In any case, Bush picked the little-known, but quite conservative, Dan Quayle. The Christian Right found little to object to in the Indiana senator.

When Robertson gave the featured address to the convention on Tuesday night, 16 August, his supporters greeted him with hundreds of signs bearing the words "Robertson For Bush." Robertson announced that he was releasing his delegates and urged them to vote for George Bush. His speech, as discussed in chapter 4, was a play on Dickens's *Tale of Two Cities*, painting a sharp contrast between the horrors of the proposed Democratic "city" and the wonders of the Republican city that was to emerge under the leadership of George Bush.[132]

After the convention, Robertson campaigned loyally, if not too prominently, on behalf of George Bush. Bush's campaign featured a number of appeals designed to mobilize an evangelical constituency without alienating other crucial voting blocks. Particularly important in this regard was his emphasis on the pledge of allegiance and his attacks on the ACLU (the ACLU is strongly disliked within the Christian Right for its litigation on behalf of a strict separation of church and state). These appeals were attractive to evangelicals but much less controversial than other Christian Right causes, particularly abortion. While Gary Wills's conclusion that Bush won the election because he "adopted Pat Robertson's cause" may involve quite a bit of exaggeration, Bush did run a campaign well suited to the evocation of evangelical support.[133]

Bush benefited as well from the fact that the exit option was not a viable one. Whatever doubts there may have been about Bush's conservatism, about his dedication to a social issue agenda, there could be little doubt that he was far closer to Christian Right positions than his Democratic opponent. Even back on Super Tuesday, at the height of Robertson's battle with the Republican party "establishment," Robertson voters had shown little inclination to defect to the Democrats. A CBS News/*New York Times* Super Tuesday exit poll found that only 2 percent of Robertson supporters claimed that they would "probably" or "definitely" vote Democratic in the general election. An impressive 65 percent were definite and another 15 percent were probable

Republicans.[134] With the Democrats presenting an unattractive alternative and Bush moving to address evangelical concerns, it should come as little surprise that Bush received between 70 and 80 percent of the evangelical vote.[135] Even without Ronald Reagan at the top of the ticket, evangelicals were firmly in the Republican camp.

Robertson's Fate, Movement Voice

> In the quest for the highest secular prize our nation has to offer, a third place finish is respectable. But my supporters were devastated. It was as if they mourned for the dead. Because they felt—as I did—that God had called me to win, not run third.
>
> —Pat Robertson

What are we to make of Robertson's third place finish? What impact did it have on the position of the Christian Right within the Republican party? Like Robertson's "devastated" supporters, many observers saw Robertson's campaign as a failure. One runs a campaign to win and Robertson did not even come close to winning. Certainly the results dealt a blow to some of the more extravagant claims made prior to the election, claims that Robertson would mobilize a vast, evangelical army able to contend seriously for the nomination.[136] Many observers took Robertson's fate as a sign that the Christian Right had failed. Michael D'Antonio provides an example of this line of thinking: "With the demise of Robertson's campaign came the death of the Christian Right's political hopes. The born again movement soon ceased to be a significant religious or social force as well."[137]

The Christian Right has obviously not disappeared; D'Antonio and many others failed to properly assess the significance of Robertson's campaign. Winning a presidential nomination is not something one should expect from a social movement leader. Let us take, as a point of comparison, the labor and feminist movements within the Democratic party. Few would deny that these movements are—or at least have at times been—quite influential within the party. Yet that does not mean that Bella Abzug, Gloria Steinem, George Meany, or Walter Reuther could have obtained the Democratic nomination. Each would have faced controversy and high "negatives" had they decided to run. Many voters would have wondered about their lack of political experience. Running against established Democratic politicians who adopted many of their causes, they might well have fared even more poorly than Robertson.

Robertson's fate does illustrate several of the points made about the Christian Right constituency in chapters 1 and 2. Religious divisions within that constituency and a lack of credibility outside it were problems for his campaign as they were for the Christian Right in general. Robertson found it difficult to attract neoevangelicals and, especially, fundamentalists to his campaign. His background as a televangelist, his divine communications, his belief in miracles and Armageddon theology, all undermined his credibility as a political figure. Like the evangelical subculture he came from, Robertson found it hard to win respect for his doctrines in a public forum.

If we examine the *way* in which Robertson lost, however, we can see that his loss is not simply an indication of Christian Right weakness. Robertson's failure to unite a politically conservative evangelical constituency behind his candidacy reflected the fact that that constituency was significantly larger than the pool of Robertson supporters. Those who dismissed the Christian Right's following based on Robertson's limited success were in for a surprise. The limited appeal of the candidate did not indicate the full potential of the movement.

A critical factor in Robertson's defeat was the fact that his Republican rivals adopted positions advocated by the Christian Right: opposition to abortion, opposition to the ERA, support for school prayer. Furthermore, they actively courted Christian Right leaders and their constituency. Thus, the *personal* defeat of Robertson was closely linked to the attention and respect Republicans were giving the Christian Right as a *movement*. The nominating battle over, the party adopted and George Bush ran on a platform the Christian Right could enthusiastically endorse.

Robertson's campaign was conducted in the shadow of the long term changes in partisan divisions discussed in chapter 4. Social issues, once only loosely related to partisan divisions, now are a defining aspect of party cleavages. The fact that the GOP had taken up the social issue causes that Robertson's supporters so fervently espoused did limit the candidate's maneuvering room, but it was also a sign that the Christian Right movement had become an established part of the Republican coalition.

A final reason not to dismiss Robertson's campaign as a failure is to be found in the resources and local activists he mobilized. Robertson demonstrated that evangelical networks could be tapped to raise large sums of money and an impressive army of local volunteers for use within the Republican party. Prior to Robertson, many Christian Right groups were top-heavy, long on publicity and direct mail solicitations but often with limited grassroots organization. The local activists who had been mobilized by groups such as the Moral Majority tended to be drawn from the ranks of fundamentalists. Robertson brought a new, heavily charismatic and Pentecostalist, wave of local activists into the political arena. Furthermore, the activists he mobilized had, by way of the campaign, been drawn into party politics. They had battled to control caucuses and party conventions. In the process, they learned electoral skills: how to raise money, the rules of order that governed party meetings, how to organize a precinct. Armed with these skills, they had taken over several state Republican parties and were a significant force in many others. In these local activists, the Robertson campaign's efforts might live on to affect the course of Republican politics for many years to come.

Chapter 6

A Voice Within: Grassroots Activism and a Place at the Republican Table

When partisan realignment on social issues was combined with mobilization of grassroots Christian Right activists brought about by the Robertson campaign, relations between the Christian Right and the Republican party entered a new era. By the late 1980s, the movement was firmly tied to the party. Exit was becoming a less and less plausible option. On the other hand, grassroots strength laid the foundation for the effective exercise of voice within the party. This chapter will examine the successes and failures met with, and the dilemmas encountered, as the Christian Right has attempted to influence party affairs.

Failed Campaigns, Transformed Parties

A year after the failure of his presidential campaign, Pat Robertson offered the following assessment of its lasting impact:

> Could it be that the reason for my candidacy has been fulfilled in the activation of tens of thousands of evangelical Christians into government? This campaign taught them that they were citizens with as much right to express their beliefs as any of the strident activists who have been so vocal in support of their own radical agenda at every level of our government. For the first time in recent history, patriotic, pro-family Christians learned the simple techniques of effective party organizing and successful campaigning.
>
> Their presence as an active force in American politics may result ultimately in at least one of America's major political parties taking on a profoundly Christian outlook in its platforms and party structure.[1]

183

Pat Robertson's claim seemed rather presumptuous for a candidate who finished a distant third in the contest for the Republican nomination. Yet, in American politics, failed campaigns can prove to be foundations for future success. Barry Goldwater's candidacy, as we saw in chapter 4, is a case in point. In 1964, Goldwater led the GOP to a humiliating defeat, capturing less than 40 percent of the vote and dragging scores of congressional candidates down with him. Many saw this defeat as the death knell of the Republican Right. Instead, it turned out that the Goldwater campaign had mobilized a new corps of conservative activists, generated a long and very useful donor list, and articulated themes that were to help fuel the GOP's growing strength in the Sun Belt states.[2] Thus Goldwater's defeat provided the basis for the eventual triumph of Ronald Reagan. A similar case can be made concerning George McGovern's 1972 campaign. McGovern suffered an equally humiliating loss (although without the same consequences for his colleagues in Congress), but the liberal activists he mobilized remained to play a leading role in Democratic party affairs for years to come. If not for a personal scandal, McGovern's campaign manager Gary Hart might well have received the Democratic presidential nomination in 1988. Will Robertson's campaign have a similar long-range impact upon his party?

In the immediate aftermath of the Robertson campaign, comparisons to Goldwater and McGovern would have seemed presumptuous. Whatever their problems in the general election, Goldwater and McGovern did manage to win their parties' nomination. Robertson came in a distant third. George Bush won the nomination in decisive fashion and swept to victory in November. While the Bush campaign reached out to the Robertsonites, there was no doubt which faction was in control of the party. Furthermore, the Christian Right as a whole appeared to be losing steam in the late 1980s. The televangelist scandals had taken a heavy toll. Many of the movement's leading organizations had died (Moral Majority) or lost their vitality (Christian Voice, Religious Roundtable). Robertson returned to his Christian Broadcasting Network in an attempt to rebuild its battered finances. Several outside observers announced the Christian Right's actual or imminent demise.[3]

However, today things look very different. The Christian Right has emerged from the late 1980s lull in activism with greater grassroots strength than ever before. Pat Robertson's Christian Coalition claims over a million and a half members and chapters in all fifty states.[4] The movement's renewed vitality is being felt within the GOP. As of the fall of 1994, an estimated eighteen state Republican parties were under Christian Right control; the movement was a "substantial" force in thirteen more.[5] The Robertson campaign, and the broader social movement it embodied, has fundamentally reshaped the Republican party.

The Newcomers

In order to understand the role the Christian Right activists mobilized by Robertson have played within the party, we need a sense of who they were, what they believed, and what motivated them. As they came into the party in the mid to late 1980s, these activists stood out from traditional Republican party "regulars." The differences and lack of understanding that separated the Robertsonites from other elements of the Republican party came out quite clearly in a series of interviews I conducted with state-level party activists in 1989.[6] These differences went well beyond the squabbles that normally divide rival party factions. Bush and Dole partisans had their differences in 1988 but once the race was over it was hard to tell them apart. The Robertsonites retained their distinctiveness.

Religion Meets Politics

Not surprisingly, the biggest differences between the Robertsonites and other elements of the party were religious. Robertson supporters attended church more often and were far more likely to consider themselves born again, evangelical, and/or fundamentalist. A large proportion were, like Robertson himself, charismatics or were Pentecostalists.[7] Bush, Kemp, and Dole supporters were often religious but their religious and political lives were kept distinct. General references to God or to "traditional values" crept into their discourse, but rarely did they invoke more specific religious doctrines or cite scripture. Among Robertson's followers, the line separating religious and political discourse was much more tenuous. Examples from the Bible were used to support arguments about campaign strategy; political meetings often began with prayer.

Differing outlooks fueled mutual suspicion. Republican party regulars felt that mixing religion and politics was improper. They feared that it would hurt the party by scaring away those of different faiths and convincing the public that they are a "bunch of kooks."[8] Their fears were heightened by the often exclusive nature of the Robertsonites' faith. Party regulars were generally comfortable with vague appeals about the importance of religion and "traditional values"; they did not look kindly upon a "Christian" politics from which they were excluded. When Robertson's Michigan campaign announced its strong showing in local caucuses by putting out a newsletter proclaiming "The

Christians have won!" many Republicans in opposing camps—faithful
Catholics, Jews, and mainline Protestants—were not amused. A high
official in the Michigan Bush campaign had this to say of the Robertson leader in his district: "Jewish party members are ruled out by her
measure. The politics of 'Christian values' is a politics of elimina-
tion and exclusion." Robertson's supporters often spoke as though the
"Christian" position on issues and candidates was clear and undebat-
able, a form of discourse that left little room for those who disagreed.
A Bush leader in Washington State complained that a minister who
had backed him in a local battle with Robertson supporters had been
subjected to harassing phone calls. Callers repeatedly claimed that the
minister was "not a Christian."

Robertson supporters viewed matters in a different light. They re-
alized that their religious views set them apart from other elements of
the party. A Robertson official in Washington State argued that outsiders had not "felt the wind" and therefore could not understand what
was animating the movement. However, they did not see why their
distinct perspective should be kept out of public life. They saw the
moral foundation provided by religion as the necessary underpinning
of a moral society and a healthy polity. Robertson's supporters believed it was the banishing of religion from American public life, seen
in such measures as the prohibition of school prayer, that had led this
nation into decline. To separate religion from politics was, in their
view, to take away the foundation upon which the American political
experiment was built. Furthermore, they said, it is an illusion. Robertson supporters argued that American politics is *already* suffused with
a religious perspective, the secular "religion" of humanism.

Robertson supporters felt that complaints about the mixing of religion and politics were, in fact, a cover for intolerance of *their* religious beliefs. Robertson's supporters were quite aware that certain
Republicans viewed them as religious fanatics and treated them ac-
cordingly. It was party regulars, they argued, who were practicing the
politics of exclusion. They suspected that the "separation of church
and state" was being used as a tool for the promotion of secularism.
Or, in the words of one Robertson supporter, "Bush's people verge on
being anti-religious."

Compromise

Robertsonites were also distinctive in their attitude toward compromise. Most non-Robertson party activists had a substantial history of
involvement in party affairs. While many had strongly held political

beliefs, they were willing to compromise to hold together coalitions and achieve victory. A substantial number looked forward to sharing in the spoils of victory at the state or national levels. They argued that the ideological rigidity of the Robertsonites made them difficult to work with and undermined the prospects of party success. In the words of one district Bush leader: "When you have the votes they work with you. When you don't they slam dunk you." If the Robertsonites were going to adopt a "take no prisoners" approach to party affairs, they argued, long-term cooperation would be difficult.

Robertson's supporters came to politics from a religious perspective hostile to compromise. Evangelical Christians (particularly fundamentalists) have spent the last century battling against religious "modernism," against those who would compromise the literal authority of scripture in an effort to stay in tune with the intellectual currents of the time. They take great pride in sticking steadfastly to their beliefs. This is how, after all, they have maintained their subculture and its values in the face of a hostile world. Given the Robertsonites' intermingling of religious and political reasoning, it came as no surprise that this attitude toward religious compromise was carried over into politics. In the words of a Michigan activist: "We are seen as inflammatory and divisive. I guess we are. But sometimes what is right is [divisive]." This attitude was reenforced by the fact that numerous Robertsonites were newcomers to politics. Like many Americans, they tended to view "politics" and the compromises it entails as corrupt. A Robertson organizer described how his followers' suspicions of state party leaders were fueled: "Anything we heard about party leaders was gospel. It was all we had. . . . We considered all politicians crooked anyways."

Social Distance

Finally, Robertson's supporters did not fit the social profile of other Republican activists. While the Robertson activists were by no means poor, they were a group of more modest income and educational attainment than other Republican activists. Differences went beyond these more concrete measures to issues of style. In 1986, Jo Freeman characterized battles between party regulars and members of the Christian Right as a battle between the "ultrasuedes" and the "polyesters." My experience at the 1988 and 1992 Republican conventions fit neatly with her observations. At the Robertson headquarters in 1988 or at the "God and Country" Rally in 1992, one came across a sartorially distinct subgroup. The activists brought in by Robertson were not the uneducated, backwoods hicks that some would stereotype them as, but their social background was not that typical of other Republican activists.[9]

Sometimes class differences were openly addressed as a source of conflict. A county coordinator for the Washington Robertson campaign declared: "We're trying to turn the Republican party from being the class of business people or the party of the rich to become the party of the people."[10] Complaints about "the country club set" cropped up on occasion in my interviews. More often the problem was not overt hostility but simple unfamiliarity. Party regulars usually had long experience in the party together. They were associated with the same clubs and political organizations. In short, they were a familiar quantity to each other. Similarly, the Robertsonites shared common religious backgrounds and organizational affiliations. Even when they had not previously met, they could find common ground in the spiritual experiences they shared. Between the two groups much less was held in common. A Bush supporter told the story of her most recent reunion. There she ran into one of her best high school friends. The friend had been "born again" and was active in an evangelical church. The two found that, despite their past ties, they had nothing in common and little to say to each other. Their experience captures the social gulf that so often divided Robertsonites from party regulars.

Movement Resurgence

Rise of the Christian Coalition

The most important organization of the present-day Christian Right, the Christian Coalition, was built upon the base laid by the Robertson presidential campaign. In 1989, that base did not look very impressive. The GOP was under the firm control of Robertson's victorious rival, George Bush. The Robertsonites, as described above, did not fit in with the party's dominant wing and appeared to be losing strength. Bruce Hawkins, Robertson's 1988 Washington campaign chair and Christian Coalition press secretary at the 1992 Republican convention, described the Robertson forces as "burned out, contributed out, and often bitter." Robertson himself feared that "local activists . . . were drifting away, their energy and enthusiasm dissipating." Signs of weakness went beyond the Robertsonites to the Christian Right as a whole. The televangelist scandals had undermined the credibility of the movement and the finances of some of its leading figures. Many of the leading organizations of the Christian Right's first decade were dead or moribund, including the Moral Majority, Christian Voice, Religious Roundtable, and the National Christian Action Coalition.[11]

At this low point in the life of the movement, Pat Robertson formed a new organization. A young Republican activist, Ralph Reed, was brought on board to manage day-to-day operations, and in the fall of 1989 the Christian Coalition was born. Its first task was to reinvigorate and organize the movement's dispirited base. This it did with remarkable success. From 25,000 members in June of 1990, the coalition grew to 150,000 members in January of 1992, and 250,000 by the time of the 1992 GOP convention. Since the convention, its growth has been even more spectacular. As of the summer of 1995, the Christian Coalition claimed "1.6 million members and supporters in 1,600 local chapters in all fifty states."

Christian Right organizations do have a history of optimistic assessments of their own strength; these numbers are likely somewhat inflated. For example, it is not entirely clear what being a "supporter" of the group entails. Skipp Porteous points out that, as of December 1994, the coalition's magazine *Christian American* had a paid circulation of 353,703, far below the organization's membership claims. (It should be noted, however, that many of these magazines are going to multimember households.) Even allowing for a margin of exaggeration, the coalition's growth has been spectacular.[12]

The Christian Coalition's organizing efforts differed from those of earlier Christian Right organizations in three main ways. First, the coalition emphasized building from the grass roots. Groups like the Moral Majority rested on an unstable base of direct mail appeals. Beneath an impressive looking centralized fundraising apparatus, local organization was often lacking. From the beginning, the Christian Coalition sought to establish a stable membership base and to involve those members in activities beyond the sending of an occasional check. The coalition's leadership schools and written materials take citizens step-by-step through processes such as setting up chapters, running petition and voter registration drives, and building alliances. The coalition's efforts in this regard are vital for the political involvement of a constituency that lacks the political experience of party regulars.[13]

Second, the coalition focused on elections. This was by no means a new activity for the Christian Right; earlier groups participated in the electoral process and claimed credit for outcomes such as the Republican victories of 1980 and 1984. However, the coalition was much more systematic in its electoral organizing. A former leader of the college Republicans and veteran of twenty-five congressional campaigns, executive director Ralph Reed helped the coalition employ technologically sophisticated, state-of-the-art campaign techniques. The coalition utilized its contacts within tens of thousands of churches and distributed tens of millions of "voter guides." The early Christian Right, according to the near universal assessment of movement activists I interviewed in the late 1980s, had aimed too high, running inexperienced candidates for the House, the Senate, or, in the case of Robertson, the presidency, without putting in the necessary groundwork first. In keeping with its grassroots focus, the Christian Coalition targeted school board and county elections as well as congressional and presidential campaigns. Low-level victories were seen as valuable in their own right, but also as important steps in the creation of a pool of candidates qualified to run for a higher-level office.

Finally, the Christian Coalition differed from earlier movement groups in its focus on the Republican party. The Robertson campaign had not only brought in a new wave of movement activists, it had targeted their activism on the internal processes of the Republican party. The Robertsonites flooded into state and local Republican party organizations. They participated in presidential primaries and caucuses and struggled with the complexities of the delegate selection process. The Christian Coalition built upon their experience. Whereas previous movement groups had had incidental dealings with the party, the coalition, from its beginning, made organizing within the party a central focus of its overall activity. Published in conjunction with the coalition's Road to Victory conference, the 1991 "Conference and Strategy Briefing" provides a telling example of the organization's party focus. The first one hundred pages of the document are devoted to the Republican party delegate selection process. State-by-state descriptions of that process are provided along with a special appendix entitled "The Iowa Model: In-Depth Preparation for Caucus Participation." The second half of the document is focused upon elections, with sections on turning out the Christian vote, key House and Senate races, and voter identification and targeted mail.[14]

The coalition's party activities are for all practical purposes confined to the Republican party. Although the organization is officially bipartisan and makes prominent references to Democratic allies such as former Pennsylvania governor Robert Casey, its ties to the Republicans are clear. The strategy-briefing document mentioned above had no section dedicated to the Democratic delegate selection process. At the 1991 Road to Victory conference, a single meeting on the Democratic selection process was scheduled. No one attended. At the 1993 Road to Victory conference, the coalition made a point of inviting then Democratic party chairman David Wilhelm. Unfortunately for the group's bipartisan reputation, he was met by booing from the audience. The rest of the conference program was filled with speeches from Republican leaders, including Bill Bennett, Pat Buchanan, Robert Dole, Newt Gingrich, Phil Gramm, Jesse Helms, and Jack Kemp. An even clearer sign of the group's party ties was a $64,000 grant from the National Republican Senatorial Committee, received in 1992.[15]

Other Groups

The Christian Coalition is the largest organization of the contemporary Christian Right and its focus on elections and parties makes it particularly relevant to this study, but it does not act alone. Particularly important in recent years has been Focus on the Family, led by Dr. James Dobson. Dobson holds a Ph.D. in psychology from the University of Southern California. His "Focus on the Family" radio program deals primarily with issues such as marriage and child rearing, but the political slant of the program is hard to miss. Dobson's audience is enormous. In the early 1990s, his was the second-largest syndicated radio show in the United States, appearing on over sixteen hundred stations.[16] In 1992, Focus on the Family operated on a $78 million budget, answered twelve hundred phone calls a day, and sent out over fifty-two million pieces of literature.[17] When Dobson takes up an issue, Congress is quickly bombarded with phone calls and letters. Dobson's Colorado Springs offices have served as the hub as that city has become a national headquarters for the Christian Right.

From 1988 through 1992, the Family Research Council (FRC), headed by former Reagan administration official Gary Bauer, was affiliated with Focus on the Family. The FRC serves as the movement's leading think tank, producing policy analysis on a variety of family-related topics. The FRC is now formally independent but works closely with Focus on the Family. Bauer, a leading Christian Right spokesman, is a frequent guest on Dobson's show.

Other major Christian Right groups include Beverly LaHaye's Concerned Women for America, Donald Wildmon's American Family Association, and Lou Sheldon's California-based Traditional Values Coalition. In addition, a number of legal groups use the courts to promote the movement's agenda. The American Center for Law and Justice (affiliated with Pat Robertson) and the Rutherford Institute are among the most notable of these. Finally, there exist a wide array of grassroots groups organized at the state or local level.

Issue by issue and campaign by campaign, different mixes of Christian Right organizations will become involved. Groups specialize, with the Christian Coalition taking the lead on elections, the American Family Association taking the lead on media boycotts, and so on. Nonetheless, it is important to realize that, impressive as its resources are, the Christian Coalition is not alone in its electoral and party work. Other Christian Right groups play an important role in mobilizing the activists and disseminating the messages that enable the movement to play a role within the Republican party.

The Christian Coalition and other movement groups have brought the Christian Right's mobilization within the GOP to a new and higher level in the 1990s. But their activism within the party has not been without problems. The social and cultural gaps that separated Robertson activists from the rest of the party in 1988 have not gone away. Their roots go back to the issues discussed in the first two chapters of this book. The Christian Right's religious language, aversion to compromise, and social base are the legacy of the evangelical religious heritage, which was discussed in chapter 1. The dilemmas it faces are rooted in the uneasy tension between subcultural values and the broader society, which was analyzed in chapter 2. While the private vitality of the evangelical subculture is the source of the movement's strength, aspects of that culture do not play well with outsiders (including nonevangelical Republicans). Yet, the Christian Right needs to work with those outsiders to achieve its goals. As the Christian Right has entered the public realm of politics, it has had to play a delicate balancing act: appealing to its base while at the same time forming the coalitions with outsiders necessary to effectively exercise its voice within the Republican party. The rest of this chapter will look at the Christian Right's success in carrying off that balancing act.

1992: Alliance and Defeat

The 1992 presidential campaign marked a deepening of the Christian Right's ties to the Republican party. Exit to the Democrats—their nomination of two Southern Baptists to top their ticket notwithstanding—was never a serious option. The Christian Right opted to exercise its voice within the Republican party and the organizational abilities of the Christian Coalition and allied groups won the movement a powerful role at the 1992 GOP Convention. That convention approved a platform even more socially conservative than those of the 1980s. The Christian Right's role in the party was exhibited for the entire nation to see.

However, 1992 was hardly an unqualified success for the Christian Right. The compromises made to gain a voice within the party were highly controversial within the movement. Media reaction to the Christian Right's role at the convention was decidedly negative. And, of course, the movement's preferred candidate, George Bush, lost the election in November—an outcome for which the Christian Right was often blamed.

Bush

An incumbent president personifies his party and is usually the central figure in its relation with social movements; so it was with George Bush and the Christian Right. Whereas the Christian Right had been enthusiastic in its support of Ronald Reagan, the movement was, in the words of one leader, "positively ambivalent" toward George Bush.[18] George Herbert Walker Bush was always an unlikely champion for the causes of the Christian Right. An Episcopalian from a wealthy Northeastern family, Bush was clearly uncomfortable with the Bible Belt enthusiasm of evangelicals. Just as a large cultural and religious gap separated the Robertsonites from GOP regulars at the state party level, so too was the Christian Right separated from George Bush. Furthermore, Christian Right leaders remembered Bush's first bid for the presidency. In 1980, he presented himself as the moderate alternative to the conservatism of Ronald Reagan. Significantly, Bush supported a woman's right to choose an abortion. Leaders of the then-emerging Christian Right were not impressed. Jerry Falwell lobbied hard to keep Bush off the GOP ticket. Bush reversed himself on abortion and even won Falwell's backing in his 1988 nomination battle. By means of an arduous courtship, George Bush won the support of the Christian Right in the 1988 general election campaign. But as he took office in 1989, the movement still had doubts about him. Many within the Christian Right felt his professions of loyalty to their causes were of questionable sincerity.

From the perspective of the Christian Right, George Bush's record in office was a mixed one. On the issue of abortion, the president's past position was a source of concern. So too were statements by party chairman Lee Atwater and Vice President Dan Quayle referring to the GOP as a "big tent," capable of accommodating conflicting views on the issue. Pro-life forces feared such language opened the way to significant weakening of the party's position on abortion; Phyllis Schlafly, in a joking remark with her supporters, referred to "tent" as a "four-letter word."[19] On the other hand, the Christian Right was generally satisfied with the Bush administration's *actions* on the abortion issue. The Bush veto stood as a bulwark against pro-choice legislation. The administration took a strong stand in its arguments before the Supreme Court, explicitly calling for a reversal of *Roe v. Wade*.[20]

The record was similarly mixed on other issues of concern to the Christian Right. Bush's selection of Clarence Thomas for a seat on the Supreme Court won the enthusiastic endorsement of the movement. While the general public was deeply divided over Thomas's nomination, Christian Right activists I have spoken to expressed uniform—and very strong—support. The Family Research Council's Gary Bauer was chairman of the Citizens Committee to Confirm Clarence Thomas. President Bush's handling of the National Endowment for the Arts (NEA) drew less support. Christian Right groups such as Pat Robertson's Christian Coalition were at the forefront of campaigns against the allegedly obscene and blasphemous art funded by the NEA under the leadership of John Frohnmayer. Bush, a personal friend of Frohnmayer's who did not see the NEA as a high priority issue, was slow to react. Under pressure from the Christian Right and the Buchanan campaign, Bush eventually fired Frohnmayer, but the issue served to underline the movement's doubts about the president.[21]

In the wake of the United States' victory in the Persian Gulf War, George Bush declared his intention to build a "New World Order." This, it turned out, caused considerable anxiety in Christian Right circles. For decades, conservative evangelical leaders had been warning against the coming danger of a "socialist, one-world order." Secular organizations of the far right, most notably the John Birch Society, had long promoted similar fears. Evangelical fears were rooted in a complex mix of nationalism and biblical prophecy (the emergence of the new world government was linked to the return of the Antichrist). Both the secular and the religious far right argued that an "establishment" elite would sell out American interests in pursuit of a unified system of global domination. George Bush's embrace of the United Nations, his links to the foreign policy establishment, and his use of the term "New World Order" provided fodder for a variety of right-wing conspiracy theories. Pat Robertson's 1991 bestseller *The New World Order* issued the following warning:

> Indeed, it may well be that men of goodwill like Woodrow Wilson, Jimmy Carter, and George Bush, who sincerely want a larger community of nations living at peace in our world, are in reality unknowingly and unwittingly carrying out the mission and mouthing the phrases of a

tightly knit cabal whose goal is nothing less than a new world order for the human race under the domination of Lucifer and his followers.[22]

While the general public heard little of the furor this issue raised, Leigh Ann Metzger, the Bush White House's outreach director for evangelicals, was kept busy reassuring the Right that no sinister intentions lay behind Bush's New World Order.[23]

It was on gay and lesbian issues, however, that the Bush administration's performance drew the sharpest—and most public—criticism from the Christian Right. Gay leaders were invited to attend a White House signing of a hate crimes bill. Bush campaign chair Robert Mosbacher met with leaders of gay and lesbian groups in early 1992. These actions certainly did not establish George Bush as a champion of gay and lesbian rights. They were, however, enough to outrage a number of Christian Right leaders. Doug Wead, Bush's own liaison to evangelicals, resigned in protest.

The administration's mixed record provoked varying responses from Christian Right leaders. The loudest protests, interestingly, came from elements of the movement known in the past for their moderation. Richard Land and James Smith of the Southern Baptist Convention's Christian Life Commission joined the National Association of Evangelicals' political director Robert Dugan, in scathing criticism of the president. These criticisms began in the wake of an April 1990 White House ceremony to which gay leaders were invited and continued through the 1992 primary season. Although other issues, most notably the National Endowment for the Arts (NEA), drove criticism of the president, homosexuality remained the principle focus. The critics were not only concerned about Bush's past meetings, they also wanted him to come out with a strong public statement opposing gay and lesbian rights.

In an attempt to deal with discontent, President Bush requested a meeting with fifteen evangelical leaders including Dugan, Jerry Falwell, and Beverly LaHaye. At the April 1992 meeting, Bush assured them that he opposed "special laws" to protect homosexual rights and affirmed his opposition to a District of Columbia domestic partners law. While leaders of the Christian Right's more directly political organizations lined up behind Bush, National Association of Evangelicals and Southern Baptist officials continued to express their dissatisfaction, publicly attacking Pat Robertson, Jerry Falwell, and Beverly LaHaye for supporting the president. Only after further reassurances from Bush—and the passage of a Republican platform with strong antigay rights planks—did the criticism die down.[24]

Failure of the Buchanan Challenge

For much of 1991, it looked as if George Bush would be renominated without a challenge. In the wake of the Persian Gulf War, Bush's approval ratings were at astronomically high levels. His nomination—and, for that matter, success in the general election—seemed assured. But, as the glow of military victory wore off, concern about the state of the economy brought Bush's approval ratings down to earth and brought a challenge for the nomination from syndicated columnist and television commentator Patrick Buchanan. How the Christian Right dealt with that challenge said a lot about its emerging role within the party.

Given the dissatisfaction with the president that existed in Christian Right ranks, Pat Buchanan's challenge from the Right might have been expected to have gained its enthusiastic support. Buchanan embraced the movement's social issue agenda, attaining notoriety with his explicit ads attacking the National Endowment for the Arts. Gary Bauer of the Family Research Council and ex-Robertson campaign chair Marc Nuttle were among those in attendance at an early meeting where Buchanan explored the possibility of entering the race.[25] Buchanan also gained the support of some lower-level Christian Right activists. Pat Robertson's 1988 Michigan and Washington state campaign chairs enlisted in the Buchanan effort.[26]

Overall, however, Buchanan met with quite limited success in his attempt to win over Christian Right leaders and their constituencies. The movement's most visible figures, such as Jerry Falwell and Pat Robertson, remained firmly in the president's camp. On the eve of critical southern primary contests, the Bush campaign distributed a letter from Robertson reaffirming his support for the president. A March 1992 poll taken at the National Association of Evangelicals' annual meeting showed Bush ahead by an 88 percent to 12 percent margin. The Georgia primary illustrated the limits of Buchanan's evangelical appeal. Despite a series of advertisements attacking Bush's handling of the NEA, Bush prevailed over Buchanan by 60 percent to 40 percent among white born-again Christians. Buchanan's showing was slightly better than the 36 percent he received among the state's voters as a whole, but George Bush nonetheless won the majority of born-agains over to his side.[27]

Why did Buchanan fail to do better among Christian Right leaders and their constituencies? First, Buchanan's nativist and isolationist tendencies probably raised questions here just as they did among the public at large. Second, the fact that Buchanan is Catholic may have undercut his appeal to some evangelical Protestants. Third, and probably most important for Christian Right leaders, Buchanan stood little chance of winning. In the words of Christian Coalition chairman Ralph Reed, "We went through one suicide mission in 1988 and we won't do it again."[28]

Party Ties

The Christian Right's unwillingness to undertake "suicide missions" reflected the fact that, by 1992, the movement had developed other, more effective, means of exercising influence. The development of the movement's grassroots capabilities gave it the ability to exercise a powerful voice within the party. Christian Coalition, in particular, was looking toward the long term, slowly building its legitimacy and power within the Republican party. Its leaders wanted to demonstrate that they were "true Republicans." These efforts would be undermined if coalition leaders challenged their party's incumbent president and threw their support to the doomed candidacy of Pat Buchanan.[29] The coalition was rewarded for its loyalty. A $64,000 grant from the National Republican Senatorial Committee represented the largest single contribution to Christian Coalition in the course of the 1992 campaign.[30]

It was the leaders based in *religious* organizations, such as the Southern Baptist Convention's Richard Land and James Smith and the National Association of Evangelicals' Robert Dugan, who were most willing to break with the president. These organizations had not developed the same ties to the GOP as their political counterparts. This gave them greater freedom to challenge party leaders. In the words of the NAE's political director Dugan, "We are not a partisan group and we can criticize both sides."[31]

Houston, Bush, and the Christian Right

The Christian Right, however, did not need to turn against the president to exercise influence in 1992. The movement became a powerful presence at the GOP's Houston convention, and won a platform very much to its liking, largely by supporting George Bush. Christian Coalition placed a high priority on getting its members selected as convention delegates. While in most states primaries determine which presidential candidate delegates will be pledged to support, they often do not determine who those delegates will be. In many cases, the delegates themselves are chosen in a separate process, in local caucuses or state party meetings. In 1988, the Robertson campaign used its strength at this level to send a number of their supporters to the convention as pledged Bush or Dole delegates. (While in most cases obligated by state law to vote for Bush or Dole on the first ballot, these delegates where free to side with Robertson on other issues.)

Christian Coalition, building on the foundation laid by the Robertson campaign, proved a powerful force in these narrow arenas in 1992. The organization worked hard to educate its members on the intricacies of the selection process and get them out to local meetings. The fact that Robertson had endorsed President Bush early on and reaffirmed his support during the primary process helped bolster the legitimacy of their requests for positions as Bush delegates. Christian Coalition leaders claim that 300 of the 2,209 delegates in Houston were members of their organization, a stronger delegate base than Robertson attained in 1988 when he was an active candidate for the nomination. With this base of delegates, Christian Coalition played an active role as state delegate caucuses picked the members of the party's platform committee. Of the committee's 107 members, 20 were members of Christian Coalition.[32]

The Christian Coalition was not alone in its organizing efforts. The Republican National Coalition for Life was started by conservative activist Phyllis Schlafly in October of 1990 for the specific purpose of defending a pro-life platform. With a board of directors featuring Christian Right luminaries Beverly LaHaye (head of Concerned Women for America) and Gary Bauer (head of the Family Research Council) and longtime conservative activist Morton Blackwell, RNC for Life was active in mobilizing pro-lifers to become delegates and platform committee members. On the first day of full committee hearings, Schlafly held a press conference to demonstrate her group's grassroots strength, presenting the platform committee with nearly 100,000 "pledges" by individuals requesting that the party retain the antiabortion language of its 1984 and 1988 platforms.[33] Thirty-five hundred of the signatures, Schlafly says, came from elected officials and individuals holding party titles. While Schlafly did not make specific claims as to how many on the platform committee were "members" of RNC for Life, she does contend that RNC for Life was on "very friendly" terms with 40 of the 107.[34]

Christian Coalition and RNC for Life did not go unopposed, however. Awakened from their slumber by the Supreme Court's Webster decision, pro-choice Republicans were active and ready to contest the abortion issue. Leading this effort were Mary Dent Crisp's National Republican Coalition for Choice and Ann Stone's Republicans for

Choice.[35] Like their opponents, NRC for Choice and Republicans for Choice attempted to educate supporters about the intricacies of the delegate selection process and get them involved. The pro-choice side—Ann Stone in particular—attained great visibility. The news media highlighted pro-choice leaders, focused on divisions within the ranks of Republican voters, and speculated as to the possibility of a floor fight on the abortion issue.

The Platform

Christian Right mobilization paid off at the GOP convention in Houston. The week prior to the main convention activities was given over to the party platform, with abortion as the key point of contention. As the Republican platform subcommittees convened on 10 August, it was clear that pro-choice forces faced an uphill fight.[36] The subcommittee on Individual Rights, Good Homes and Safe Streets dealt with the platform's abortion language. The subcommittee chair was Mary Potter Summa. A member of Phyllis Schlafly's Eagle Forum and a former legislative assistant to Jesse Helms, Summa was pregnant at the time of the meeting, a fact she made known to dramatic effect in her arguments for a pro-life position. The pro-choice forces found little support in the subcommittee; the vote was seventeen to three in favor of keeping the platform's call for a constitutional ban on abortion.

In the full committee, pro-choice forces planned a series of five amendments, moving from one they felt would be hardest to pass (striking all abortion language from the platform) to that they felt would be easiest (adding "big tent" language acknowledging party differences on abortion). The plan had involved difficult negotiations to bring coordination to the independent-minded pro-choice platform committee members.[37] The plan met with little success. When the amendment to strike the platform's abortion language came up, the pro-life side demanded a roll call vote. The amendment failed eighty-four to sixteen. The New England states, traditional home of liberal Republicanism, provided a six to four (two absent) vote in favor of the amendment but in other regions of the country opposition was overwhelming. The vote was a demoralizing blow to the pro-choice side, demonstrating that efforts to alter the platform were likely to prove futile. In Phyllis Schlafly's words, "They were blown out of the water." Later votes were not recorded but further pro-choice amendments lost by what appeared to be very large margins. Even an attempt to add language expressing sympathy with victims of rape and incest was voted down handily by a pro-life majority fearful of anything that could be interpreted as a weakening of the platform's abortion language.[38]

The platform committee did eventually offer a nonbinding resolution acknowledging party differences on abortion and other issues. But this resolution was a token gesture; it did not go into the platform; it did nothing to alter the sweeping victory of the pro-life side. Ann Stone, chairwoman of Republicans for Choice, does, however, believe that the resolution helped undermine her efforts to get the twenty-seven votes from the platform committee needed to bring the issue to the convention floor. Demoralized by lopsided defeats and under serious pressure from the Bush campaign, some pro-choice committee members were ready to settle for the resolution and give up the fight.[39]

Why were the results so one-sided? The grassroots organizing efforts of conservative, pro-life activists played a key role, helping produce a platform committee with a strongly pro-life membership. While the pro-choice side held successful press conferences, the effectiveness of its grassroots delegate selection campaign was open to question. In a telling development, Republicans for Choice leader Ann Stone's own attempt to become a convention delegate failed when Christian Coalition activists flooded the district party meeting she attended and kept her from being sent to the state convention.[40] As voting results indicate, the pro-choice side was not well represented on the platform committee. Stone claims that, going into the hearings, 35 of the 107 members had given her a firm commitment to back "big tent" language. However, the first and only recorded abortion vote was on a much stronger amendment (striking all abortion language from the platform). This received only sixteen votes. After this, pro-choice members were demoralized and, in any case, their votes were not recorded.

In addition to the pro-life and the pro-choice activists, a third force was at work during the platform hearings, the Bush campaign. Nominees generally play critical roles in the platform process but the exact nature of that role is often hard to pin down. That certainly is the case here.[41] Some things are clear concerning the role of the Bush campaign. Despite "big tent" hints from Quayle, Bush himself never wavered from his pro-life position. The campaign had a free hand to select the platform committee chairman and sent a pro-life message by selecting Senator Don Nickles of Oklahoma. Even minor things, like the assignment of space for groups during the convention, pointed to the fact that the pro-life side was being favored. During the hearings, point man Bo Calloway did not waver in his opposition to pro-choice amendments. Clearly the Bush campaign was in favor of retaining strong anti-abortion language but its role in selecting and manipulating the committee is less clear. Given the strongly conservative cast of the committee, little manipulation may have been needed.

After the platform hearings ended, pro-choice forces attempted to win over the six state delegations needed to bring the abortion issue to the floor of the convention. Few nominees relish the thought of a floor fight marring their convention, and the Bush campaign did some serious arm twisting to keep delegations in line. With that pressure, the pro-choice side was limited to four states (Maine, Massachusetts, New Mexico, and the Virgin Islands). Votes were very close in three additional states (Vermont, Rhode Island, and New Jersey) but close was not enough and the attempt to modify the platform's uncompromising pro-life language ended in failure.[42]

While attention was focused on abortion during the platform hearings, the Christian Right's grassroots mobilization paid off in other areas as well (see table 6.1). Most striking was the language on gay and lesbian issues. The 1988 Republican platform, for all its moral conservatism, was silent on gay and lesbian rights.[43] The draft platform that served as the starting point for the 1992 platform committee broke that silence by defending the military's policy of excluding homosexuals from service. Several more provisions were added during the platform hearings themselves. The party proclaimed itself opposed to same-sex marriages, adoptions by same-sex couples, and the extension of antidiscrimination legislation to homosexuals. It added language denouncing corporations that cut off support to the Boy Scouts (the scouts have faced protests due to their discriminatory policies against gays). The platform language on AIDS was amended to call for education stressing abstinence, to denounce the distribution of condoms or clean needles, and to call for legislation making it a criminal act to knowingly transmit the AIDS virus.

The antigay and antilesbian language appears to have been inserted with little input from the Bush campaign. Martin Mawyer, president of the Christian Action Network, claims that his group was behind two of the amendments. Earlier in the year he had approached the Bush campaign with the idea of adding antigay language to the platform and had been "led to believe that change would be difficult," that it was too late to alter the platform's language. Mawyer eventually contacted Ralph Reed of Christian Coalition for advice on introducing the amendments. When they were introduced, Mawyer was surprised to see them pass with no evidence whatsoever of resistance from the Bush campaign. Given a platform committee stacked with

Table 6.1
Provisions Concerning Social Issues Added
to GOP Platform during Platform Hearings

Gay and lesbian related issues

• "We oppose efforts by the Democrat Party to include sexual preference as a protected minority receiving preferential status under civil rights statutes at the federal, State, and local levels." (p. 29)

• "We oppose any legislation or law which legally recognizes same-sex marriages and allows such couples to adopt children or provide foster care." (p. 29)

• "We encourage State legislatures to enact legislation which makes it a criminal act for anyone to knowingly transmit the AIDS virus. . . . We reject the notion that the distribution of clean needles and condoms are the solution to stopping the spread of AIDS. Education designed to stop the spread of this disease should stress marital fidelity, abstinence, and a drug-free lifestyle." (p. 27)

Family

• "Republicans oppose and resist efforts by the Democrat Party to redefine the traditional American family." (p. 10)

• A paragraph lauding the two-parent family added on p. 11.

• "Today more than ever, the traditional family is under assault." (p. 8)

Religion

• Reference to the country's "Judeo-Christian tradition" added. (p. 21)

Source: Booklet version of the 1992 Republican Platform distributed at the 1992 Republican National Convention.

Note: Other new passages support home schooling as an option for welfare children (p. 34), call on state legislators to take legal action against pornography (p. 30), denounce assisted suicide (p. 39), and call for changes in the RICO laws (p. 76). (The RICO laws have been used to prosecute Operation Rescue.)

social conservatives, this lack of resistance led to a platform that dramatically staked out new ground for the party. On abortion, social conservatives had triumphed by holding the line, sticking to the position of past conventions and to the draft platform. On gay and lesbian issues, the party was going well beyond its previous stands.[44]

The platform committee's promotion of the Christian Right agenda was not limited to the issues of abortion and homosexuality. Language was added to support home schooling, oppose attempts to "redefine" the family, take stronger action against pornography, and protect Operation Rescue against prosecution under the RICO laws. The platform was amended to warn against an "assault" on the traditional family. A plank on school prayer that had begun with the words "Mindful of our rich religious pluralism" was amended to add a reference to our "Judeo-Christian heritage." These amendments, combined with the platform's positions on homosexuality and abortion, gave the Christian Right as much or more than it could have hoped for. From its perspective, the platform was more appealing than those it had embraced in 1980, 1984, and 1988. Bruce Hawkins, convention press secretary of Christian Coalition, put it this way: "We won. Nobody thought we could do better than 1988 but this platform is more precise, more focused." Pat Robertson, speaking to the God and Country Rally at the convention, celebrated the passage of "the most conservative platform in decades."[45]

Convention Images

Many argue that American party conventions have become little more than extended commercials. If the GOP's Houston convention was a commercial, one of the "products" on display was a Republican party closely tied to the themes and leaders of the Christian Right. Many argue that that product did not sell well. But before we look at sales, we need to examine how that product was constructed and why it was offered to the public.

The product—an image of Christian Right/GOP alliance—was created, in part, by the platform but other factors promoted the image as well. The delegates affiliated with the Christian Right were a visible presence throughout the convention and media reports relayed their perspectives to a national audience. Christian Coalition and RNC for Life attracted attention with two of the largest of the rallies held during the course of the convention. Christian Coalition's God and Country Rally, featuring Vice President Quayle, Pat Robertson, Ralph Reed, Phyllis Schlafly, and Pat Boone, drew an overflow audience to the

Astrodome Hotel's Sam Houston Ballroom on 17 August. The following day, RNC for Life held a $75 a head "Definitely Texas" gala re-
ception featuring the vice president, Phyllis Schlafly, Pat Robertson,
Jerry Falwell, Gary Bauer, John Sununu, Beverly LaHaye, Henry Hyde,
and "special guest" conservative talk show sensation Rush Limbaugh.
At each event a sizable press contingent was on hand. During convention sessions, Christian Right leaders such as Jerry Falwell and Pat
Robertson received places of honor, sitting in the presidential and vice-
presidential boxes.[46]

Convention speakers reenforced the image of Christian Right/GOP
ties. Fundamentalist preacher James Kennedy was invited to give a
fiery invocation. Pat Robertson was given a prominent spot to warn:
"When Bill Clinton talks about family values, he is not talking about
either families or values. He is talking about a radical plan to destroy
the traditional family and transfer its functions to the federal government."[47] Pat Buchanan made his famous prime-time declaration
of cultural war. Dan Quayle sounded a similar theme, telling listeners that "the gap between us and our opponents is a cultural divide." The convention's Wednesday night session was "family night,"
a chance to feature candidate's spouses and to push a less combative
version of the cultural message. While warm, fuzzy images of the
candidates and their loved ones were certainly forthcoming, so too was
Marilyn Quayle's challenge to women's liberation. Mrs. Quayle told
America that "most women do not want to be liberated from their
essential nature as women."[48]

These statements were not unprecedented. Conservative appeals to
"family" values had certainly been made at previous GOP conventions.
The family theme was only one among many at the convention, having to compete with Congress bashing, credit taking for the end of
the cold war, and attacks on Bill Clinton's record in Arkansas. Nonetheless, the harsh tone of the family-value rhetoric and the proclama-
tion of cultural "war," when combined with the platform and the very
visible presence of the Christian Right at the convention, led to an
unusually potent image of Christian Right influence. President Bush
strengthened his identification with the movement when, immediately
following the convention, he spoke to a gathering of ten thousand
religious leaders and denounced the Democrats for leaving "three simple letters: G.O.D." out of their platform.[49]

Why was an image of close Christian Right/GOP ties the one broadcast? In the 1980, 1984, and 1988 campaigns, the Republican party
managed to satisfy the Christian Right without linking itself to the

movement in quite so visible a manner. The movement's activists were mobilized on behalf of the presidential campaign but the party did not suffer the full costs of identification with an unpopular constituency. What changed in 1992? Why did the party allow its appeals to the Christian Right to become so visible and so inflammatory?

One reason lies in the development of the potent Christian Right grassroots organization. With so many delegates and platform committee members coming from Christian Right organizations, or at least supporting the movement's social agenda, attempts to moderate the party's positions would have been difficult to enforce. Furthermore, a large presence at a convention brings with it the possibility of disruption. As the news media scours contemporary party conventions for something that is not scripted and predictable, nothing attracts their attention like a good fight. A threat of disruption is potent because few candidates want such a fight to distract from the carefully scripted message of their convention showcase. The Christian Right's intense commitment to its cause (especially the pro-life cause) helped make threats of disruption real. More so than other elements of the GOP, Christian Right Republicans are willing to put their issues above loyalty to the party. Ann Stone, leader of Republicans for Choice, felt that calculations concerning possible disruptions worked to her disadvantage. The Bush campaign, she argues, "knew our people wouldn't throw fits. Our people aren't willing to do anything. They are too civilized."[50] Stone thus sees her opponents' potential "incivility" as a crucial contributor to their success.

The mobilization of pro-choice Republicans such as Ann Stone was another contributor to the visibility of movement-party ties. In 1988, George Bush and the Republican party ran on a platform as adamantly pro-life as that of 1992. Yet the platform hearings generated nowhere near the level of controversy or coverage of those of 1992. Without an active pro-choice movement to publicize the issue, the party was able to quietly give the Christian Right what it wanted. With pro-choice Republicans holding rallies and threatening floor fights, this quiet option was much harder to exercise in 1992.

Several problems specific to George Bush's 1992 campaign also worked to keep movement-party ties visible. A comparison with his 1988 campaign and convention helps illustrate his difficulties. First, Bush was suspect in the eyes of the Christian Right. Unlike Ronald Reagan, he would have to prove himself worthy of their support. In 1988, Bush was able to gain acceptance by wrapping himself in Reagan's mantle. With Reagan four years into the past and a record of his own that had drawn criticism from conservatives, Bush was in a much weaker position to resist the desires of the Christian Right at the convention. Second, in 1992 Bush had less to distract attention from his concessions to the Christian Right. In 1988, the focus of attention was George Bush's selection of a running mate, then it was the dramatic language of his acceptance speech. Concessions to the Christian Right in the platform could slip by without undue attention.[51]

The 1992 Bush campaign added to its problems by failing to integrate its appeals to the Christian Right into language that would play to a wider audience. The flag, the pledge of allegiance, prison furloughs, and the ACLU were central issues at the 1988 convention. Appeals on these issues resonated with the social conservatism of the Christian Right, particularly the attacks on one of the movement's most hated foes, the ACLU. But flags, pledges, and criminals locked securely away in prisons have much wider appeal, especially when they play into a general strategy that can paint one's opponent as a liberal out of touch with American values. In 1992, whether because of more skillful ideological positioning on the part of Bush's opponent or less adept strategy on Bush's part, the focus was more squarely on controversy over abortion, gay rights, and Christian Right leaders themselves.[52] The convention did try to wrap its appeal on social issues in warm and fuzzy images of the candidates and their families, but this does not appear to have successfully diverted attention from the controversy beneath.

Significance

The 1992 Republican convention and platform illustrated a deepening of the trend discussed in earlier chapters: the long-term realignment of the parties on the social issues of concern to the Christian Right. The parties used to be silent on issues such as abortion and gay rights. Slowly these issues have worked their way into the party platforms, the parties have staked out less equivocal positions on them, and those positions now offer the public quite distinct alternatives. Those alternatives were on clear display in the summer of 1992. A month prior to the Republican convention, the Democratic platform had reaffirmed the party's support for a woman's right to choose an abortion and taken a strong stand in defense of gay and lesbian rights. A very visible gay and lesbian presence at the podium and in the convention audience reenforced the identification of the party with groups opposed by the Christian Right. If it was not clear already, the 1992 platforms and conventions firmly established the Republicans as the party of social issue conservatism and the Democrats as the party of social issue liberalism.

The 1992 convention was significant for another reason as well. It made the connection between the GOP and the Christian Right very visible to the general public. In previous years, the party had fairly successfully managed to target its appeals. On the one hand, the party adopted positions supported by the Christian Right on issues such as abortion. The party utilized the communications networks of the movement to broadcast specialized messages to an evangelical audience. It benefited from movement-led get-out-the-vote drives. On the other hand, the party's links to the Christian Right were not a prominent part of the message it broadcast to the general public. Instead, Ronald Reagan and George Bush presented themselves as foes of big government, anticommunists, and agents of prosperity.

The party's targeted approach made sense. Evangelicals are profoundly dissatisfied with contemporary cultural trends and possess impressive organizational resources. At the same time, evangelical arguments often lack public credibility. A targeted approach allowed the party to tap into dissatisfaction in the evangelical subculture and to make use of its organizational resources, while minimizing offense to the general public. The prominence of the Christian Right at the 1992 convention undermined this strategy. It was hard for the general public to miss the GOP's close links to the controversial leaders and positions of the Christian Right.

The almost universal judgment of the mainstream media was that the convention had been an unmitigated disaster for the party, a judgment reenforced by George Bush's subsequent defeat in the general election. As we shall see shortly, there are good reasons to question this judgment. As the Christian Right has grown in strength, the negative publicity of association with it may be outweighed by the assistance the movement can bring the party.

As the Christian Right gains strength, it draws greater attention to itself. The Christian Coalition, in its early days, was given to "stealth" campaigns. Resources would be mobilized behind state or local candidates without alerting the opposition. In the rather dramatic words of Ralph Reed: "I want to be invisible. I do guerilla warfare. I paint my face and travel at night. You don't know its over until you're in a body bag. You don't know until election night."[53] Eventually opponents catch on. Today, the Christian Coalition's actions and its role in the party are better publicized. The movement may still be a net plus for the party, but the visibility of Christian Right/party ties does create difficulties for the GOP.

On to November

After the convention, the Christian Right rallied behind the Republican ticket just as it had in 1988. On 22 August, the GOP announced the formation of the Evangelical Leaders and Laymen Coalition for Bush-Quayle '92, featuring movement luminaries such as Jerry Falwell and Tim LaHaye as cochairs. Christian Coalition and other movement organizations swung into action. The coalition mobilized its 300,000 members, conducted voter-registration drives, and distributed forty million "voter guides" in over forty thousand churches. (Technically nonpartisan, the voter guides were clearly designed to promote conservative candidates and positions.) Other Christian Right groups—including Concerned Women for America, the National Association of Evangelicals, the Christian Life Commission of the Southern Baptist Convention, and local affiliates of Focus on the Family—pitched in as well. Christian Right groups campaigned for a wide array of local candidates and initiatives, as well as for the Bush-Quayle ticket.[54]

The efforts of the Christian Right were not enough to save George Bush. The incumbent president received only 38 percent of the vote in a three-way race. Bill Clinton received 43 percent and independent Ross Perot got 19 percent. The on-and-off campaign of Perot complicated decisions for many voters, but the pro-choice independent was never a serious option for the Christian Right. In the end, white evangelical voters followed Christian Right leaders in rallying behind the losing Bush ticket. Table 6.2 tells the story. Bush received 63 percent of the white evangelical vote. If one narrows the focus to the Christian Right's core constituency, white evangelicals who attend church regularly, Bush's support rises to 70 percent. That is an impressively high figure, given the low level of Bush's overall support in a three-way race.

Another measure indicates the importance of the evangelical vote to the GOP. George Bush depended on evangelicals for 38 percent of his overall vote. Without heavy evangelical support, Bush's defeat could have been a rout. Republicans at the congressional level received strong evangelical support as well, with 73 percent of regularly attending evangelicals casting their vote for GOP House candidates. This support helped the party make modest gains at the congressional level. Party identification figures demonstrate the strength of evangelical attachment to the Republican party. Over the last several decades, evangelicals have gone from a heavily Democratic constituency (which often defected to the GOP at the presidential level) to a

Table 6.2
Evangelicals in the 1992 Election: Presidential Vote

	Bush	Clinton	Perot
General population	38	43	19
White Evangelicals			
All	63	22	15
Regular church			
attenders	70	18	12

Percentage of Candidates' Vote Coming from Different Religious Traditions

	White evangelical	White mainline	Catholic	Secular	Other*
Bush	38	24	22	11	5
Clinton	18	17	26	18	21
Perot	20	26	29	19	6

Vote for House of Representatives

	% Republican
White Evangelicals	
All	67
Regular church attenders	73

Party Identification

	% Republican	% Democrat
White Evangelicals		
All	50	23
Age 18–29	59	19
Age 30–44	54	19
Age 45–59	44	24
Age 60+	42	39

Source: On the presidential and congressional vote see Lyman Kellstedt, John Green, James Guth, and Corwin Smidt, "Religious Voting Blocs in the 1992 Election," in *The Rapture of Politics,* ed. Steve Bruce, Peter Kivisto, and William Swatos, Jr. (New Brunswick: Transaction, 1995), 95; on the presidential share of the vote from different religious traditions see John C. Green, James L. Guth, Lyman A. Kellstedt, and Corwin E. Smidt, "Murphy Brown Revisited: The Social Issues in the 1992 Election," in *Disciples & Democracy: Religious Conservatives and the Future of American Politics,* ed. Michael Cromartie (Published jointly Washington, D.C.: Ethics and Public Policy Center/Grand Rapids: Eerdmans, 1995), 49; and on party identification see Hertzke and Fowler, *Religion and Politics in America* (Boulder: Westview Press), 99.

*"Other" consists largely of Black Protestants.

firmly Republican one. Particularly encouraging for the Republicans is the identification of younger voters. While older evangelicals retain a significant level of support for the Democrats, new generations are coming into the electorate overwhelmingly Republican. The 1992 election demonstrated the scope of evangelical realignment. Evangelicals had become a core GOP constituency, sticking with the party even in defeat.

If the GOP held on to evangelicals, it lost the support of other religious groups. From 1988 to 1992, the party's greatest declines in support occurred among Catholics and mainline Protestants. Did an emphasis on the social issue concerns of the Christian Right drive them away? Did the Republican convention scare off social issue liberals? The answer to these questions appears to be "no" or at least "not to any great extent." Voters who attached a high level of importance to social issues (abortion, gay rights, and family values) tended to take conservative positions on those issues and to support George Bush. Bush's problem was that a much larger portion of the electorate was concerned about the state of the economy and these voters went heavily for Clinton. Voters who made their voting decisions shortly after the Republican convention did support Clinton by a significant margin, but they do not appear to have been driven heavily by social issue concerns. While the party might have fared better with a more targeted social issue message, it did not lose the election on the basis of those issues.[55]

Out of Power—And Prospering

In the wake of the Republican's 1992 defeat, the Christian Right rejected charges it was to blame. Pointing to the movement's impressive mobilizational efforts and the loyal support of evangelical voters, Christian Right leaders argued that they had earned the right to a significant voice in party affairs. This argument was strengthened by the movement's stunning postelection growth. A good enemy can be a powerful organizing tool. In the early 1980s, environmental groups found that out as Ronald Reagan's controversial interior secretary James Watt did wonders for their membership rolls. The Clinton administration served a similar function in galvanizing evangelicals. In office, Clinton quickly issued executive orders to ease restrictions on abortion and proposed lifting the ban on gays and lesbians in the military. His surgeon general, Joycelyn Elders, caused controversy with her forthright views on sex education and drug legalization. The Christian

Right's constituency was not pleased.[56] In the rather dramatic words of Christian Coalition executive director Ralph Reed:

> Clinton's greatest legacy will be a reawakened grassroots movement for common sense. The conservative community, largely asphyxiated during the Bush years, awoke from its slumber like Rip Van Winkle on steroids after the Clinton inaugural. Membership in pro-family organizations is up dramatically, attendance at conferences and seminars is rising. . . . The Christian Coalition entered the Clinton era with 250,000 members and activists; that number now approaches 1.4 million.[57]

By the first half of 1995, Christian Coalition was claiming a membership of 1.6 million.[58] This number may be exaggerated, but there is little doubt that Christian Right organizations have prospered in the Clinton era.

A particular area of movement strength has been at the state party level. Christian Right activists have been active within state Republican parties going back to the movement's beginnings. In the early 1980s, several state parties were taken over by Christian Right forces. The first big upsurge in Christian Right involvement in state party affairs occurred in the mid to late 1980s and was tied to Pat Robertson's presidential campaign. Robertson and Bush forces battled for control of local parties as part of their larger struggle for the nomination. However, once initiated into the world of state and local party politics, many Christian Right activists stayed. As the grassroots strength of the Christian Right has grown in the 1990s, so too has the movement's influence within state and local parties.

The most comprehensive overall evaluation of Christian Right strength at the state and local level has been provided by *Campaigns and Elections* magazine. The magazine's staff interviewed party officials, journalists, academics, campaign activists, and political consultants in the summer of 1994. They concluded that the Christian Right was dominant in eighteen state party organizations and a substantial force in thirteen more.[59] These characterizations are open to question. There is no clear-cut line that separates "members" of the Christian Right from ideologically similar "nonmembers." State party organizations slip in and out of movement control. Nonetheless, this represents a very impressive level of strength across the country. While Christian Right strength is greatest in the South, states in the dominant category included California, Oregon, Washington, Alaska, Idaho, Hawaii, Iowa, and Minnesota. Christian Right strength is low in the New England and Middle Atlantic states.[60]

The Christian Right's foothold in state party organizations is a valuable one, but its importance should not be overestimated. Control of state party organizations does not necessarily mean selection or control of the party's elected officials. Control of state parties can help partisans of a presidential candidate write somewhat more advantageous rules for their favorites. Movement activists organized in a state party can be influential in a caucus setting. However, as discussed in chapter 3, state party organizations have lost their control over the presidential nominating process. Primary electorates, not state party leaders, are now the dominant players in nomination politics. At congressional and state level as well, control of the party organization does not mean control over nominations. Primary elections determine the vast majority of nominations for the House, Senate, governor, and state legislative positions. At the presidential level, the Christian Right must achieve success in primaries to be truly influential.[61] Takeover of state parties is thus probably more important as an indicator of grassroots Christian Right strength than as a phenomenon in its own right.

1994: Remarkable Success
and Continuing Limitations

Grassroots strength played a significant role in the Republican landslide of 1994. The GOP won historic victories, augmenting its strength in state legislatures and governors' mansions, recapturing the Senate, and, most dramatically, breaking the Democrats' forty-year hold on the House of Representatives. As in 1992, the Christian Coalition and other movement groups mounted a massive grassroots effort to get out the vote for GOP candidates. An estimated four million activists were mobilized and perhaps fifty million potential voters contacted by the movement. The Christian Coalition distributed thirty-three million "voter guides," Focus on the Family distributed nine million, and Concerned Women for America an additional two million.[62] Movement affiliated television and radio programs provided further aid. As a frequent listener to Christian radio and viewer of Pat Robertson's "700 Club," I was struck by the vehemence and consistency of their pro-Republican, anti-Clinton message. In 1994, this powerful partisan message was disseminated throughout the evangelical subculture.

The results were impressive. Regular church attending evangelicals' vote for House Republican candidates rose 12 percent from the already high levels of 1992; 38 percent of the members of this group reported "being contacted by a religious group, having political information available at church, or being urged to vote for a party or candidate by church leaders." Those contacted were significantly more likely to vote and to vote Republican. In a number of close races, the Christian Right's effort may have been the key to GOP victory. Thirty Republican House candidates won by less than 5 percent in districts where Christian Right campaign involvement was heavy.[63]

The Republican landslide of 1994 drew upon a number of sources. Groups other than evangelicals swung to the GOP as well (notably Catholics).[64] Nonetheless, the Christian Right could claim significant credit for the party's success—and the influence within the party their efforts on its behalf had earned them. The 1994 elections deepened further the trends seen in earlier elections: ever-closer Christian Right ties to the Republican party, realignment to the GOP among evangelical voters, and the decline of exit to the Democrats as a viable option. The events of 1994 also meant something new for Christian Right/ Republican relations. With the Republican takeover of Congress, movement relations with the party will be at least somewhat less focused on relations with presidents and presidential candidates.

Yet for all the Christian Right successes, there were some notable movement failures in 1994. These failures illustrate some of the Christian Right's continuing, and deeply rooted, weaknesses. The most watched race of 1994 was almost certainly the Virginia Senate race pitting the state's incumbent Democrat Chuck Robb against Republican candidate Oliver North. Unlike most states, Virginia often uses party conventions to nominate candidates. North likely could not have won a primary, but the state convention played to the strength of his conservative and Christian Right supporters. Their grassroots organization was well suited to pack a state convention. North received the nomination and campaigned with the full support of the Christian Right. In my many years of research, I have seen few figures evoke the kind of enthusiasm in the movement that North did. Money poured into his campaign and a grassroots army was mobilized, plastering the state with North road signs. The year 1994 was a very Republican one; Chuck Robb was a weak, scandal-ridden opponent; North outspent Robb four to one; Virginia is a conservative state, home to Pat Robertson and Jerry Falwell. Nonetheless, North lost.

What happened? Some of North's problems, most notably his notoriety from the Iran-Contra affair, were not directly linked to the Christian Right.[65] But his links to the movement hurt as well. Virginia voters had very negative opinions of Jerry Falwell and Pat Robertson. Robb ran ads linking them to North and the Christian Right's ties to the North candidacy were well publicized throughout the campaign. North's defeat had much in common with the 1993 defeat of the GOP's candidate for lieutenant governor, Michael Farris. Farris, a home school advocate who had formerly held positions with the Moral Majority and Concerned Women for America, was a product of the state's Christian Right. His ties to the movement were emphasized in the campaign and Farris lost as the rest of the Republican statewide ticket swept to easy victories.[66]

The Christian Right also met with defeat in the 1994 Minnesota governor's race. The race featured a two-step nomination process. A June party convention endorsed candidates, but actual nominations were decided in a primary three months later. The incumbent, Republican governor Arne Carlson, was popular with Minnesotans overall, but his pro-choice and pro–gay rights stance did not endear him to the Christian Right forces that controlled the state party. Turnout to the caucuses that elected delegates to the state convention was low—about 1 percent of the state's voters participated. Christian Right forces dominated the process. They denied Carlson their endorsement, turning instead to little-known Christian Right figure Allen Quist. Quist was quickly tagged with the Christian Right label and embarrassed himself with a statement that men are "genetically predisposed" to head families. Despite the heated opposition of the movement and the state party organization it controlled, Governor Carlson easily won the primary and went on to a two to one victory in the general election.[67]

The Virginia and Minnesota results illustrate some important limitations of the Christian Right. First, the movement is much stronger in low-turnout arenas like state party conventions (where organization is the critical factor) than it is in higher turnout arenas like primaries and general elections (where broader popularity is needed). Second, serious potentially damaging divisions between Christian Right activists and other elements of the party remain. The differences that separated Robertsonites from party regulars have not been overcome. In Virginia, Republican moderates refused to support North, their party's nominee. Republican former attorney general Marshall Coleman entered the race as an independent. The state's Republican senator, John Warner, declared North unfit to serve in the Senate and threw his endorsement to Coleman.[68] The split between Christian Right and pro-Warner forces continues to cause turmoil in the Virginia GOP. Third, candidates perceived to be *from* the Christian Right have a much harder time than outside candidates *sympathetic* to the movement.[69]

This last point is an important one. Candidates closely allied with the movement can win. As Michael Farris went down to defeat in

Virginia, GOP gubernatorial candidate George Allen won easily with movement backing. He combines a support for Christian Right causes with an emphasis on fiscal conservatism and tough anticrime measures that appeal well beyond the movement. As Allen Quist was losing in Minnesota, Republican candidate Rod Grams won a Senate seat with Christian Right support. Grams's voting record in the House had won him a 100 percent rating from the Christian Coalition but, unlike Quist, he was not perceived to be a Christian Right candidate. Across the country in 1994, numerous candidates allied with the movement won election. Over one-fourth of the members of the GOP House freshman class were themselves members of evangelical denominations. The Christian Right can elect politically and religiously sympathetic candidates. What it must avoid is candidates whose identification with the Christian Right taps into the general public's discomfort with the movement. Outside a few narrow arenas, the Christian Right is not capable of victory on its own. While the GOP has come to depend upon the movement's ability to mobilize evangelical voters, the Christian Right needs the Republican party as a vehicle to form the broad-based coalitions the movement is incapable of forming on its own.[70]

Conclusion:
A Tale of Two Contracts

On 17 May 1995, the Christian Coalition unveiled its "Contract with the American Family." The ten-point plan, designed as a supplement to the Republican party's "Contract with America," included a "religious equality" amendment to the Constitution, as well as provisions to provide family tax credits, to slash federal spending for the arts, humanities, and education, to protect "parental rights," and to restrict abortion. The contract's unveiling attracted attention. Ralph Reed, the coalition's executive director, was joined at his Washington news conference by an array of top Republican leaders, including House Speaker Newt Gingrich, presidential hopeful Senator Phil Gramm, and Senate majority whip Trent Lott. The Senate majority leader, Robert Dole, met with Christian Coalition leaders later in the day. The "Contract with the American Family," and the events surrounding its introduction, neatly tie together many of the themes of this study.

The Contract and the Christian Right Today

Social Agenda

The ten provisions of the contract fit well with the arguments concerning Christian Right motivations made in chapter 2. The central concern that drives the movement is the desire to pass the values of the evangelical subculture on to the next generation. The fear that animates movement members is that their children will, in the words of movement leader Gary Bauer, be "peeled away, seduced by the popular culture."[1] Therefore, Christian Right activism has focused upon those institutions that pass values on to the next generation: schools, media, churches, and, above all, family. This is also the focus of the Contract with the American *Family*. Its provisions are designed to reenforce institutions that the movement feels it can control, expand evangelical influence in other institutions, and restrict the power and funding of institutions deemed hostile to evangelical values.

Families are to be bolstered with a $500 tax credit per child, provisions to offset the tax code's marriage penalty, and a "Homemakers' Rights Act," which would make it easier for homemakers to provide for retirement. The coalition also called for a constitutional amendment to "ensure parents' rights over the care and nurturing of their children are not violated."[2]

The contract's first three items concern education. The religious equality amendment is aimed primarily at expanding religious expression in the public schools. Items two and three call for "transferring funding of the federal Department of Education to families and local school boards," and school choice. The public schools and the Department of Education have long been targets of Christian Right criticism for subjecting their children to what they consider a "secular humanist" course of study. The religious equality amendment is a response to that perceived secularism. The contract's other education provisions work to take power from the federal government and give it to local school boards, which the movement feels are more likely to be sympathetic to its concerns. If local public schools remain hostile, the Coalition's measures also funnel money to private schools (through a school choice plan) and thereby provide further defense of the educational prerogatives of evangelical families.

Hostile cultural messages are limited by restricting pornography and ending funding for federal cultural agencies: the Corporation for Public Broadcasting and the National Endowments for the Arts and Humanities. Provision eight calls for unspecified measures to "enhance contributions to private charity" as part of a larger plan to replace the welfare state with "a system of private and faith-based compassion."[3] Again, the aim is to undermine the power of federal institutions in favor of institutions believed more sympathetic to movement values.

Measure five, restricting abortion, does not fit perfectly into the cultural transmission framework. Abortion is still the movement's most important issue and it has a life of its own that goes well beyond questions of cultural transmission. That being said, it is worth noting that the abortion issue is closely intertwined with debates concerning the family and sexual roles within it. The Christian Right's challenge to abortion rights cannot easily be separated from the movement's celebration of motherhood and "traditional" family structures. Abortion rights and, more generally, feminism are seen by the movement as threats to the family structures they depend upon to transmit their values.[4]

The Contract with the American Family nicely illustrates the concerns that have driven and will continue to drive the Christian Right. The movement is fueled by a desire to defend evangelical religious and sexual norms by means of a program designed to restructure the societal institutions that affect the transmission of those norms to the next generation. At one level, this program seems unexceptional: most people care about passing on their values. Yet a comparison with the House Republicans' "Contract with America" illustrates the distinctive character of the Christian Right's program. That contract, a centerpiece of the 1994 congressional campaign, for the most part stays clear of the social issues emphasized by the Christian Coalition. Its focus is upon political institutions and economics: reform of Congress, term limits, tax cuts, slashing regulation, restriction of lawsuits, cutting spending, and welfare reform.[5]

Points of agreement between the two contracts certainly exist. Both contracts include tax credits for families with children and call for tougher measures against pornography and crime. The two contracts also agree on the definition of the enemy: an overly large and intrusive federal government. The House Republicans fear government as a threat to taxpayers and business; the Christian Coalition sees it as a threat to the values of evangelical families. Nonetheless, the difference in emphasis between the two contracts is striking. The Christian Right has entered the Republican party and the party has moved to the right on social issues to accommodate it; an effective working relationship between the movement and the party may or may not be maintained, but the movement and its concerns remain distinctive within the party. There is little prospect that this will change in the near future.

Organizational Power

Not only is the Christian Right a distinctive bloc within the Republican party, it is also a powerful one. The Republican leaders present at the contract's unveiling were paying tribute to the movement's influence. Nor was this press conference an isolated incident. In the early stages of the 1996 presidential nomination battle, most of the major contenders worked hard to win the support of Christian Right organizations and activists. The September 1995 Christian Coalition

Convention featured addresses by Lamar Alexander, Pat Buchanan, Richard Lugar, Bob Dole, and Phil Gramm.[6] If we think back twenty years, we can see what a change this represents. White evangelical Protestants were largely unorganized. Candidates certainly made appeals to white evangelical *constituencies*, but they did not have to contend with grassroots evangelical *organizations*.

The late 1970s and early 1980s saw the rapid development of Christian Right organizations such as the Moral Majority and Christian Voice, but their impact on the party was limited. Two factors were crucial in limiting their influence. First, early organizations depended heavily on outside leadership and funding. The Moral Majority was organized by New Right activists such as Paul Weyrich. The ACTV (American Coalition for Traditional Values), a prominent movement organization during the 1984 campaign, depended on funding from Republican party sources.[7] Evangelical leaders like Jerry Falwell and Pat Robertson were political neophytes; in the Christian Right's early stages, they often acted under the tutelage of more experienced New Right and party leaders. It was not easy for these newcomers to stake out their own positions and challenge those who had guided their entry into politics. Second, early Christian Right groups generally lacked effective grassroots organization. While Jerry Falwell and his Moral Majority captured the attention of the nation's media, they lacked the local organization needed to take over state parties or influence the outcome of caucuses and primaries.

Pat Robertson, Ralph Reed, and the Christian Coalition are now in a very different position, one that illustrates the organizational developments analyzed in chapters 4 through 6. Since the early 1980s, Christian Right leaders have learned the political ropes, emerged from under the tutelage of the New Right and the party, and adjusted their strategies in the light of experience.[8] Christian Coalition and other movement organizations have also utilized religious resources to develop a powerful grassroots base. Atop this organizational base, movement leaders can approach the party from a position of considerable independence and potential power. The attentiveness Republican leaders showed Ralph Reed and his contract no doubt has much to do with the fact that the Christian Coalition, perhaps exaggeratingly, claims 1.6 million "members and supporters" and over 1,600 local chapters.[9] And it is not alone. James Dobson's Focus on the Family, Beverly LaHaye's Concerned Women for America, and a myriad of state and local groups all possess the organizational resources to play a significant role within the party.

Realignment, Exit, and Voice

Protestations of nonpartisanship notwithstanding, the Christian Co-alition is firmly tied to the Republican party. The Contract with the American Family was presented as a supplement to the House Repub-licans' Contract with America. The leading figures present at its un-veiling were overwhelming Republican. The only Democratic official in attendance, U.S. Representative Mike Parker of Mississippi, switched parties later in the year.

A telling example of the Christian Coalition's identification with the GOP came in January of 1995. In the wake of the Republican takeover of Congress, Ralph Reed told the Detroit Economic Club:

> We now assume the twin burdens of majority status. First, the re-quirement of responsibility and reasonableness in governance. . . . Second, the burden of seeking what is good for the entire nation, not just our particular constituency. I believe that our shoulders are broad enough, our hearts are big enough, and our spirits are humble enough to carry the responsibility we now bear.[10]

Not only did Reed identify himself firmly with the Republicans (note the "we" with which the quote begins), he also assumed the perspec-tive of party leaders rather than that of his "particular constituency."

As in the area of organizational power, a look back twenty years is instructive. In the mid-1970s, white evangelicals were an unorganized swing constituency. In 1976, Democrat Jimmy Carter's victory was, to a significant degree, the result of his ability to win back the sup-port of evangelicals who had strayed from the Democratic fold in previous elections. As we have seen in previous chapters, white evan-gelicals since that time have been voting—and identifying—more and more Republican. The Christian Right movement that sprang from white evangelical ranks has become even more firmly tied to the Republicans. As the parties have staked out clearly defined positions on the social issues of concern to the Christian Right, the Democratic option has grown less and less appealing. Democratic president Bill Clinton, supporter of abortion rights and (at least tentatively) of the right of gays and lesbians to serve in the military, has little hope of gaining movement backing.

Possibilities for major party exit have declined. Republican leaders have little reason to fear that the Christian Right will bolt to the Democrats. White evangelicals have become one of the party's core constituencies, a group that sticks with the party when, as in 1992, other groups defect. Republican leaders still must face the threat of exit in the form of decreased turnout or third party defection. However, carrying out either threat has serious dangers for the movement. Should Christian Right organizations fail to mobilize their followers, low turnout would undermine candidates sympathetic to their cause across a wide range of offices and affect the success of ballot measures of concern to the movement. Third parties are notoriously difficult to sustain in the American political system. Furthermore, open support for a third party would threaten the foothold the Christian Right has gained within the GOP.

The Christian Coalition's contract is clearly an element of a "voice" strategy. While some threat of exit remains, the coalition's recent actions are primarily geared toward enhancing its influence within the party. This requires the organizational resources needed to participate effectively in the state party conventions, caucuses, and primaries. The coalition's domination of many state party organizations, its large membership, local chapters across the nation, and ability to deliver millions of "voter guides" all contribute to the strength of its voice within the party. However, as I have argued previously, more than organizational resources is required. To effectively exercise the voice option, the Christian Right must accept the compromises inherent in coalition building and must demonstrate respect for Republican party norms. Ralph Reed has worked hard to moderate the coalition's public language and reach out to form coalitions with Catholics, Jews, and African Americans.[11] He has attempted, with mixed success, to broaden the coalition's issue focus. Instead of scaring potential allies off with talk of a Christian nation, Reed portrays his evangelical constituents as an oppressed minority, akin to African Americans of the pre–Civil Rights era.[12]

In a party whose norms dictate suspicion of outside group loyalties, Reed, Robertson, and the Christian Coalition have worked hard to establish their credentials as loyal Republicans. Dissatisfaction in Christian Right ranks notwithstanding, Robertson endorsed the party's incumbent president, George Bush. Christian Coalition members who attended the 1992 national convention as delegates did so as Bush delegates. The Christian Coalition strongly supported the House Republican Contract with America; in January 1994 the coalition launched a million dollar campaign to stir up support for the contract. In the early days of the Republican Congress, Ralph Reed repeatedly stressed his willingness to hold off on contentious social issues, if that was necessary to advance the GOP's economic agenda. Eventually, the coalition would put forward its social issue agenda in the form of the Contract with the American Family. However, the contract was presented only after the movement had established its strength within, and loyalty to, the GOP. Even then Reed was careful to characterize the contract's provisions as "suggestions," not as demands upon the party.[13]

Ongoing Dilemmas

If the politics surrounding the contract are indicative of the Christian Right's agenda, organization, and partisan affiliation, they also help illuminate the continuing problems the movement faces as it tries to exercise influence within the GOP. Ralph Reed's political approach has faced challenges from within the Christian Coalition. Members have not proven particularly enthusiastic about Reed's attempts to move beyond social issues; local activists continue to express themselves in language that scares off potential allies. Nor have coalition members easily accepted compromising their demands to advance the interests of the party. Pressure from below was probably behind Reed's most notable deviation from his overall strategy: a February 1994 implied threat to abandon the GOP should it put a pro-choice candidate on the presidential ticket. Reed quickly backpedaled, claiming that no threat was intended.

More direct threats have come from outside the Christian Coalition. James Dobson, of the Focus on the Family radio ministry, insisted that the Republicans would have to address the "moral issues" in the 1996 campaign if they wanted to avoid mass defection by religious conservatives. Rather than stressing party loyalty, Dobson has flirted with third party options. Reed's willingness to postpone action on school prayer and his contract's failure to call for a Constitutional amendment to ban abortion have not always been well received by other elements of the Christian Right.[14]

Resistance to Reed is indicative of a continuing dilemma faced by the movement: the imperatives of pursuing voice within the party run against those of appealing to and mobilizing the movement's core constituency. This dilemma is not unique to the Christian Right; most movements face tensions between strategies designed for external audiences and those that will appeal to the movement's base.

As its name implies, the Christian Right is a religiously based movement. The values it defends are closely intertwined with religious belief and its mobilization has relied heavily on the preexisting networks provided by churches, television and radio evangelists, and other parachurch organizations. Activating these networks and appealing to the values of the movement's core constituencies requires an explicitly religious approach that often comes into conflict with the imperatives of alliance formation.

The contrast between evangelical vitality in the public and private spheres is a key aspect of this dilemma. In the face of the challenges of modernity, American evangelicalism has retained its vitality, but that vitality is largely confined to the private sphere (see chaps. 1 and 2). Evangelicalism has maintained its hold over the faithful, offering them solace in the face of adversity and guidance in their personal lives. Tapping into this religious base has proven a key to the Christian Right's success. However, in the "public" sphere—in the worlds of science, bureaucracy, academia, and the national media—evangelicalism has had markedly less success.[15] These worlds now operate according to a secular logic that leaves limited room for religiously based arguments.

The world of partisan politics is part of this public sphere. American politicians do invoke the name of God. Some embrace a "civil religion" that speaks of America's special role in history.[16] Politicians call for greater morality and praise the social benefits brought about by the nation's churches. Nonetheless, all this political religious talk has a vague, generic quality to it, best captured in a famous statement by President Dwight Eisenhower: "America makes no sense without a deeply held faith in God—and I don't care what it is."[17] More specific appeals to religion meet with less favor. Political actors who cite Scripture as the basis for their public positions are likely to be looked upon with disfavor. Some observers have denounced this separation of religious and political discourse; others defend it as essential to the healthy functioning of democracy in a nation of multiple faiths.[18] Whatever the merit of the competing arguments on this issue, the position of the Christian Right's constituency is clear. It wants to discuss political issues in specific, scriptural terms. Unlike Eisenhower, it cares "what"—passionately. Specific religious language is what has mobilized the Christian Right's religious organizational base. Recasting the movement agenda in more general or even secular terms, putting forth pragmatic arguments for cultural conservatism and "traditional values," makes the movement's message more salable in the public, political sphere, but the movement's base does not easily relinquish its religious language. A secular strategy carried too far is likely to undermine the religious enthusiasm that fuels the movement.

A final aspect of the dilemma is rooted in attitudes toward compromise. Evangelicals have maintained their subculture by refusing to compromise their beliefs in the face of the pressures of modernity.

This aversion to compromise is strongest among fundamentalists; it is not surprising that the movement's more recent success at alliance building has been achieved under the leadership of the heavily Pentecostalist and charismatic Christian Coalition. Not only are these groups somewhat less rigid on doctrinal matters, the cross-denominational nature of the charismatic religious movement provides a groundwork for political bridge building. Thus, for example, charismatic Catholics have played a key role as the coalition has attempted to reach out to the Catholic community.

Prospects

Based on the analysis of preceding chapters, I will boldly put forward a decidedly unbold looking prediction: the Christian Right will not go away; it will not succeed either. After years of fluctuating evaluations, from imminent theocratic takeover to repeated pronouncement of the movement's demise, it is time to recognize that both the movement's strengths and its limitations are deeply rooted. Its strength is rooted in a well-organized and politicized evangelical subculture; its limitations are rooted in the dilemma described in the preceding section. To explore the Christian Right's future prospects, I will examine the movement's attempts to deal with that dilemma and then move on to review more generally the possibilities for the effective exercise of voice within the party.

Solutions?

Can the Christian Right resolve the dilemma described above? Can the movement mobilize a base partial to uncompromising, specific religious appeals while, at the same time, building effective coalitions in a largely secular political sphere? The short answer is no. The Christian Right has found no easy way around the dilemma.

In one respect, the dynamic described above can work to the Christian Right's benefit. An uncompromising base constituency can be utilized to strengthen a movement's bargaining position. As movement leaders such as Ralph Reed bargain with party officials, they can stress that *they* would like to cooperate but that the "troops" are restless. This restlessness could potentially take the form of exit, of staying home or bolting to a rival party. The threat of exit can augment the power of voice within the party. If, for example, the Republicans should reverse their pro-life position or embrace gay rights, exit by the Christian Right's constituency is a real possibility. This possibility clearly weighs on the mind of platform writers and candidates. Unless some possibility of exit exists, party leaders may be tempted to take the movement's demands for granted. (The position of African Americans within the Democratic party provides an example of this.)[19]

Advantages to be derived from the movement's "dilemma" should not, however, be overestimated. Religious rhetoric that scares away potential allies is rarely beneficial to the movement. Refusal to compromise often undermines coalition building and efforts to establish the movement's legitimacy within the GOP. While a threat of exit confers bargaining advantages, exit itself carries a high cost.

One solution to the dilemma is simply to broadcast different messages to internal and external audiences. This has been a common strategy since the early days of the Christian Right. In the Christian Coalition, this strategy is embodied in the split between executive director Ralph Reed and president Pat Robertson. In his public appearances and in his book *Politically Incorrect*, Reed puts forward a moderate version of the Christian Right's message. He reaches out to Catholics and Jews, African Americans, and Latinos. He eschews talk of a "Christian nation." Increasingly, it is Reed who is put forward as the public voice of the coalition. Robertson was not even present for the unveiling of the contract with the American Family. Robertson has not disappeared; he continues to host his "700 Club" television show, write books, and send out mailings to his evangelical audience. While there is much overlap between his message and Reed's, Robertson expresses himself in a very different manner. Robertson speaks a much more specifically religious language, replete with references to Scripture and his personal communications with God. If Reed can engage in moderate coalition building with outsiders while Robertson rallies the movement base, perhaps the Christian Right can have the best of both worlds.

Unfortunately for the Christian Right, this approach is difficult to carry out in the face of outside scrutiny. What one says to rally the troops cannot be kept secret from a broader audience. Opponents of the Christian Right, such as People for the American Way, have consistently utilized statements aimed at the movement's religious constituency to discredit its leaders among the broader public. Unusual, extreme, and theocratic statements of national and local Christian Right leaders have repeatedly been used against the movement in public debate. When Pat Robertson announced his presidential campaign, People for the American Way was ready with a video of potentially damaging statements, including a claim to have turned away a hurricane through the force of prayer. More recently, press attention has focused on Robertson's book *The New World Order*. Its rehashing of anti-Semitic conspiracy theories has proven a continuing source of embarrassment.[20]

Another solution increasing in popularity is an appeal to minority rights. Movement leaders have come to adopt a language more common to movements of the left. Decrying "Christian bashing," they claim that they are the victims of discrimination. Societal elites, they argue, feel free to ridicule and restrict Christians in a manner that would be unacceptable if the target were racial minorities. Thus, Ralph Reed's *Politically Incorrect* contains chapter titles such as "To the Back of the Bus: The Marginalization of Religion" and "The New Amos and Andy: How the Media Portrays People of Faith." This strategy has a number of advantages. It resonates with evangelicals who feel themselves a beleaguered and set upon minority in a hostile land. At the same time, it is an effective approach outside the movement's base. It puts opponents on the defensive; few Americans are happy to accept the label of anti-Christian bigot. This strategy associates the Christian Right with the heroism and legitimacy of the Civil Rights movement. It reassures wary outsiders that the movement's followers are victims worthy of sympathy rather than potential oppressors. Finally, instead of injecting religious arguments into a public sphere where they are likely to be deemed inappropriate, this strategy advances claims in the dominant language of a secular public sphere: rights-based liberalism.

Yet this strategy has its drawbacks as well. First, the Christian Right has questionable standing to invoke the memory of the struggle for civil rights. Movement leaders old enough to have been around for that struggle were generally on the wrong side. Jerry Falwell fought to keep his church segregated.[21] Pat Robertson did not challenge the segregationist stand of his father, Senator A. Willis Robertson of Virginia. Christian Right political heroes such as Jesse Helms, Ronald Reagan, and Strom Thurmond actively opposed civil rights legislation. On issues such as affirmative action, the Christian Right continues to take stands at odds with those of today's civil rights organizations. Second, and even more important, the rhetoric of minority rights does not capture the true ambitions of the movement. Movement members certainly feel that they are discriminated against, but they do not see themselves simply as one minority among many, each of whose rights and beliefs must be respected. Their claims are inherently universalistic. Theirs is the *one true faith* without which nations—and individuals—founder. No matter how hard leaders try to refocus the debate in terms of minority rights, these universalistic claims continually well up from the grass roots to undermine their appeals.

While the above mentioned "solutions" may prove useful for the Christian Right, the underlying dilemma remains. Attempts to exercise voice in the public realm of party politics will continue to be undermined by the imperatives of appealing to the party's base. This was brought home to me forcefully at a recent academic conference. Three of us, it turned out, had interviewed the same Virginia Christian Right leader and gotten the same argument from him. The local movement, he said, had recently acted in ways that had scared off potential allies and sabotaged potential political success. He insisted that the movement had learned its lesson and would not act in such a manner again. The only problem with this story is that we three academic observers had heard it over the course of nearly a decade. For some reason, the movement could not quite learn its lesson. If we recognize the deep-rooted nature of the movements's dilemma, this failure of learning becomes more understandable.

Party Terrain

Different parts of the American party system offer very different levels of access to movements such as the Christian Right. While the movement has had significant success in caucuses and in gaining control of state parties, it is not as well positioned to influence the outcome of primary elections. As a general rule, the movement is stronger where the "scope" of conflict is narrow. Where the number of participants is low, the Christian Right's formidable organization has given it significant influence. Thus, we saw Pat Robertson's disproportionate 1988 success in caucus states, the Senate nomination of movement ally Oliver North at the 1994 Virginia GOP convention, and the Christian Right's takeover of many state parties. In these cases, a relatively small number of well-organized and well-disciplined people can pack local meetings and take control of the situation. Recent growth in the movement's grassroots organization, most notably the expansion of the Christian Coalition, should enhance the movement's power in such situations.

Where the scope of conflict is broader (i.e., where more participants are involved), the movement has been less successful. Pat Robertson's caucus strength did not carry over into primary states; facing a very weak opponent, Oliver North could not prevail in the general election. The Christian Right's control of state parties far exceeds its control over congressional candidates, the vast majority of whom are selected by means of primaries. In broader arenas, the movement must face the fact that its popularity does not match its level of organization. That does not mean it can never succeed. Ralph Reed's efforts at coalition building and moderating the movement's image aim to gain it the popular support necessary to prevail in broader arenas. However, the imperatives of appealing to the movement's base constituency continually work to undermine such a strategy.

Success in primaries and general elections is closely tied to the characteristics of candidates. Candidates who can appeal to the Christian Right without being identified as *from* the Christian Right can build coalitions that go well beyond what the movement itself could produce. Whereas candidates such as Michael Farris in Virginia, Allen Quist in Minnesota, and Pat Robertson at the national level scare off potential allies and seriously divide the GOP, others, such as Virginia governor George Allen and President Ronald Reagan, have proven quite capable of appealing to the Christian Right and to a broader constituency.

Over the long run, the Christian Right's influence within the party will depend on the coalition building efforts of groups such as the Christian Coalition and on the success of coalition building within the Republican party. While movement organization can bring victory in narrower arenas, these victories are not as significant as they might appear. By international standards, American party organizations are weak. Official party organizations at the local, state, and even national level have limited influence on nominations and on the party's elected officials. Seizing control of party organizations can not substitute for the far more difficult task of building the alliances and public support needed for victory in primaries and general elections. Flooding presidential nominating caucuses can certainly help the Christian Right's favored candidates, but it is important to remember that caucuses selected only 16 percent of the delegates to the 1992 Republican National Convention.[22]

A Limited but Very Significant Movement

In conclusion, the portrait this book paints is one of a deeply rooted but limited political movement, one that is likely to be with us for a long time to come. This is not the most dramatic of conclusions but, if we look back just twenty years in time, its significance becomes more apparent. At that time, evangelical Christians were a quiescent constituency. Political involvement was low and rarely organized along religious lines. Since that time religious networks have been tapped, a significant segment of the evangelical community organized, and a powerful movement created. That movement has entered the world of partisan politics, helping promote its social issue concerns to a prominent place in partisan debate and developing an intimate alliance with one of America's major parties. As the plausibility of exit from that party has declined, the Christian Right has augmented its capacity for voice within the party. Like the women's, labor, civil rights, and environmental movements, the Christian Right has become an established player on the stage of American politics. And, for the moment at least, the Christian Right is enjoying significantly more success. For better or worse, that is no small accomplishment.

Notes

Introduction

1. See John Persinos, "Has the Christian Right Taken Over the Republican Party?" *Campaigns and Elections* 15 (September 1994): 20–24.

2. See Joseph Conn, "The Airwaves Ayatollahs," *Church and State* 47 (1994): 3, 7–10; and Jerome L. Himmelstein, *To the Right: The Transformation of American Conservatism* (Berkeley: University of California Press, 1990), 117.

3. National Religious Broadcasters, *Official Convention Program* (Washington, D.C.: National Religious Broadcasters, 1994), 27, 31.

4. The quotation is from a 31 January 1994 "Dear Friend" letter from Alliance Defense Fund president Alan Sears.

5. The name has since been changed to the *National* Council of Churches.

6. In 1960, the FCC ruled that stations could count *paid* religious programming toward their public service obligations. Stations, not surprisingly, cut back on the free airtime they offered to nonevangelicals and sold more time to evangelical broadcasters. See Steve Bruce, *Pray TV: Televangelism in America* (London: Routledge, 1990); and Jeffrey Hadden and Anson Shupe, *Televangelism: Power and Politics on God's Frontier* (New York: Henry Holt and Company, 1988).

7. By 1977, 92 percent of all religious television broadcasts consisted of paid programming (Hadden and Shupe, *Televangelism*, 52).

8. Bruce, *Pray TV*, 31.

9. See Robert Wuthnow, *The Restructuring of American Religion* (Princeton: Princeton University Press, 1988).

10. See Mancur Olson, *The Logic of Collective Action* (Cambridge: Harvard University Press, 1971).

11. See Allen Hertzke, *Echoes of Discontent* (Washington, D.C.: Congressional Quarterly Press, 1993); and Kenneth Wald, Dennis Owen, and Samuel Hill, Jr., "Churches as Political Communities," *American Political Science Review* 82 (1988): 531–48.

12. See Laurence Barrett, "Pulpit Politics," *Time* (31 August 1992): 34–43; and Ellen M. Rosenberg, *The Southern Baptists: A Subculture in Transition* (Knoxville: The University of Tennessee Press, 1989).

13. See Robert Wuthnow, "The Political Rebirth of American Evangelicals," in *The New Christian Right*, eds. Robert Liebman and Robert Wuthnow (New York: Aldine Publishing Company, 1983), 167–85.

14. The evidence concerning evangelical turnout is mixed. Depending on the survey and election one looks at, evangelical turnout can be slightly higher or lower than that of the public as a whole, but the pattern of earlier decades, in which evangelical turnout was significantly lower, no longer exists. See Corwin Smidt, "Evangelical Voting Patterns: 1978–1988," in *No Longer Exiles*, ed. Michael Cromartie (Washington, D.C.: Ethics and Public Policy Center, 1993), 85–117.

15. National Religious Broadcasters, "NRB Resolution on Boris Yeltsin" (press release, 29 January 1994).

16. National Religious Broadcasters, "Official Statement from National Religious Broadcasters Concerning Presidential Invitation" (press release, 29 January 1994).

17. See James L. Guth, "A New Turn for the Christian Right? Robertson's Support from the Southern Baptist Clergy" (paper presented at the annual meeting of the Midwest Political Science Association, Chicago, Ill., April 1989).

18. See James Guth, John Green, Lyman Kellstedt, and Corwin Smidt, "God's Own Party: Evangelicals and Republicans in the 1992 Elections," *The Christian Century* 110 (1993): 5, 172–76.

19. A key problem is sorting through and finding relevant press materials. The newspaper archives at the Library of Congress and the well-organized clipping files at the Data Center in Oakland and at the Washington headquarters of the People for the American Way all proved to be invaluable resources.

Chapter 1

1. The reader interested in digging further can find a wealth of historical scholarship dealing with the issues discussed here. Sidney Ahlstrom's *Religious History of the American People* (New Haven: Yale University Press, 1972) and A. James Reichley's *Religion in American Public Life* (Washington, D.C.: The Brookings Institution, 1985) provide excellent general accounts; Nathan Hatch's *The Democratization of American Christianity* (New Haven: Yale University Press, 1989) provides a fascinating argument concerning the populist roots of much of American Protestantism; George Marsden's *Fundamentalism and American Culture: The Shaping of Twentieth-Century Evangelicalism 1870–1925* (New York: Oxford University Press, 1980) covers the origins of fundamentalism; Paul Boyer's *When Time Shall Be No More* (Cambridge: Harvard University Press, 1992) provides an overview of American prophecy belief; Timothy Weber's *Living in the Shadow of the Second Coming: American Premillennialism 1875–1925* (New York: Oxford University Press, 1979) chronicles the impact of dispensational premillennialism; Ellen Rosenberg's *The Southern Baptists* covers developments in what has become American Protestantism's largest denomination; Robert Wuthnow's *The Restructuring of American Religion* provides an analysis of the post–World War II period.

2. See, in particular, Hatch, *Democratization of American Christianity*.

3. The new biblical criticism posed two threats. First, it was felt that these doctrines would undermine belief and promote secularism. Once the literal truth of certain passages was open to question, what was to prevent that questioning from proceeding on to the basic tenets of the faith? If one could doubt the story of Jonah and the whale, why not the story of the Resurrection? Second, even if the basics of the faith were maintained, the new biblical criticism shifted the locus of authority from the lay reader to academic experts. And it was, after all, a revolt against the monopoly of biblical interpretation by clerical experts that had helped fuel the Protestant Reformation.

4. See David H. Bennett, *The Party of Fear: From Nativist Movements to the New Right in American History* (Chapel Hill: University of North Carolina Press, 1988), 160–61.

5. Historian David Bennett describes the connection in this fashion:

In some places, it is true, there would be modest rivalry between fundamen- talist groups and the new organization, but in most areas the appeals of fundamentalism and nativism in the 1920s were compatible. For the frater- nal order many now would join would provide community even as it offered a way of cleansing the country and checking destructive forces that threat- ened the nation, the moral order, and the life of white, Protestant America. This was the Ku Klux Klan. (Bennett, *Party of Fear*, 208)

6. For example, Frances Willard, longtime president of the Women's Chris- tian Temperance Union, was active in a leading suffrage organization, an editor of a Christian Socialist journal, and served as chair at the first convention of the Populist party. (See Joseph R. Gusfield, *Symbolic Crusade: Status Politics and the American Temperance Movement*, 2d ed. [Urbana: University of Illinois Press, 1986], chap. 4.) Willard clearly represented the more radical wing of the tem- perance movement but it is important to remember that support for Protestant moral norms was, in the nineteenth century, often compatible with what are today considered "progressive" causes.

7. See Boyer, *When Time Shall Be No More*, Marsden, *Fundamentalism and American Culture*, and Weber, *Living in the Shadow of the Second Coming*.

8. While Jones, Jr., opposed involvement in political activity, many did not heed his advice: graduates of BJU are now to be found playing leadership roles within the Christian Right.

9. Thus, for example, it is difficult to place America's largest Protestant denomination, the Southern Baptists, firmly within either of these two categories. It straddles both and is subject to heated internal controversy. In recent years, a very conservative faction, dedicated to a strict version of biblical inerrancy and the political agenda of the Christian Right, has managed to wrest control from moderates and move the denomination in a more fundamentalist direction. It is similarly difficult to determine the exact point where neoevangelism fades into the moderate elements of mainline Protestantism. While defining precise cutting points along a continuum of orthodoxy is an inexact process, the differences as one moves from separatist fundamentalism to liberal ecumenism are profound

ones. Attention to these differences is critical to a proper understanding of the politics of the Christian Right.

10. As opposed to the discredited fundamentalists, Graham was the confidant of presidents and for decades a constant presence on the list of America's ten most admired men.

11. See, for example, Acts 2:4 and 3:6-7.

12. See table 1.1 and Margaret Poloma, *The Charismatic Movement* (Boston: Twayne Publishers, 1982), 11. Overall membership in Pentecostal denominations is difficult to determine because, like fundamentalism, the movement is marked by large numbers of independent, unaffiliated churches.

13. The fundraising and publicity apparatuses of the televangelists bear a striking resemblance to the operations of contemporary political campaigns. This point will be developed in chapter 4.

14. The mainline churches' loss of control of the airwaves was also linked to an FCC ruling of the early 1960s that allowed stations to count *paid* religious programming toward their public service obligations. Instead of giving time to Catholics, Jews, and the National Council of Churches, stations increasingly decided to sell time to conservative Protestant evangelists (see Steve Bruce, *Pray TV*, 30).

15. Roof and McKinney, *American Mainline Religion: Its Changing Shape and Future* (New Brunswick: Rutgers University Press, 1987).

16. Roof and McKinney, *American Mainline Religion*, 82–183.

17. See Lyman Kellstedt, John Green, James Guth, and Corwin Smidt, "Religious Voting Blocs in the 1992 Election," in *The Rapture of Politics*, eds. Steve Bruce, Peter Kivisto, and William H. Swatos, Jr. (New Brunswick: Transaction Publishers, 1995), 89. The authors identify evangelicals by the denominations they belong to. Therefore, their measure does not include charismatic members of nonevangelical denominations.

18. Corwin Smidt, "Evangelical Voting Patterns: 1978–1988," finds evidence of a slight increase in evangelical numbers in the 1976–1988 period.

19. For sophisticated discussions of the nuances of measurement strategies, see Kenneth Wald and Corwin E. Smidt, "Measurement Strategies in the Study of Religion and Politics," in *Rediscovering the Religious Factor in American Politics*, eds. David C. Leege and Lyman A. Kellstedt (Armonk, N.Y.: M. E. Sharpe, 1993); and Clyde Wilcox, *God's Warriors* (Baltimore: The Johns Hopkins University Press, 1992), chap. 3.

20. See George Gallup, Jr., and Jim Castelli, *The People's Religion: American Faith in the 90's* (New York: Macmillan, 1989), 93.

21. While African-American religious beliefs are very often evangelical in nature, their historical experience and political beliefs are sharply different from those of white evangelicals.

22. See Smidt, "Voting Patterns," 90; and see Kenneth Wald, *Religion and Politics in the United States* (New York: St. Martin's Press, 1987), 200; and L. Kellstedt, P. Kellstedt, and C. Smidt, "Evangelical and Mainline Protestants in the 1988 Presidential Election" (paper presented at the annual meeting of the American Political Science Association, San Francisco: 30 August–2 September 1990).

23. For example, a 1980 Gallup Poll found that 72 percent of the members of evangelical Protestant denominations believed the Bible was literally true versus 35 percent of the members of mainline denominations (figures for white respondents only). The difference is striking, but it still leaves us with significant numbers of respondents whose beliefs do not "match" their denomination. See Paul Lopatto, *Religion and the Presidential Election* (New York: Praeger Publishers, 1985), chap. 2.

24. A key to this development was the Federal Communications Commission's 1960 decision to allowed *paid* religious programming to count towards a station's public interest obligations. Instead of offering free airtime (which had been given predominantly to the more "respectable" mainline Protestant denominations and to the Catholic Church), stations could now make a profit by selling that airtime. Free airtime declined precipitously, from 47 percent of all religious programming in 1959 to only 8 percent in 1977. (See Kimberly Neuendorf, "The Public Trust Versus the Almighty Dollar," in *Religious Television: Controversies and Conclusions*, eds. Robert Ableman and Stewart Hoover [Norwood, N.J.: Ablex, 1990], 77.) As evangelicals were far more successful than their opponents at the fundraising necessary to support paid religious programming, this change worked strongly to their advantage.

25. See Mark Noll, *The Scandal of the Evangelical Mind* (Grand Rapids, Mich.: Eerdmans, 1994).

26. Dugan is director of the Office of Public Affairs for the National Association of Evangelicals. The quote is from Vern McLellan, *Christians in the Political Arena* (Charlotte, N.C.: Associate Press, 1986), 97.

27. Jerry Falwell, *Strength for the Journey* (New York: Simon and Schuster, 1987), 377.

28. Matthew Moen argues that the Christian Right has, over the last decade, moved toward a much greater reliance upon minority rights rhetoric (Matthew Moen, "From Moralism to Liberalism," chap. 6 in *The Christian Right and Congress* [Tuscaloosa: The University of Alabama Press, 1992]).

29. Particularly noteworthy has been the influence of "reconstruction theology." This strand of postmillennialism calls Christians to an active societal role; church hegemony is to be achieved through human action, not through divine intervention. The exact extent of the movement is difficult to gauge. As many of the tenets of reconstruction theology are extremely controversial—particularly its call for the imposition of a legal system based on the proscriptions of the Old Testament—reconstructionists do not tend to publicize their affiliations. My interviews did reveal reconstructionists among Robertson's supporters. For further information see Rob Boston, "Thy Kingdom Come: Christian Reconstructionists Want to Take Dominion over America," *Church and State*, 6–12; and Sara Diamond, "Life in the Spirit," chap. 4 in *Spiritual Warfare: The Politics of the Christian Right* (Boston: South End Press, 1989).

30. The most important prophecies in popular premillennialism are linked to the Middle East, the alleged site of the coming battle of Armageddon. The founding of the state of Israel, it is claimed, was a key step in the fulfillment of biblical prophecy, indicating that the endtime is imminent. In these interpretations of

prophecy, the endtime is portrayed as a period of incredibly destructive conflict, possibly involving nuclear war. If a candidate aspiring to the presidency believed such conflict was coming—and that that conflict was the will of God—it could obviously have disturbing implications. Grace Halsell's *Prophecy and Politics: Militant Evangelists on the Road to Nuclear War* (Westport: Lawrence Hill & Company, 1986) stresses the potential dangers of the Christian Right's prophetic beliefs. The most popular statement of these premillennial beliefs is provided in the works of Hal Lindsey. His *Late Great Planet Earth* (Grand Rapids: Zondervan Publishing House, 1970) was immensely popular, selling eighteen million copies in the 1970s, outselling all other books (except the Bible) in the United States for that decade. By 1990, twenty-eight million copies of the book had been printed. See Halsell, 4, and Boyer, *When Time Shall Be No More*, 5, on sales figures.

31. On the background of local Moral Majority leaders see Robert Liebman, "Mobilizing the Moral Majority," in *The New Christian Right*, eds. Robert Liebman and Robert Wuthnow (New York: Aldine Publishing Company, 1983), 49–73. On Robertson's campaign, see Clyde Wilcox, *God's Warriors*, chaps. 7 and 8.

32. See James Davison Hunter, *Culture Wars: The Struggle to Define America* (New York: Basic Books, 1991); Wade Clark Roof and William McKinney, *American Mainline Religion*; and Robert Wuthnow, *Restructuring of American Religion* (see chap. 1, n. 2) and *The Struggle for America's Soul* (Grand Rapids: Eerdmans, 1989).

33. Pat Robertson and John Cardinal O'Connor were among those who signed the document. It called for cooperation between the two groups in pursuit of a number of social issue goals. See "Evangelicals and Catholics Together: The Christian Mission in the Third Millennium," *First Things* 43 (May 1994): 15–20.

34. Paul Weyrich, interview by author, 15 March 1989. Weyrich argued that while fundamentalists had become much more willing to work with Catholics over the last decade, animosities between fundamentalists and Pentecostalists/charismatics were showing much less of a tendency to subside.

35. See Karl Marx, *The Eighteenth Brumaire of Louis Bonaparte* (New York: International Publishers, 1963), 15.

Chapter 2

1. The best sources for early explications of the status politics approach are the articles found in Daniel Bell, ed., *The New American Right* (New York: Criterion Books, 1955); and Daniel Bell, ed., *The Radical Right* (Garden City: Anchor Books, 1963). Seymour Martin Lipset and Earl Raab, *The Politics of Unreason* (Chicago: The University of Chicago Press, 1978), first published in 1970 and later updated to cover events of the 1970s, provide an in-depth explication of the status approach, used to analyze right-wing movements throughout American history.

2. In fact, the status approach emphasized the role of conservative Protestantism well before the rise of the Christian Right. Richard Hofstadter, one of the leading status theorists, declared:

The little we know from the press about the John Birch Society, the Christian Crusade of Dr. Fred Schwarz, and the activities of the Reverend Billy Hargis has served to remind us how much alive fundamentalism still is in the United States. . . . To the three sources of right-wing sentiment that are commonly enumerated—isolationism (or anti-Europeanism), ethnic prejudice, and old fashioned "liberal" economics—one must add the fundamentalist revolt against modernity, and not by any means as a minor partner. (Richard Hofstadter, "The Pseudo-Conservative Revolt," in *The Radical Right*, ed. Daniel Bell [Garden City: Anchor Books, 1963], 103)

3. See Michael Paul Rogin, *The Intellectuals and McCarthy* (Cambridge: MIT Press, 1967) for a general critique of the status theory. Rogin and Nelson Polsby ("Toward an Explanation of McCarthyism," in *Politics and Social Life*, eds. N. Polsby, R. A. Dentler, and P. A. Smith [Boston: Houghton Mifflin, 1963], 809–24) both question the accuracy of the theory's explanation of McCarthyism. Steve Bruce (*The Rise and Fall of the New Christian Right* [Oxford: Clarendon Press, 1988]) provides a spirited attack on attempts to apply status explanations to the Christian Right.

4. See Kenneth D. Wald, Dennis E. Owen, and Samuel S. Hill, Jr., "Evangelical Politics and Status Issues," *Journal for the Scientific Study of Religion* 28, no. 1 (1989): 1–16.

5. See Wald, Owen, and Hill, Jr., "Evangelical Politics and Status Issues," 2. They combine an "orthodox formulation" of the status approach that sees status movements as "a vengeful effort by declining cultural groups to restore lost prestige" with the approach of other scholars who "have insisted that supporters of the Christian Right believe—realistically—that their way of life is under assault and therefore mount rational counterattacks on behalf of the institutions, processes, and values which sustain their lifestyle." My critique of status politics is aimed primarily at its "orthodox" formulation. I am in general agreement with the second approach, which should become clear as the argument proceeds. See also Michael D' Antonio, *Fall from Grace: The Failed Crusade of the Christian Right* (Boston: South End Press, 1989).

6. Daniel Bell, "The Dispossessed," in *The Radical Right*, ed. Daniel Bell (Garden City: Anchor Books, 1963), 2–3.

7. See Richard Hofstadter, "The Pseudo-Conservative Revolt," in *The Radical Right*, ed. Daniel Bell (Garden City: Anchor Books, 1963), 84.

8. Thus *The Politics of Unreason* is the title of Lipset and Raab's study of status-based movements.

9. For example, Hofstadter states "in the mind of the status driven it is no special virtue to be more American than the Rosenbergs, but it is really something to be more American than Dean Acheson or John Foster Dulles—or Franklin Delano Roosevelt" (Hofstadter, "Pseudo-Conservative Revolt," 92).

10. Gusfield, in his study of the temperance movement, *Symbolic Crusade*, provides a more moderate version of the status politics argument. He claims that government prestige granting is a normal aspect of politics and that status politics need not assume dangerous and irrational forms. Yet Gusfield shares the approach

of other status theorists in his insistence that status campaigns are not "really" about what they claim to be about. In his case, the temperance issue is seen primarily as a tool used by displaced groups in their attempts to regain lost prestige. See Bruce, *Rise and Fall*, chap. 1, for a well-argued critique of the Gusfield position.

11. Lipset and Raab's argument was updated in "The Election and the Evangelicals," *Commentary* 71 (1981): 25–32. For more recent discussion of a status approach applied to the Christian Right see Charles L. Harper and Kevin Leicht, "Explaining the New Religious Right: Status Politics and Beyond," in *New Christian Politics*, ed. David Bromley and Anson Shupe (Macon: Mercer University Press, 1984), 101–12; John Simpson, "Moral Issues and Status Politics," in *The New Christian Politics*, ed. Robert Liebman and Robert Wuthnow (New York: Aldine Publishing Company, 1983), 187–205; and Wald et al., "Evangelical Politics" (chap. 2, n. 4). These discussions all use a much looser definition of "status politics" and do not make the associations with irrationality implied by Crawford, Lipset, and Raab.

12. Crawford, Lipset, and Raab wrote during the movement's early stages; they lump both what I call the New Right and what I call the Christian Right together under the "New Right" label.

13. Alan Crawford, *Thunder on the Right* (New York: Pantheon, 1980), 148–49.

14. The status framework's emphasis on the irrationality of social movement action was also rooted in the dominant social movement theories of the 1950s and 1960s. Under the rubric of "collective behavior," these theories lumped social movements together with mobs, fads, and crazes. (As an example of this, see Neil Smelser's *Theory of Collective Behavior* [New York: The Free Press, 1962— chapter headings include "The Panic," "The Craze," and "The Hostile Outburst.") A sharp line was drawn between the healthy functioning of pluralist democracies and irrational outbreaks of collective behavior. Collective behavior was seen to be rooted in the displaced individuals of "mass society," individuals subject to demagogic appeals, hysteria, and authoritarianism. For examples of such an approach, see William Kornhauser, *The Politics of Mass Society* (Glencoe: The Free Press, 1959); Eric Hoffer, *The True Believer* (New York: Harper and Row, 1951); and Smelser, *Collective Behavior*. See Doug McAdam, *Political Process and the Development of Black Insurgency* (Chicago: University of Chicago Press, 1982) for a critique of what he refers to as "classical" social movement theory.

15. Two works that would fit into this category are Michael D'Antonio's *Fall from Grace* and Ronald's Inglehart's *Culture Shift in Advanced Industrial Society* (Princeton: Princeton University Press, 1990). D'Antonio concludes: "In the end, defeated and exhausted, the Christian Right crusade of the 1980s could be seen as America's longing look backward at religious absolutism. It was, it seems, only a pause in the secularizing process that has been underway since the turn of the century" (242). Inglehart comes to a similar conclusion—the Christian Right is seen as making little headway against a trend toward "postmaterialism" and an accompanying decline in traditional religious values. Inglehart declares:

All the evidence we have seen points toward a pervasive tendency toward secularization. Clearly, the proprayer and antiabortion movements do have devoted partisans. But the revival of religious issues reflects a reaction among a dwindling traditionalist sector, rather than a general shift toward cultural conservatism among the population at large. (205)

16. Hunter, *American Evangelicalism: Conservative Religion and the Quandry of Modernity* (New Brunswick, Rutgers University Press, 1983), 60.

17. These efforts have been particularly successful in Latin America, where the spread of evangelical Protestantism is becoming increasingly worrisome to the Catholic Church. An excellent account of these events is provided in David Stoll's *Is Latin America Turning Protestant?* (Berkeley: University of California Press, 1990). Recent events in the former Soviet Bloc are opening the way for massive evangelistic efforts in that region as well.

18. See Kenneth D. Wald, *Religion and Politics in the United States*, 2d ed. (Washington, D.C.: Congressional Quarterly, 1992), 238–41.

19. See Hunter, *American Evangelicalism*; James Davison Hunter, *Evangelicalism: The Coming Generation* (Chicago: University of Chicago Press, 1987); and Frances Fitzgerald, *Cities on a Hill* (New York: Simon and Schuster, 1986); and David Harrington Watt, *A Transforming Faith: Explorations of Twentieth Century American Evangelicalism* (New Brunswick: Rutgers University Press, 1991), 154.

20. Theories of "modernity" have been central to religious sociology in general and to accounts of American evangelicalism in particular. My account builds on the work of a number of previous theorists, most notably Peter L. Berger, *The Sacred Canopy: Elements of a Sociological Theory of Religion* (New York: Anchor Books, 1967); Hunter, *American Evangelicalism* and *Evangelicalism*; Robert Booth Fowler, *Unconventional Partners* (Grand Rapids: Eerdmans, 1989); Anthony Giddens, *Modernity and Self-Identity* (Stanford: Stanford University Press, 1991); Bruce Lawrence, *Defenders of God: The Fundamentalist Revolt against the Modern Age* (New York: Harper & Row, 1989); and David Martin, *A General Theory of Secularization* (New York: Harper & Row, 1978).

21. My utilization of the concepts of modernity and modernization in the analysis of a First World case should not be taken as an endorsement of "modernization theory" as it applies to developing (or as is often the case nondeveloping) countries. Embedded in a world economy already dominated by the developed nations, these countries face a far different situation than that faced hundreds of years ago by the pioneers of capitalist development. Therefore, it is not clear that the Third World will—or even should try to—retrace the steps of the First.

22. Hunter, *American Evangelicalism*, 12.

23. See Wuthnow, *Struggle for America's Soul*, for an excellent discussion of the expansion of the state into areas that were once church domains. Wuthnow is particularly concerned with the role of the church as part of a voluntary sector "public sphere" serving as a counterforce to the market and the state.

24. See Alexis de Tocqueville, *Democracy in America: Volume I*, 319.

25. See Wald, *Religion and Politics*, 2d ed., 9. Jon Butler, *Awash in a Sea of Faith* (Cambridge: Harvard University Press, 1990), provides an interesting

analysis that suggests that levels of belief and religious practice have generally risen over the course of American history.

26. The changing positions of the established and insurgent forces can be seen in the relative strength of two denominations: "The Congregationalists, which had twice the clergy of any other American church in 1775, could not muster one-tenth the preaching force of the Methodists in 1845" (Hatch, *Democratization of American Christianity*, 4).

27. Hatch, *Democratization of American Christianity*, 14.

28. Martin, *General Theory of Secularization*, 28. Martin is contrasting American Protestantism with its much different European counterparts.

29. See Martin for an excellent discussion of the differing fate of the church in the United States and Europe.

30. R. Laurence Moore, *Selling God: American Religion in the Marketplace of Culture* (New York: Oxford University Press, 1994).

A work entitled *The Salesman from Nazareth* declares:
   The Salesman from Nazareth knew His business. Which, in no small measure, accounts for His success. He simply had to know His stuff. His prospects challenged him at every step He took. So did His competitors. When He said, "Verily I say unto you . . . " He knew what He was talking about. (Josef Daikeler, quoted in Carol Flake, *Redemptorama* [New York: Penguin Books, 1984], 149)

Robertson's short spots often feature individuals who have gone astray. Lives plagued by drugs, alcohol, or marital problems are miraculously turned around when the individual finds Christ. The parallel between Christ and the consumer product is very apparent; one almost expects the announcer to promote the "new and improved" version. See also Razelle Frankel, *Televangelism: The Marketing of Popular Religion* (Carbondale: Southern Illinois University Press, 1987) on market techniques and the history of revivalism.

31. See Berger, *Sacred Canopy*, chap. 5.

32. Warren I. Susman, *Culture As History: The Transformation of American Society in the Twentieth Century* (New York: Pantheon Books, 1984), provides an excellent account of the shift in American culture from an ethos of puritan self-control, emphasizing "character," to an ethos of consumption, emphasizing the development of "personality."

33. The works of Tim LaHaye, one of the Christian Right's leading figures, provide a good illustration of this trend. Titles include *How to Win Over Depression, How to be Happy Though Married, Spirit-Controlled Temperament, Spirit-Controlled Family Living,* and *The Act of Marriage.* (The latter two works were coauthored with his wife Beverly, herself a leading figure in the Christian Right.) Titles of these works are taken from Tim LaHaye, *The Battle for the Mind* (Old Tappan: Fleming H. Revell Company, 1980). The LaHayes also offered "family life seminars" and "temperament analysis" for the faithful.

34. Discussing the rise of the therapeutic within evangelicalism, David Harrington Watt declares:

By the 1960s, popular evangelicalism had been profoundly influenced by its encounter with modern psychology. A stress on the here and now, a lack of concern with the afterlife, and a constant emphasis on the importance of self esteem—these were some of the hallmarks of popular evangelicalism in the 1960s and 1970s. (*A Transforming Faith*, 154)

35. For an extended discussion of the adaptation of evangelical doctrine in keeping with the constraints of modernity see Hunter, *American Evangelicalism*.

36. Dean M. Kelley, *Why Conservative Churches Are Growing* (New York: Harper & Row, 1972). My argument in this section also has much in common with that of Fowler, *Unconventional Partners*.

37. In this argument he draws heavily on Peter Berger's seminal work, *The Sacred Canopy*.

38. Strict churches, in the study, are generally conservative ones. Kelley does point out, however, that "strict" churches need not necessarily be conservative; the content of the beliefs about which one is "strict" can vary greatly. Thus, for example, the radical charismatic movement associated with *Sojourners* magazine, with the serious demands it makes on its members to sacrifice for the poor, to accept the burdens of peace and social justice struggles might be seen as a "strict" church of the Left. So too might the base communities of liberation theology. (These two examples are mine, not Kelley's.)

39. Gary Bauer, interview by author, 6 March 1989.

40. The 1980s and 1990s are not included only because Watt's study is limited to the period of 1925–1976. My observations indicate that the focus on the family has not abated; Watt, *Transforming Faith*, 85.

41. Ed McAteer, interview with author, 13 February 1989.

42. See Rosenberg, *Southern Baptists*.

43. This racial conservatism is particularly pronounced among those evangelical leaders associated with the Christian Right. Other evangelical leaders, especially those in the neoevangelical camp, tend to more liberal positions.

44. Roof and McKinney, *American Mainline Religion*, 217–21.

45. I obtained a copy of this flier at the 1989 National Religious Broadcasters convention. It showed graphs tracing SAT scores, crime, and sexually transmitted disease rates. In each case things began to get worse roughly around the time of the Supreme Court's decision. Of course, this methodology proves little; any event of this period—from the assassination of President Kennedy to the Beatles appearance on the Ed Sullivan show—could be just as easily linked to these trends.

46. Flake, *Redemptorama*, 46.

47. See Bruce, *Rise and Fall*, 42–43.

48. To what extent is the Christian Right a response to the invasion of a *segregated* subculture? Sorting out the role played by race from those played by religious, family, and cultural concerns is not easy. Certainly, many figures now associated with the Christian Right opposed the Civil Rights movement in the 1960s. (See, for example, Falwell, *Strength for the Journey*, chap. 11.) The movement has opposed key elements of the more recent civil rights agenda, most notably, affirmative action and sanctions against South Africa. Yet most movement lead-

ers now profess support for equal rights, and some African Americans play a prominent role in evangelical circles—most notably Ben Kinchlow, longtime cohost of Pat Robertson's "700 Club." Based on my own experience with the movement, I do not doubt that it contains a number of outright racists, and a much larger number of racial conservatives whose motives might reasonably be open to question. I do, however, dissent from views that see the movement as *primarily* motivated by racial concerns, views that see religious and cultural issues as mere "cover" for a racial agenda. Religious and cultural issues are central to the movement and receive far greater attention from its leaders and its activists than do positions—whatever they may be—on racial issues. See Peter Skerry, "Christian Schools Versus the I.R.S.," *The Public Interest* 61 (fall 1980): 18–41, for a critique of efforts to explain the Christian schools movement along purely racial lines.

49. Kristen Luker, *Abortion and the Politics of Motherhood* (Berkeley: University of California Press, 1984), 127.

50. See James Traub, "CBN Counts Its Blessings," *Channels* (May/June 1985) in *The Pat Robertson File* from the Data Center, Oakland, Calif.

51. Simpson, "Moral Issues."

52. Simpson's choice of questions leads to a finding of very high levels of moral conservatism (about 70 percent) in the American populace. Steve Bruce, *Pray TV*, points out that using a somewhat different set of questions, one can come to a far smaller estimate of support for moral conservatism. Bruce also—quite rightly—points out that support for a selection of issues championed by the Christian Right need not imply approval of the movement. Nonetheless, these problems seem unlikely to undermine the validity of Simpson's findings concerning the *relative* moral conservatism of different groups.

53. Roughly similar pictures are painted by Roof and McKinney, *American Mainline Religion*, chap. 6, and George Gallup, Jr., and Jim Castelli, *The People's Religion*, chap. 6.

54. See Hadden and Shupe, *Televangelism*, chap. 11.

55. In explaining the forces against which evangelicals are contending, several outside commentators—and even a few Christian Right figures—have drawn on academic theories depicting the rise of a "new class." This new class, it is claimed, is based not on control of labor power, ownership of small business or of capital; rather its defining characteristic is *expertise*. Its members make their living through the creation and manipulation of symbols: in the media, and academia, and among policy experts and social workers. The new class is often held to be part of a far-reaching process of expanding social regulation on the part of the state. This aspect of the theory—along with the undeniable social liberalism of those commonly held to compose the new class—fit well with a picture of liberal forces encroaching upon the Christian Right constituency. While the general picture they draw is accurate, I have doubts about the extent to which this culturally liberal segment can profitably be considered a *class* with unified purpose or even with a common set of latent interests. For examples of the new class approach as applied to the politics of the Christian Right, see Hunter, *American Evangelicalism*; Barbara Hargrove, "Religion and the New Mandarins," in *Secularization and Fundamentalism Reconsidered: Religion and the Political Order*, vol. 3, ed. Jef-

frey Hadden and Anson Shupe (New York: Paragon House, 1989), 215–29; and Samuel T. Francis, "Message from MARS," in *The New Right Papers*, ed. Robert Whitaker (New York: St. Martins Press, 1982), 64–83. Even Christian Right leader Tim LaHaye (*Battle for the Mind*, 146–47) invokes Daniel Bell's discussion of the new class as he delineates the outlines of the secular humanist menace.

56. See McAdam, *Black Insurgency*, and Theda Skocpol, *States and Social Revolutions* (New York: Cambridge University Press, 1979).

57. Gary Bauer, interview by author, 6 March 1989.

58. Alan Peshkin's *God's Choice: The Total World of a Fundamentalist Christian School* (Chicago: The University of Chicago Press, 1986) provides a fascinating case study of the difficulties faced by Christian schools as they try to mold young minds in the face of a world hostile to many of their beliefs.

Christian School Action, founded by Robert Billings in 1977 as a response to IRS efforts to take away tax exemptions from Christian schools, was one of the first organizational efforts of what was to become the Christian Right. (See Moen, *Christian Right and Congress* [Tuscaloosa: The University of Alabama Press, 1989], 27.) Billings also stressed the importance of the school issue in my interview with him (21 January 1989).

59. The National Religious Broadcasters (NRB), founded in the 1940s to help get evangelicals onto the airwaves, has flourished and now plays a critical role in Christian Right politics.

60. On the battle for control of the Southern Baptist Convention, see Nancy Tatom Ammerman, *Baptist Battles: Social Change and Religious Conflict in the Southern Baptist Convention* (New Brunswick: Rutgers University Press, 1990), and Rosenberg, *Southern Baptists*.

61. Dobson surveys what he sees as a mighty array of Left and secular forces threatening "Judeo-Christian" precepts in America. He then asks:

Where, then, are the strongholds of the Judeo-Christian ethic? Only two bulwarks remain, and they both face unrelenting pressure from the left. The first is the Christian church. . . . The second repository of Judeo-Christian values is the institution of the family. Alas the beleaguered, exhausted, oppressed, and overtaxed family now stands unprotected against a mighty foe . . . it should be clear why these two institutions are under such vicious attack from so many quarters today. They alone stand in opposition to vast cultural changes, planned and promoted by social engineers. (James Dobson and Gary Bauer, *Children at Risk: The Battle for the Hearts and Minds of Our Kids* [Dallas: Word Publishing, 1990], 22–23)

62. Discussing the dangers he perceives in secular childcare, Gary Bauer provides insight into the role of family in Christian Right thought.

In its final report in 1970, The White House Conference on Children made this startling statement. "Day care is a powerful institution. A day care program that ministers to a child from 6 months to 6 years of age has over 8,000 hours to teach him values, fears, beliefs and behaviors."

We agree overwhelmingly! Indeed that is what concerns us about rail-
roading large numbers of today's preschoolers into government sponsored
day care centers. The temptation to teach this generation a new system of
values—one that contradicts the views of their parents—will be almost
irresistible. It will place in the hands of the cultural elite—whom we now
see as our cultural adversaries—all the tools necessary to destroy the Judeo-
Christian system of values in a single generation. (Dobson and Bauer, *Children
at Risk*, 122)

63. Beverly LaHaye, head of the Christian Right group Concerned Women for
America, put her criticism of feminism this way:

I don't believe you can be a Christian feminist because the words contradict
each other. Christian is serving others, feminist is looking out for my own
rights, my own self, me. . . . The feminist woman has her priorities all
messed up but the traditional woman keeps her family the number one
priority. (Interview by author, 23 March 1989)

64. See, for example, Falwell, *Strength for the Journey*, chap. 13.
65. Two excellent works have dealt with this issue: Luker's *Abortion and the
Politics of Motherhood* and Faye Ginsberg's *Contested Lives: The Abortion Debate
in an American Community* (Berkeley: University of California Press, 1989).
66. See Luker, *Abortion*, 158–75, and Ginsburg, *Contested Lives*, chaps. 10
and 12.
67. Anti-abortion advocates argue that disrespect for life in the case of the
fetus will lead to a more general disrespect, manifesting itself in such practices
as euthanasia.
68. In particular, the Christian Right constituency was mobilized in support
of the contra war against the Sandinista government of Nicaragua. With the re-
placement of the Sandinistas and, more generally, with the end of the Cold War,
the foreign policy concerns of this constituency are more difficult to predict.
Some Christian Right leaders are turning to a more isolationist stance. The movement's foreign policy agenda also appears to be focusing more on evangelism—
especially in Latin America and the former Soviet Bloc.
69. See John Green and James Guth, "Robertson's Republicans: Christian Activists in Republican Politics," *Election Politics* 4 (1987): 9–14; John McGlennon,
"Religious Activists in the Republican Party," paper presented at the annual meeting
of the Midwest Political Science Association. Chicago, 13–15 April 1989; and
Corwin Smidt and James Penning, "A House Divided: A Comparison of Robertson
and Bush Delegates to the 1988 Michigan Republican State Convention," *Polity*
23 (1989): 127–38.
70. For example, Tim LaHaye's *The Battle for the Mind*, one of the better
known examples of the "secular humanism" argument, claims that 275,000 dedicated humanists hold the media, the schools, indeed nearly the entire country
under their control (181). The complexities of contemporary politics are reduced
to a simple clash between Christian and humanistic worldviews.

71. See Michael Lind, "Rev. Robertson's Grand International Conspiracy Theory," *The New York Review of Books* 42, no. 2 (1995): 21–25.

72. A strongly stated and influential case for a politics of cultural conservatism built on a secular foundation, see The Institute for Cultural Conservatism, *Cultural Conservatism: Toward a New National Agenda* (Washington, D.C.: Free Congress Education and Research Foundation, 1987) from an offshoot of Paul Weyrich's Free Congress foundation.

Chapter 3

1. Critics of party reform include: Jeane Kirkpatrick, *Dismantling the Parties* (Washington, D.C.: American Enterprise Institute, 1979); Nelson Polsby, *The Consequences of Party Reform* (New York: Oxford University Press, 1983); Austin Ranney, *Curing the Mischief of Faction* (Berkeley: University of California Press, 1975); and Byron Shafer, *Quiet Revolution: Reform Politics in the Democratic Party, 1968–1972* (New York: Russell Sage Foundation, 1984). Defenders of party reform include Denise Baer and David Bositis, *Elite Cadres and Party Coalitions* (Westport: Greenwood Press, Inc., 1988); and William J. Crotty, *Decision for the Democrats* (Baltimore: Johns Hopkins University Press, 1978). Howard L. Reiter, *Selecting the President* (Philadelphia: University of Pennsylvania Press, 1985), is among those who argue that the impact of party reform has been overstated.

2. See Leon Epstein, *Political Parties in the American Mold* (Madison: The University of Wisconsin Press, 1986), 97.

3. See William G. Mayer, "Caucuses: How They Work, What Difference They Make," in *In Pursuit of the White House*, ed. William G. Mayer (Chatham: Chatham House Publishers, 1996), 122.

4. The 13 percent–18 percent range for the Democrats reflects the 5 percent of the delegates who were chosen in Texas, which used a mixed caucus-primary system. A few states utilize "advisory" primaries, with actual delegates chosen in caucuses. I have counted these as caucus states (see Mayer, "Caucuses," 122).

5. See Mayer, "Caucuses," 116.

6. See Mayer, "Caucuses," 126–28.

7. On campaign finance, see Clyde Wilcox, "Financing the 1988 Prenomination Campaigns," in *Nominating the President*, ed. Emmett H. Buell, Jr., and Lee Sigelman (Knoxville: The University of Tennessee Press, 1991).

8. See, for example, Tom Rosenstiel, *Strange Bedfellows* (New York: Hyperion, 1993).

9. See Baer and Bositis, *Elite Cadres*.

10. See Polsby, *Consequences*, for a well-argued statement of the antireform case.

11. See Reiter, *Selecting the President*.

12. See Albert O. Hirschman, *Exit, Voice, and Loyalty* (Cambridge: Harvard University Press, 1970), 4.

13. See Anthony Downs's *An Economic Theory of Democracy* (New York: Harper and Row, 1957) for an analysis of party strategy based primarily on exit considerations.

14. See Hirschman, "On Spatial Duopoly and the Dynamics of Two Party Systems," chap. 6 of *Exit, Voice, and Loyalty*.

15. One suspects that Hirschman's omission is linked to the difficulty of distinguishing such withdrawal from the exercise of voice by party activists. This is a real problem, but limiting analysis to the exit of voters misses much that is of importance in the case of the Christian Right.

16. Hirschman, *Exit, Voice, Loyalty*, 4.

17. A representative statement in this regard is the following: "There are *a great many ways* in which customers, voters, and party members can impress their unhappiness on a firm or a party and make their managers highly uncomfortable; only a few of these ways and not necessarily the most important ones, will result in the loss of sales or votes, rather than in, say, loss of sleep by the managers" (Hirschman, *Exit, Voice, Loyalty*, 73–74). What these "great many ways" are remains something of a mystery.

18. Hirschman, *Exit, Voice, Loyalty*, 86. Boycott partakes of exit in that customers quit buying a firm's product, but it contains elements of voice because this exit is conditional, linked to specific demands for improved performance.

19. In the last two decades, the Democratic and Republican National Committees and their affiliated congressional committees have experienced remarkable fundraising success. Professional, centralized party organizations now play a greater role in congressional elections and in getting the parties' messages out to the general public. However, these committees do not have the role in the presidential nominating process once held by local grassroots party organizations. On the impact of the rise of central party organizations, see Xandra Kayden and Eddie Mahe, Jr., *The Party Goes On: The Persistence of the Two-Party System in the United States* (New York: Basic Books Inc., 1985); and Paul Herrnson, *Party Campaigning in the 1980s* (Cambridge: Harvard University Press, 1988).

20. See Olson's *Logic of Collective Action* for a discussion of the political importance of groups organized for nonpolitical ends. Olson argues that organizing solely for political ends often makes little sense for individuals. Therefore it is easier to keep members in groups that perform important nonpolitical functions (such as the satisfaction of religious needs) and transfer organizational resources over to political functions than it is to organize individuals for political ends. See Razelle Frankl, *Televangelism: The Marketing of Popular Religion*; Allen Hertzke, *Echoes of Discontent*; Jeffrey Hadden and Anson Shupe, *Televangelism*; and Kenneth Wald, Dennis Owen, and Samuel Hill, Jr., "Churches as Political Communities," for specific discussions of the political uses of religious organizations.

21. See John Green, "The Christian Right and the 1994 Elections: A View from the States," *PS: Political Science and Politics* 28, no. 1 (March 1995): 5–8.

22. See Steve Bruce, *Pray TV*, 175–6.

23. For arguments to this effect at the state level, see John Green, "The Christian Right and the 1994 Elections: A View from the States"; and Clyde Wilcox, Mark J. Rozell, and J. Bradford Coker, "The Christian Right in the Old Dominion: Resurgent Republicans or Holy War?" *PS: Political Science and Politics* 28, no. 1 (March 1995): 15–18.

24. My thinking on conflicts between organizational needs and strategic requirements has been helped greatly by Jane Mansbridge's *Why We Lost the ERA* (Chicago: Chicago University Press, 1986). My thanks go to my colleague Kay Schlozman for insisting that I read it.

25. Similar problems exist at lower levels in the electoral system. Republican candidates in state and local races often want the Christian Right's electoral resources mobilized on their behalf but also want to avoid being publicly linked to the movement and its controversial leaders. To deal with this difficulty, Jerry Falwell once suggested that a candidate he was backing feel free to denounce him publicly if the candidate thought it would help with the voters.

26. See John Persinos, "Has the Christian Right Taken Over the Republican Party?"

27. As critics have pointed out, Hirschman's argument assumes that voice is the only viable alternative to exit. When exit is cut off, however, some individuals may simply suffer in silence rather than utilize the often expensive option of voice. See Brian Barry, "Review Article: *Exit, Voice, Loyalty,*" *British Journal of Political Science* 4 (1974): 79–107.

28. For an excellent critique of Hirschman, see Brian Barry, "Review Article," especially his discussion of loyalty (95–99).

29. Jo Freeman, "The Political Culture of the Democratic and Republican Parties," *Political Science Quarterly* 101, no. 3 (1986): 327–56; and "Whom You Know vs. Whom You Represent," in *The Woman's Movements of the United States and Western Europe,* ed. Mary Katzenstein and Carol Mueller (Philadelphia: Temple University Press, 1987).

30. Threats of group exit may involve either threats to defect to an opposing party or to drop out of party activities, pursuing goals as a nonpartisan interest group.

31. One of the ways in which the Christian Right stands out from the Republican norm is in its choice of clothing. Freeman describes the clash between the "ultrasuedes" and the "polyesters" ("Political Culture," 351). Such an observation may seem trivial but it is just one mark of social distinctions that are quite real. From my experience at the 1988 and 1992 Republican conventions, it was clear that Christian Right activists and party regulars inhabited very different social worlds. For empirical data on differences between Robertson and Bush supporters see Duane Oldfield, "Pat Crashes the Party: Reform, Republicans, and Robertson," working paper (Berkeley: Institute of Governmental Studies, 1990), 10–15; and Green and Guth, "Robertson's Republicans."

32. Robertson's 1988 rhetoric and demands took a very different form than Jesse Jackson's. Robertson went to great lengths to stress his *Republican* affiliation and loyalties. His demands at the Republican convention tended not to be made on behalf of an oppressed Christian Right constituency. Instead, Robertson would advance his positions by affiliating them with a dominant faction, claiming that his vision was the true Republican (or more specifically, Reaganite) vision, applicable to all Americans. On the strategic choices facing Jackson, or any other Black presidential candidate, see Ronald Walters, *Black Presidential Politics* (Albany: State University of New York Press, 1988). For a comparison of Jackson and Robertson, see Hertzke, *Echoes of Discontent.*

Chapter 4

1. There is some ambiguity as to Robertson's exact position. Biographer David Harrell, Jr., presents Robertson as an enthusiastic Carter supporter (*Pat Robertson: A Personal, Political, and Religious Portrait* [San Francisco: Harper and Row, 1987], 176). John Donovan's authorized biography, *Pat Robertson: The Authorized Biography* (New York: Macmillan, 1988), contains Robertson's claim that he made a last-minute decision to vote for Ford (181), a claim I have heard Robertson make on the campaign trail. Obviously, a claim to have voted for Ford is convenient for a man running for the Republican presidential nomination; we may never be sure exactly what Robertson did in the privacy of the voting booth. Whoever he in fact voted for, it is clear that Robertson, like many other conservative evangelicals, quickly grew disillusioned with *President* Carter.

2. Press release of Robertson's speech to the Republican National Convention, 16 August 1988. This speech can also be found at the end of Pat Robertson, *The Plan* (Nashville: Thomas Nelson Publishers, 1989).

3. Press release, "Remarks by Reverend Pat Robertson Given before the Republican Convention on August 19, 1992."

4. Press release, "Address to the Republican National Convention by Patrick J. Buchanan."

5. Press release, "Prepared Text of the Acceptance Address by the Vice President."

6. The biggest changes involved more explicit language opposing gay rights. See chap. 6 for more details.

7. In 1950, the Federal Council of Churches was renamed the National Council of Churches, the name it retains to this day.

8. See Joel Carpenter, "Uneasy in Zion," in *Evangelicalism and Modern America*, ed. George Marsden (Grand Rapids: Eerdmans, 1984), 178 (n. 58), for representative samples of McIntire's assaults on the NAE. One article in the ACCC journal *Christian Beacon* was entitled "NAE Leader Defends Communist Front Preachers." On dissemination see Benjamin R. Epstein and Arnold Forster, *The Radical Right: Report on the John Birch Society and Its Allies* (New York: Vintage Books, 1966), 10, 70.

9. See Epstein and Forster, *The Radical Right*, 25.

10. Bruce, Pray TV, 165.

11. Wilcox, *God's Warriors*.

12. This statement was made at a national affairs briefing attended by over ten thousand Christian Right activists and, significantly, by presidential candidate Ronald Reagan. Reagan won enthusiastic backing as he declared his support for the group, but Smith's comment remained a continuing source of embarrassment (see Rosenberg, *Southern Baptists*, 192).

13. Billy James Hargis, *Why I Fight for a Christian America* (Nashville: Thomas Nelson Publishers, 1974), 36.

14. Lipset and Raab, *Politics of Unreason*, 275.

15. Bruce, *Pray TV*, 166.

16. Hargis, *Christian America*, 165.

17. See Hargis, *Christian America*, 160. From my experience with Christian Right gatherings and reading Christian Right literature, this verse is far and away the movement's favorite. Its appeal goes beyond Hargis and the Christian Right as well. Richard G. Hutcheson (*God in the White House: How Religion Has Changed the Modern Presidency* [New York: Macmillan, 1988], 136) reports that Jimmy Carter planned to use this passage in his inaugural address until aides prevailed upon him to delete it.

18. See Hargis, *Why I Fight for a Christian America*, 154.

19. See LaHaye, *Battle for the Mind*, 181–85. LaHaye even has a graphic showing America in chains, subject to the control of these 275,000.

In LaHaye's words, "What the Bible is to Christians, the Humanist Manifesto is to humanists. It represents the official position of the humanist movement and is accepted by the faithful as the current mandate on humanist beliefs, values, and goals. . . . This amazing document blueprints their takeover of the twenty-first century" (see LaHaye, *The Battle for the Mind*, 85). The manifestos do represent important intellectual trends but they, and specifically humanist organizations, are much more a reflection than a cause of these trends.

The invocation of the Illuminati is indirect. The conspiracy is not specifically mentioned but the name of Weishaupt, the alleged originator of the Illuminati, is included in a list of subversive humanist authors (see LaHaye, *Battle for the Mind*, 25).

20. The quote is the only attributed endorsement on the back cover of the paperback edition.

21. For more detailed accounts of the origins of the Christian Right, see Crawford, *Thunder on the Right*; Conway and Siegelman, *Holy Terror* (New York: Dell Publishing Company, 1984); Diamond, *Spiritual Warfare*; and Richard Viguerie, *The New Right: We're Ready to Lead* (Falls Church, Va.: The Viguerie Company, 1980).

22. See Jerome L. Himmelstein, *To the Right*, 84–94, for an argument that the New Right was not nearly so new as many believed.

23. On New Right/GOP tensions, see Paul Weyrich, "Blue Collar or Blue Blood? The New Right Compared with the Old Right," in *The New Rights Papers*, ed. Robert Whitaker (New York: St. Martin's Press, 1982). See also Richard Viguerie, *The Establishment vs. the People: Is a New Populist Revolt on the Way?* (Chicago: Regnery Gateway, Inc., 1983). Viguerie helped third party candidate George Wallace raise $7 million to retire his 1972 campaign debt (Himmelstein, *To the Right*, 82–83). In Richard Viguerie's words: "Conservatives must learn to disregard meaningless party labels" (Crawford, *Thunder on the Right*, 245).

Although Schlafly's activism on behalf of right-wing causes went back to the Goldwater days and she shared many of the traits of the New Right leaders, her organization—the Eagle Forum—tended to maintain its independence from interlocking networks of the New Right.

24. John Green, "A Look at the 'Invisible Army': Pat Robertson's Campaign Contributors" (paper prepared for the Annual Meeting of the American Association for the Advancement of Science, San Francisco, Calif., 14–19 January 1989), 13.

25. Phillips has since converted to Christianity.

26. On Billings, see Conway and Siegelman, *Holy Terror*, 112. In a personal interview on 15 March 1989, Weyrich describes his suggestion that Billings move to Washington to further his efforts to promote the interests of private Christian schools. To Weyrich's surprise, Billings showed up on his doorstep some time later, having sold his house in Florida and moved to Washington. Billings asked for Weyrich's advice in setting up the NCAC, described by Weyrich as the first Christian Right organization.

Robert Billings talked about the IRS in an interview by the author, 21 January 1989. The immediate cause of the dispute was an attempt by the IRS to revoke the tax-exempt status of schools it believed practiced racial discrimination, but it was clear from my interview that Billings saw this as only part of a broader ranging effort to regulate private Christian schools.

Ed McAteer's comments are from a telephone interview by the author, 13 February 1989.

27. McAteer, interview. See also Conway and Siegelman, *Holy Terror*, 114.

28. Viguerie, *The New Right*, 56.

29. The meeting was put together by Ed McAteer. The pollster involved was Lance Torrance.

30. Weyrich, interview.

31. Moen, *Christian Right and Congress*, 67–68.

32. Weyrich's groups remain healthy. So too does Phyllis Schlafly's Eagle Forum, one of the few New Right affiliated groups to attract a large grass-roots following. It should be noted, however, that Schlafly's success has been built largely on the social issue concerns that animate the Christian Right. One can see Eagle Forum as a group straddling the line between the New and Christian Right—a position Paul Weyrich took in my interview with him.

33. Weyrich, interview.

34. Scholar Paul Lopatto, *Religion in the Presidential Election*, divided Protestants into three denomination-based categories: conservative, moderate, and liberal. The "conservative" category is roughly equivalent to the usage of "evangelical" in this book. Figures on evangelical voting from 1960–1980 in this chapter are, unless otherwise noted, the figures for Lopatto's conservative Protestant category.

35. Duane Oldfield and Aaron Wildavsky, "Reconsidering the Two Presidencies," *Society* 26 (July/August 1989): 54–59.

36. Goldwater's position on racial issues is captured in the following statement, written in 1960:

It is wise and just for Negro children to attend the same schools as whites . . . [however] . . . the federal constitution does *not* require the states to maintain racially mixed schools. Despite the recent holding of the Supreme Court, I am firmly convinced—not only that integrated schools are not required—but that the Constitution does not permit any interference whatsoever by the federal government in the field of education. (Thomas Byrne Edsall and

Mary D. Edsall, *Chain Reaction: The Impact of Race, Rights, and Taxes on American Politics* [New York: W. W. Norton and Company, 1991], 40-41)

37. The states were Mississippi, Alabama, Georgia, South Carolina, and Louisiana. Goldwater's only other success came in his home state of Arizona (see Edward G. Carmines and James A. Stimson, *Issue Evolution: Race and the Transformation of American Politics* [Princeton: Princeton University Press, 1989], chap. 2).

38. See Carmines and Stimson, *Issue Evolution*, chap. 4.

39. See David W. Rhode, *Parties and Leaders in the Postreform House* (Chicago: University of Chicago Press, 1991), especially chaps. 3 and 6.

40. Donald Bruce Johnson, ed., *National Party Platforms: Volume II, 1960–1976* (Urbana: University of Illinois Press, 1978), 683.

41. Feminist leaders attempted to insert a pro-choice plank into the platform but this was defeated. The McGovern organization was afraid an abortion plank would damage the candidate in the general election (see Freeman, "Whom You Know vs. Whom You Represent").

42. Johnson, ed., *National Party Platforms: 1960–1976*, 796.

43. Johnson, ed., *National Party Platforms: 1960–1976*, 796.

44. Lopatto, *Religion and the Presidential Election*, 55.

45. See Warren Miller and M. Kent Jennings, *Parties in Transition* (New York: Russell Sage Foundation, 1986); and Robert W. Kweit and Mary Grisez Kweit, "The Permeability of Parties," in *The Life of the Parties*, eds. R. Rapoport, A. Abromowitz, and J. McGlennon (Lexington: The University Press of Kentucky, 1986).

46. The ERA lost in a platform subcommittee vote and won by a narrow fifty-one to forty-seven margin in the full committee (see Freeman, "Whom You Know vs. Whom You Represent").

47. The Democratic abortion plank, reflecting candidate Carter's personal ambivalence on the subject, reads as follows: "We fully recognize the religious and ethical nature of the concerns which many Americans have on the subject of abortion. We feel, however, that it is undesirable to attempt to amend the U.S. Constitution to overturn the Supreme Court decisions in this area." The Republican platform acknowledges the difficulty of the issue, and the contradictory positions held by party members, but goes on to declare: "The Republican Party favors a continuation of the public dialogue on abortion and supports the efforts of those who seek enactment of a constitutional amendment to restore protection of the right to life for unborn children" (see Johnson, *National Party Platforms: 1960–1976*, 976).

48. Johnson, *National Party Platforms: 1960–1976*, 973–74.

49. A. James Reichley, "Pietist Politics," in *The Fundamentalist Phenomena*, ed. Norman J. Cohen (Grand Rapids: Eerdmans, 1990. Reichley argues that the pro-Carter impact of evangelicals was important in northern states such as Pennsylvania as well as in the South. See also Lopatto, *Religion and the Presidential Election*.

50. Donald Bruce Johnson, ed., *National Party Platforms of 1980* (Urbana: University of Illinois Press, 1982), 183, 203, 62.

51. As the 1976 platform proudly pointed out, the Republicans had—in 1940—been the first of the major parties to endorse the ERA.

52. Johnson, *National Party Platforms of 1980*, 43–44, 55, 182, 183, 186.

53. For decades the platforms of both parties had routinely contained clauses decrying discrimination on the basis of race, gender, ethnicity, religion, and so on. In 1980 the Democrats added "sexual orientation" to this list (see Johnson, *National Party Platforms of 1980*, 61).

54. See Johnson, *National Party Platforms of 1980*, 184.

55. Nelson Polsby and Aaron Wildavsky, *Presidential Elections*, 7th ed. (New York: The Free Press, 1988), 131.

56. Arthur H. Miller, Christopher Wlezien, and Anne Hildreth, "A Reference Group Theory of Partisan Coalitions," *The Journal of Politics* 53, no. 4 (1991): 1134–49.

These figures for 1972 reflect a fairly traditional set of group associations with the party, indicating that the groups associated with McGovern had not yet been associated with the Democratic party as a whole.

57. Viguerie, *The New Right*, 17.

58. Lopatto, *Religion and the Presidential Election*, 55.

59. William A. Rusher, *The Rise of the Right* (New York: William Morrow and Company, Inc., 1984), 267.

60. These figures were members of the Committee on Conservative Alternatives, a group set up to "evaluate the Republican party and a new party as alternative channels for future conservative political activity" (see Rusher, *The Rise of the Right*, 271).

61. Details on the 1976 third party effort are drawn primarily from Rusher, *The Rise of the Right*, chap. 11.

62. One foreseeable development might cause elements of the Christian Right to bolt to a third party. That is a rejection by the GOP of its current opposition to abortion. Abortion is the movement's top priority, the issue on which activists' passions run strongest. Furthermore, the abortion issue has been central to party/movement negotiations. The party's reneging on its "commitment" in this area would lead to an extremely strong reaction.

63. Personal interview with Robert Dugan, political director of the National Association of Evangelicals and a participant in these many meetings, 16 March 1989. Dugan did not remember the exact date the first meeting was held. It was either during December of 1979 or January of 1980. Charles Judd, who went from a position at the RNC under chairman Brock to a later position as executive vice president of Jerry Falwell's Moral Majority, also had strong words of praise for Brock's efforts to reach out to evangelicals (Personal interview, 26 June 1989).

64. Dugan's comments are from a speech given as a member of a panel, "The Religious Factor in the 1988 Elections," at the 1988 National Religious Broadcasters Convention.

65. Dugan, interview.

66. On the National Affairs Briefing, see Rosenberg, *Southern Baptists*, 192; and Hadden and Shupe, *Televangelism*, 212–13.

67. Rosenberg, *Southern Baptists*, 192.

68. Moen, *Christian Right and Congress*, 75–76.

69. For the role of the Right in Republican victories see Seymour Martin Lipset and Earl Raab, "The Election and the Evangelicals"; and Robert Zweir, "The New Christian Right and the 1980 Elections," in *New Christian Politics*, eds. David Bromley and Anson Shupe (Macon: Mercer University Press, 1984). On the role of the economy see D. Roderick Kiewiet and Douglas Rivers, "The Economic Basis of Reagan's Appeal," in *New Directions in American Politics*, eds. John Chubb and Paul Peterson (Washington, D.C.: The Brookings Institution, 1985); Polsby and Wildavsky, *Presidential Elections* (see figure 1.2 on the close relationship between economic performance and incumbent fortunes); and Himmelstein, *To the Right*, 173. On NCPAC and Christian Voice see Zweir, "New Christian Right," 173 and 193, and Gillian Peele, *Revival and Reaction: The Right in Contemporary America* (Oxford: Clarendon Press, 1984), 123.

70. See Himmelstein, *To the Right*, 239. Himmelstein looks at the rates of defection of 1976 Carter supporters in the 1980 election. He finds that "born-again" and non–born-again supporters of Carter in the first election abandoned him at the same rate in the second.

71. Moen, *Christian Right and Congress*, 109.

72. See Moen, *Christian Right and Congress*, chap. 7; and Allen Hertzke, *Representing God in Washington: The Role of Religious Lobbies in the American Polity* (Knoxville: The University of Tennessee Press, 1988), chap. 6; see also Moen, *Christian Right and Congress*, chap. 9 on the impact of the Christian Right on the congressional agenda.

73. See Moen, *Christian Right and Congress*, 27–28.

74. Viguerie, *Establishment vs. the People*, 219.

75. A few Christian Right leaders did sign, notably Gary Jarmin and Tim and Beverley LaHaye. See the "Statement of Conservative Leaders," a ten-page document dated 21 January 1982.

76. Hutcheson, *God in the White House*, 193.

77. Pictures with the president would often appear in mailings sent to viewers. To the extent the New Right had a constituency, it was based on direct mail political appeals and to get money it helped to rile people up, to denounce unconscionable evils and betrayals of the true cause. The televangelists had followings that had been drawn in primarily for religious reasons; they had to worry that attacks on a popular president might drive away their flocks.

78. Funding is discussed in Diamond, *Spiritual Warfare*, 66; and organization information came from Gary Jarmin, ACTV national field director, personal interview, 22 March 1989. For registration numbers see Wald, *Religion and Politics*, 194–95.

79. See Himmelstein, *To the Right*, 122. Lopatto's data—the source for most of my previous figures on the evangelical share of the vote—ends in 1980. This figure is based on somewhat different methodology and may not be precisely comparable, but it should be noted that the same poll found Reagan's white evangelical support at only 63 percent in 1980.

80. Lyman Kellstedt, "Evangelicals and Political Realignment," in *Contemporary Evangelical Political Involvement*, ed. Corwin Smidt (Lanham, Md.: University Press of America, 1989).

81. Himmelstein, *To the Right*, 124.

82. See Carmines and Stimson, *Issue Evolution*, for an excellent discussion of "issue evolution" as it applies to the issue of race. See their chapter 7 for a discussion of the time lag between the assumption of opposing positions by party elites and subsequent realignment by the general public.

83. Himmelstein, *To the Right*, 123.

84. See Himmelstein, *To the Right*; and J. Guth, J. Green, L. Kellstedt, and C. Smidt, "God's Own Party: Evangelicals and Republicans in the 1992 Election," 172–76.

85. Corwin Smidt and Paul Kellstedt, "Evangelicals in the Post-Reagan Era" (paper presented at the Citadel Symposium on Southern Politics, The Citadel, 8–9 March 1990), 26.

86. Tim LaHaye, interview by author, 28 March 1989.

87. James A. Reichley, "Post-Reagan Politics," *The Brookings Review*, winter 1987, 22.

88. LaHaye, interview.

Chapter 5

1. See Matthew Moen, *The Transformation of the Christian Right* (Tuscaloosa: The University of Alabama Press, 1992), for an extended discussion of this transformation.

2. From Pat Robertson, *The Plan*, 21.

3. See T. R. Reid, "Robertson Says God Guides White House Bid: 'I Am Going to Be the Next President,'" *Washington Post*, 15 February 1988.

4. Thomas B. Edsall, "TV Preacher Eyes GOP Nomination," *Washington Post*, 19 August 1985.

5. Particularly important in this regard was the liberal lobbying group People for the American Way.

6. See *Pat Robertson: Who Is This Man?*, prod. Constance Snapp, Eagle Media Group, and Americans for Robertson, 1988, videocassette.

7. Snapp and Americans for Robertson, *Who Is This Man?*.

8. Snapp and Americans for Robertson, *Who Is This Man?*.

9. From my experience watching the Robertson campaign and reading its literature, I would argue that the video is quite representative. Its themes are quite similar to the widely distributed audiocassette "What I Will Do As President."

10. Later in the video, Dean Jones compares Robertson's religious convictions to those of James Madison, George Washington, and other Founding Fathers. Jones then declares: "I cringe at the thought of the day when the seats of authority in this land are filled by people without those convictions, without spiritual vision. It will be the death knell of this nation" (Snapp and Americans for Robertson, *Who Is This Man?*).

11. A critical issue in mobilizing activists for Robertson was abortion. In the minds of these activists, the issue of abortion was closely linked to these more general problems of morals and faith. Abortion comes up in the video as part of a montage of pictured social ills that follow in the wake of the nation's turn away from faith but it is not as prominent in the video as it was in the minds

of Robertson activists. On the centrality of the abortion issue for Robertson activists, see John McGlennon, "Religious Activists in the Republican Party," and Corwin Smidt and James Penning, "A House Divided."

12. R. Marc Nuttle, interview with author 21 June 1989. Press accounts based on interviews with Nuttle during the course of the campaign accord quite closely with my interview, conducted a year after its end. (See, for example, Wayne King, "Robertson Bid Relying on Caucuses and Fervor," *New York Times*, 15 March 1987, and Paul Taylor, "Robertson Campaign Persists Amid Setbacks," *Washington Post*, 31 March 1987. While Nuttle listed these three aspects of the Robertson strategy in my interview with him, the descriptions of each aspect provided here draw from a number of sources and are not necessarily derived from that interview. Hertzke, *Echoes of Discontent*, also provides a good account of the Nuttle-Robertson strategy.

13. See, for example, David Maraniss, "Democrats Switching to Fight for Robertson," *Washington Post*, 12 February 1987.

14. Stewart M. Hoover, *Mass Media Religion: The Social Sources of the Electronic Church* (Newbury Park: Sage Publications, 1988), chap. 4.

15. See Hadden and Shupe, *Televangelism*, 275.

16. For example, Robertson was very active in the Christian Right's effort to defeat the 1988 "Grove City" bill. Designed to reverse Supreme Court rulings that had narrowed the antidiscrimination protection provided under Title IX of the 1972 Education Act Amendments, the Grove City bill was seen by the Christian Right as a threat to the freedom of action of religious schools. Despite the Christian Right's opposition, Congress passed the bill, overriding a veto by then president Reagan.

17. Robertson's presidential campaign helped inspire a number of biographies. John B. Donovan, *Pat Robertson: The Authorized Biography*, faithfully chronicles Robertson's career. Much more insightful is David Harrell, *Pat Robertson: A Personal, Political, and Religious Portrait*. Harrell does an excellent job of situating Robertson within the religious and political currents of the day. Hubert Morken, *Pat Robertson: Where He Stands* (Old Tappan: Fleming H. Revell Company, 1988), downplays biography to provide a generally sympathetic explication of Robertson's beliefs. For a much more critical view of Robertson that focuses on his role at CBN, see Gerard Thomas Straub, *Salvation For Sale: An Insider's View of Pat Robertson's Ministry* (Buffalo: Prometheus Books, 1988). For Robertson's own account of his early years, see Pat Robertson, *Shout It from the Housetops* (Plainfield, N.J.: Logos International, 1972). (In the 1988 campaign a controversy arose over this book when it was discovered that the new edition deleted certain potentially embarrassing passages. So be forewarned if you find a more recent version.) Hertzke, *Echoes of Discontent*, provides valuable biographical material on Robertson and interesting comparisons with the campaign of Jesse Jackson.

18. "Nightline," 8 October 1987. Quoted from Morken, *Where He Stands*, 237.

19. Robertson's position can be seen in a 1985 edition of *Charisma* magazine; its readers voted him the most influential figure in the charismatic movement. See Harrell, *Pat Robertson*, 107, on this poll and chaps. 6 and 11–15 for an excellent discussion of Robertson's religious history.

20. Pat Robertson, *Beyond Reason: How Miracles Can Change Your Life* (New York: Bantam Books, 1984).

21. Pat Robertson (with Bob Slosser), *The Secret Kingdom* (New York: Bantam Books, 1982). See also Matthew 3:2.

22. This diversity is partly denominational: charismatics are to be found in a wide array of denominations, from the Southern Baptists to mainline Protestantism and the Catholic Church. The charismatic movement has also been able to appeal to an ethnically diverse constituency, particularly in its outreach to Hispanics.

23. See Wilcox, *God's Warriors.*

24. See Harrell, *Pat Robertson,* 138–43.

25. One area in which Robertson's views could be controversial involves his move from premillennialism to views closer to postmillennialism and the influence a postmillennialist doctrine known as Christian Reconstructionism at Robertson's Regent University (see Harvey Cox, "The Warring Visions of the Christian Right," *The Atlantic Monthly* 276, no. 5 [1995]: 59–69).

26. In his 1972 autobiography, Robertson claims God told him that a minister should not get involved in electoral politics. When the autobiography was reissued during Robertson's presidential campaign, this passage had mysteriously disappeared from the book (see T. R. Reid, "Robertson Corrects Details of His Life," *Washington Post,* 8 October 1987).

27. As noted in chapter 4, some accounts claim that Robertson privately shifted his allegiance to Gerald Ford just prior to the general election.

28. See Harrell, *Pat Robertson.*

29. Paul Weyrich, interview with author, 15 March 1989.

30. Ed McAteer, phone interview, 13 February 1989.

31. Leading figures on the original Moral Majority board included Charles Stanley, Greg Dixon, and Tim LaHaye (all Baptists), along with conservative Presbyterian James Kennedy. Baptist Jerry Falwell was president (see Diamond, *Spiritual Warfare,* 60). Despite the Moral Majority's repeated claims to represent moral conservatives from a variety of different religious persuasions, its local organizations were almost entirely built upon a foundation of fundamentalist independent Baptist churches (see Hadden and Shupe, *Televangelism,* 174).

32. Shakarian's FGBMFI is one of the central organizations in the charismatic surge of the last few decades. "Full Gospel" refers to teachings that include the gifts of the Holy Spirit (see Poloma, *The Charismatic Movement*).

33. See Pat Robertson, *America's Dates with Destiny* (Nashville: Thomas Nelson Publishers, 1986), 282.

34. McAteer says that one of his motivations for starting the Roundtable was that the Moral Majority (which he had helped found) was becoming too narrowly fundamentalist in its religious base (McAteer, personal interview).

35. Weyrich, personal interview. Weyrich said that Robertson had never given him a clear explanation as to why he withdrew, other than to state that he had unspecified "misgivings."

36. McAteer, personal interview. McAteer reminded Robertson of this letter when Robertson announced his presidential bid.

37. See Harrell, *Pat Robertson*, 187.

38. In a breakdown of the content of the programs of ten leading televangelists, Robert Abelman finds that in both 1983 and 1986, Pat Robertson's show had far and away the highest proportion of political messages. Not surprisingly, in 1986, as Robertson began to prepare for his presidential bid, political content was substantially higher than in 1983 (see Robert Abelman, "Who's Watching, For What Reasons?" in *Religious Television: Controversies and Conclusions*, ed. R. Abelman and S. Hoover [Norwood: Ablex Publishing Corporation, 1990], 109–29).

39. Robertson served as head of the Council in 1985 and 1986 (see Harrell, *Pat Robertson*, 188).

40. See Dudley Clendinen, "Robertson's Evangelist Bandwagon," *San Francisco Chronicle*, 2 October 1986; and Beth Spring, "One Step Closer to a Bid for the Oval Office," *Christianity Today* 30, no. 15 (1986): 39–45.

41. D'Souza explains: "Many of Jerry Falwell's people are tired of being treated as outcasts; they want to be accepted by the rest of the country, and if a moderated political approach to personalities can help achieve that, some are willing to live with it" (Dinesh D'Souza, "Jerry Falwell Is Reaching Millions and Drawing Fire," *Conservative Digest* [December 1986], 5–12). For a fascinating account of Falwell's attempts to moderate his stance and achieve respectability see Frances Fitzgerald, *Cities on a Hill*; see also Hadden and Shupe, *Televangelism*, 179.

Falwell claims that he urged Ronald Reagan *not* to choose Bush as his running mate in 1980 but that his impression of Bush had improved in the intervening years (see Jerry Falwell, "Who Should Succeed Reagan? Some Preliminary Thoughts," *Policy Review* 37 [summer 1986]: 32–41); see Michael Kramer, "Are You Running With Me, Jesus?," *The San Francisco Chronicle*, 7 September 1986, for the Falwell comment).

42. The support of the LaHayes did not turn out to be as helpful as Kemp had hoped. Tim LaHaye was forced to resign his position as a "national co-chairman" of the Kemp campaign shortly after assuming it when newspapers publicized his past statements critical of Catholics and Jews (see Maralee Schwartz and Charles R. Babcock, "Kemp Supporter Has Controversial Religious Views," *Washington Post*, 5 December 1987). Beverly LaHaye broke with the campaign at a later point when an overzealous Kemp aide put out a statement under her name that implied criticism of Robertson. The statement was sent out to the Concerned Women for America mailing list—LaHaye claims the use of her list was unauthorized—and led to a strong reaction from CWA members who backed Robertson. Protesting her treatment by campaign staffers, Beverly LaHaye resigned her position as an honorary Kemp cochair in an attempt to stem the damage the controversy was doing to CWA (Beverly LaHaye, personal interview, 23 March 1989).

43. CWA arrived at this figure by counting as a member anyone who had ever contributed, regardless of their current membership status (see Diamond, *Spiritual Warfare*, chap. 3).

44. Note that the LaHayes' personal stance did not necessarily mirror the position of the members of the organizations they led. Beverly LaHaye says a poll of CWA members found 55 percent supporting Robertson to only 25 percent for Kemp and 10 percent for Bush (personal interview).

45. Beverly LaHaye, personal interview, 23 March 1989.

46. In my 22 March 1989 interview with him, Jarmin stressed that these were personal endorsements and did not represent a position taken by Christian Voice as an organization. Christian Voice, Jarmin, and Grant are controversial within the Christian Right due to their association with the Reverend Sun Myung Moon and thus the backing of Grant and Jarmin may have been something of a mixed blessing within evangelical circles.

47. Robert Billings, personal interview, 21 January 1989. This is only a partial list of the many positions Billings has held. Not well known to the general public, Billings was a central figure in the development of the Christian Right. His other positions included executive director of the National Christian Action Coalition, chairman of the Christian Schools Political Action Committee, vice chairman of the Committee for the Survival of a Free Congress, and executive director of Intercessors for America.

48. Personal interviews, Jarmin, McAteer, and Billings stressed the attractiveness of rival candidates and remarked that, below the top leadership level, it was still difficult to get fundamentalists to work with charismatics.

49. The convention was held in late January/early February 1988, just prior to the Iowa caucuses. My impressions concerning levels of support are admittedly unscientific, based as they are upon several days of mingling, listening to levels of applause, and doing a running count of buttons worn by the four thousand attendees. Kemp had far less open support than Robertson; I saw and talked to extremely few supporters of Bush or Dole.

50. Beverly LaHaye, personal interview.

51. See, for example, John Mashek, "Dole Campaign Wooing Robertson Supporters," *Atlanta Journal Constitution*, 27 October 1987.

52. Quote is from Doug Wead, "The Republican Party and the Evangelicals (Twice Abridged Verision)," Internal Bush Campaign Document, 31 July 1988, 23.

53. Wead, "Republican Party."

54. Wead, "Republican Party."

55. The material in this paragraph comes from Wead, "Republican Party."

56. See Wead, "Republican Party," 29. The campaign's thinking about Kemp shifted as well. By late 1987, Kemp was seen as drawing votes from Dole. Thus, having Robertson damage Kemp, perhaps knocking him quickly from the race, began to look like a less-appealing option.

57. R. Marc Nuttle, personal interview.

58. See Charles Babcock, "Robertson: Blending Charity and Politics," *Washington Post*, 2 November 1987.

59. Hadden and Shupe, *Televangelism*, 254.

60. See Babcock, "Blending Charity."

61. In September of 1986 the Freedom Council's executive director Greg Jackson claimed the group had spent $400,000 in Michigan and was planning to spend $150,000 each in Florida and North Carolina by the end of the year (see Beth Spring, "Pat Robertson in Michigan: Vying for Evangelical Voters," *Christianity Today* 30, no. 12 [1986]: 52–56).

The links between the Freedom Council and the Robertson campaign came out in my interviews. In late 1986, Kerry Moody, Northeast director of the Freedom Council, claims he tried to turn down a request to work for the Robertson campaign, expressing his desire to stay on with the council. Robertson campaign chair Marc Nuttle replied: "That's not a choice you can make. You will work in the campaign!" Several weeks later Moody heard that the Freedom Council had been shut down. He went to work on the Robertson campaign (Kerry Moody, interview by author, 2 February 1989). Robertson himself was president of the Freedom Council until 1985. Jerry Curry, who succeeded him, resigned in April 1986, feeling the council had grown too close to Robertson's presidential effort (see Charles Babcock, "Robertson Accused of Using Tax-Exempt Group for Politics," *Washington Post*, 6 April 1987). Curry was replaced with longtime Robertson associate Bob Slosser, president of CBN University and coauthor of one of Robertson's books. The head of the Michigan Freedom Council, Marlene Elwell, went on to become the Midwestern regional director of Robertson's presidential campaign. The Northeastern director of the Freedom Council went on to become Northeastern regional director of the Robertson campaign.

The Freedom Council was a 501 c/4 organization (this status allows political activity but not the support of particular candidates) and filed for the even more restrictive 501 c/3 status in early 1986 (see Jeff Gerth, "Tax Data of Pat Robertson Groups Are Questioned," *New York Times*, 10 December 1986). For discussion of CBN donation to the Freedom Council, see Babcock, "Blending Charity." For more on the Freedom Council controversy, see Spring, "Pat Robertson in Michigan," and Gerth, "Tax Data." To try to hush the controversy, former employees were offered $100 to sign a confidentiality agreement that banned them from discussing the council's activities (see Jeff Gerth, "Robertson and Confidentiality," *New York Times*, 19 March 1987).

62. See E. J. Dionne, Jr., "Robertson and GOP in Michigan to Send Rival Slates to Convention," *New York Times*, 31 January 1988.

63. The origins of the 1988 selection process are a point of contention among the various sides in Michigan. Many reporters—and representatives of campaigns other than George Bush's—described the system as a ploy of Bush supporters. The idea, supposedly, was that it would be a system dominated by the state party organization, an organization solidly behind George Bush. For example, this is the argument made by Michigan Dole chair Colleen Engler, who claims to have been part of the panel that devised the caucus plan (personal interview, 24 April 1989). State party chair Spencer Abraham disputes this claim. The caucus system, he says, was what was in place prior to the adoption of a primary in 1972. When the primary was repealed in 1983, things simply went back to the old caucus rules. The rules for 1988 were the same ones that applied in 1984 (personal interview, 1 May 1989). Whatever the true origins and motivations of the plan, it is clear that the Robertson leaders I talked to thought the 1988 system was a new one and that they—and Robertson—were unaware of its details until the June 1985 banquet described in the text (personal interviews with Marlene Elwell, 28 April 1989, and James Muffet, 27 April 1989, both with the Freedom Council and then the Robertson campaign). James Muffet's comments are from interview by author, April 1989. For expenditures see Spring, "Pat Robertson in Michigan," 55.

64. From an April 1989 interview with Marlene Elwell, Midwest Freedom Council director and later Midwest director of the Robertson campaign. (The quote refers to Lori Packer, who soon learned a great deal about precinct delegates.)

65. See Hadden and Shupe, *Televangelism*, 250–51.

66. See Richard L. Berke, "Gain for Robertson in Later Michigan Tally," *New York Times*, 15 February 1987.

67. The Dole campaign hoped to gain some benefit simply by staying out of the fray. Michigan Dole chair Colleen Engler declared: "We're just sitting here waiting for everybody to get angry with everybody else . . . and then to come to us" (from David Shribman, "System Devised by Michigan GOP is Gross Old Politics," *Wall Street Journal*, 17 July 1987).

68. Both quotes are from Shribman, "System Devised by Michigan GOP." The first statement is Shribman's.

69. Americans for Robertson, "A New Vision for America" (text of a 17 August 1986 speech by Pat Robertson distributed as part of a press package at the 1988 Republican National Convention), 5.

70. See Hadden and Shupe, *Televangelism*.

71. The total number of signatures is open to some dispute. After the 1988 election, the list of 3 million was sold to the Republican National Committee. T. R. Reid, "'Invisible Army' Won Few Battles," *Washington Post*, 17 December 1988, claims that the list contained only 1.8 million names and that the RNC was dissatisfied with it, eventually obtaining it for a reduced price. Robertson campaign chair Marc Nuttle (interview with the author 21 June 1989) denied that the RNC was dissatisfied. He claims that the list did indeed contain over 3 million names in its original form. By the time the list was sold, some of the names were over two years old, thus it was only natural that some of the names and addresses were no longer valid. However, Nuttle says that even after "cleaning up," the lists contained 2.5 million valid entries. Interestingly, Robertson tells a story that gives some support to Reid's 1.8 million number. He claims, "our final computer print out (which was not completed until the end of 1988) showed the names of 1,800,000 households where there were 3 million people!" Robertson also contends that there were many additional names on a special "miracle list" that was never used. (Robertson, *The Plan*, 106.)

72. On fundraising see Federal Election Commission, "Presidential Primary Spending at $200 Million Mark," press office release, 18 August 1988; Anthony Corrado, "The Changing Environment of Presidential Campaign Finance," in *In Pursuit of the White House*, ed. William Mayer (Chatham: Chatham House Publishers, 1996), 220–53; and Ralph Z. Hallow, "Robertson Laying the Groundwork," *Insight*, 23 February 1987, 24.

73. Robertson himself makes a similar claim in his book *The Plan*. "Unfortunately, I didn't have the time or the money to process more than a small portion of the huge volume of people, get them organized by precinct, and contact them on a state by state basis" (Robertson, *The Plan*, 106).

74. "A" is the campaign's Northeast regional director Kerry Moody. "B" is Carolyn Sundseth, outreach director of the Robertson campaign. From a joint interview with the author, 2 February 1989.

75. See Hallow, "Robertson Laying the Groundwork."

76. See Robertson, *The Plan*, 105. John Green finds that Robertson had to spend far more than Bush to elicit his many small contributions: "The Robertson campaign . . . apparently spent nearly twice per dollar raised on fundraising expenses as the Bush campaign." See John Green, "A Look at the 'Invisible Army': Pat Robertson's Campaign Contributors" (paper presented at the annual meeting of the American Association for the Advancement of Science, San Francisco, January 1989), 14.

77. See Myra MacPherson, "Pat Robertson and the Beauty Contest," *Washington Post*, 16 November 1987.

78. James Muffet, interview.

79. See Bob Secter, "Pat Robertson Shuns Taint of TV Ministers," *Los Angeles Times*, 6 July 1987.

80. Although Operation Blessing was a charitable relief organization, it also had a very controversial political side to it. One of the organization's major projects was providing money and supplies to the contra rebels in Nicaragua. See Vicki Kemper, "In the Name of Relief," *Sojourners* 14, no. 9 (1985): 12–20. Robertson's own campaign video features a visit to a Contra camp as a featured part (Snapp and Americans for Robertson, *Who Is This Man?*).

81. This very authoritarian form of religious organization required the believer to place a wide range of personal decisions under the control of a spiritual "shepherd." Robertson led the attack on this practice in the 1970s, but in the 1980s, leaders of the shepherding movement began to appear on his show again. See Diamond, *Spiritual Warfare*, chapter 4, for a discussion of the practice of shepherding.

82. Robertson's version of "prosperity theology" is relatively restrained and dignified compared to some rival televangelists. For example, Robert Tilton calls his show "Success in Life" and laces it with numerous, none too subtle, appeals to viewer greed.

83. Robertson and other advocates of prosperity theology often rely on Luke 6:38 "Give, and it will be given unto you." Giving to religious causes ends up being quite profitable to the donor. (See, for example, pages 33–34 of Robertson's *Beyond Reason*. The passage from Luke is invoked in the story of Clyde Bass of Tulsa. Despite his "limited income," Clyde makes a "substantial pledge" to a religious organization. Clyde's glaucoma disappears almost immediately and he is able to see again!)

84. Jerry Falwell has been a particularly vociferous critic of prosperity theology.

85. On access to God, see Donovan, *Pat Robertson*, 46. Robertson not only claimed he was being told to buy a television station; God gave him the exact price to offer for it. See Robertson and Slosser, *The Secret Kingdom*, 193, on God's stock market advice. See also Reid, "Robertson Says God Guides White House Bid."

Much of the *The Plan* by Robertson is structured around the question, if God told Robertson to run, why did he lose? In answering this question Robertson provides his advice as to how the reader can understand God's plan for his/her life. The quote early in this chapter, in which Robertson hears the voice of God telling him to run, is taken from *The Plan*.

86. On the air Robertson declared: "Storm, we command you to turn north and then go east. Your winds shall die down and go harmlessly into the ocean in the name of Jesus." (Quoted from Dinesh D'Souza, "Pat Robertson's World: In the Beginning There Was Hurricane Gloria," *American Spectator*, November 1986, 16–19. The hurricane did in fact turn north, sparing Virginia Beach and CBN. Unfortunately, it struck further up the Atlantic coast, costing a number of lives. This 1985 storm, Hurricane Gloria, was not the first that Robertson claimed to have diverted (see Robertson, *The Plan*, 63).

87. See Grace Halsell, Prophecy and Politics, 4.

88. See Morken, *Where He Stands*, chap. 12: "Prophecy: Robertson Defends It."

89. These prophecies are discussed in Robertson and Slosser, *The Secret Kingdom*, chap. 15, "The Coming King." On the mark of the beast, see also Revelation 13:16, 17.

90. If Robertson had been elected, this question might not have remained theoretical. The Iraqi invasion of Kuwait and the subsequent Persian Gulf war led to an explosion of prophetic speculation in some segments of the evangelical community.

91. See Hadden and Shupe, *Televangelism*, 231–32.

92. The Freedom Council letter is discussed in Hertzke, *Echoes of Discontent*, 266. On Bennett's reaction see Jim Castelli, "Pat Robertson: Extremist," booklet put out by People for the American Way Action Fund, 2.

93. Oral Roberts and the Reverend Robert Schuller (host of the "Hour of Power") leaped in to defend Bakker and denounce Swaggart. Evangelist John Ankerberg backed Swaggart.

94. Robertson did his best to downplay the personal connection he had once had with the Bakkers. They had not supported his candidacy but their history *was* closely linked to his. Jim and Tammy had gotten their start with Robertson and CBN. The fundraising techniques they pioneered at CBN played a key role in helping the fledgling network expand in the 1960s. In his 1972 autobiography, Robertson lavished praise on the two but, after the scandal, he insisted that he had had questions about their conduct even then. In the early 1970s the Bakkers left Robertson's network to found PTL (Art Harris and Michael Isikoff, "Robertson's Bakker Connection," *Washington Post*, 6 February 1988). In the televangelist scandal's first three months, it was the subject of no less than eleven editions of the *Nightline* news program, a figure that most world crises would be hard pressed to match. And these programs did wonders for the show's ratings (Hadden and Shupe, *Televangelism*, 6).

Billy Graham and Jerry Falwell were the only leading figures to retain their initial levels of support through the scandal. Graham remained popular and above the fray. Falwell's ratings were similarly low before and after the scandal (see n. 96, below). Gallup Poll results are in Schneider (1987).

On the financial difficulties of TV ministries in the wake of the scandals, see Randy Frame, "Surviving the Slump," *Christianity Today* 33, no. 2 (1989): 32–34.

95. See Wayne King, "Presidential Polls Prompt 'Repackaging' of Robertson," *New York Times*, 23 June 1987.

96. See William Schneider, "The Republicans in '88," *The Atlantic* 259, no. 6 (July 1987).

97. In the November poll, just months before the voting was to start, 41 percent of registered Republicans knew too little about Kemp to form an impression; 67 percent knew too little about du Pont.

98. The data in this and the preceding paragraph are from Martin Plissner, "Presidential Politics—Ten Weeks to the Iowa Caucuses," *CBS News/New York Times Poll*, for release 30 November 1987; Martin Plissner, "Campaign '88—A Year to Go," *CBS News/New York Times Poll*, for release 27 October 1987; and Louis Harris, "Negative Vote Pivotal in Super Tuesday Balloting," *The Harris Poll*, for release 3 March 1988.

99. See Lloyd Grove, "Robertson, Taking Aim at the Critics," *Washington Post*, 22 February 1988.

100. Robertson, *The Plan*, 145.

101. For ill-advised statements, see Castelli, "Pat Robertson: Extremist"; Michael Kramer, "Are You Running with Me Jesus?"; and Wallace Turner, "Robertson Upsets GOP Regulars with Attacks on Key Republicans," *New York Times*, 19 October 1987. North's remark is in Mark Z. Barabak, "Robertson Sticks to His Story about Discussion with North," *San Francisco Chronicle*, 15 July 1987. It is not clear why North would have revealed to Robertson the nature of his highly secret mission. In his resumé, Robertson claimed to have done "graduate study" at the University of London—in fact he took one introductory summer art course. He claimed to be on the board of directors of a Virginia Bank—in fact he was a member of a local advisory board with no directoral authority (see T.R. Reid, "Robertson Corrects Details of His Life").

102. See Hertzke, *Echoes of Discontent*, 148. I do not know which poll is the source of Nuttle's figures.

103. Hertzke, *Echoes of Discontent*, 149.

104. See Shribman, "System Devised by Michigan GOP."

105. See E. J. Dionne, Jr., "Robertson and GOP in Michigan to Send Rival Slates to Convention."

106. An additional factor cited on behalf of the defectors concerned the state committee's decision to exclude the 1,200 GOP nominees. Many felt that this decision by the Robertson-Kemp alliance violated a promise made earlier between the various factions in Michigan (Thomas B. Edsall, "Robertson Says Kemp Sold Out in Michigan," *Washington Post*, 30 January 1988). My interviews with Michigan activists revealed considerable disagreement as to exactly what had been promised by whom.

107. See Edsall, "Robertson Says Kemp." The implications of Robertson's boast were emphasized by one of the leading defectors, Saul Annuzis, in an interview with author 27 April 1989.

108. See Thomas B. Edsall, "Bush Wins Plurality in Michigan," *Washington Post*, 31 January 1988.

109. See Shribman, "System Devised by Michigan GOP."

110. *Gallup Poll*, 6 January 1988. See also Bill Peterson, "Robertson Takes His 'Invisible Army' on Tour," *Washington Post*, 19 January 1988.

111. See "1988 Republican Primary Results and 1988 First Round Caucus Results," *Congressional Quarterly* 46, no. 3 (1988): 2254–255.

112. Much to the consternation of the Dole campaign, less attention was paid to their candidate, the actual victor.

113. R. Marc Nuttle, interview.

114. See Robertson, *The Plan*, 110-11.

115. Early reporting showed Bush the winner. Robertson supporters voted "uncommitted" in the initial round of the caucuses to hide their strength but they eventually won the majority of the state's convention delegates.

116. Robertson scored less well in the Kansas caucus (Dole won 98 percent of the vote), the Wyoming caucus (Robertson was third with 9 percent), and the Vermont primary (third place with 5 percent of the vote). All figures in this and the preceeding paragraph are from "Republican Primary Results and 1988 First Round Caucus Results."

117. Robertson, *The Plan*, 142.

118. Interview by author with member of Robertson's campaign staff.

119. See "Republican Primary Results."

120. Figures in this and preceeding paragraph are from "Republican Primary Results and 1988 First Round Caucus Results."

121. See "Republican Primary Results and 1988 First Round Caucus Results."

122. Both comments made on the "700 Club," 17 May 1988.

123. The fifteen-million member SBC contains a variety of religious currents within it and does not fit neatly in either the fundamentalist or neoevangelical category.

124. See Wilcox, *God's Warriors*, 155, for the figures in this paragraph.

125. See Corwin Smidt and James Penning, "A House Divided." See also John Green and James Guth, "Robertson's Republicans."

126. Neil Bush later apologized claiming that the term "cockroach" was meant as a compliment to the Robertsonites' work ethic. Bush said he should have used the words "worker bees" (*Baltimore Sun*, 25 November 1987—quoted from *Campaign Hotline*—American Political Network, Inc., 25 November 1987).

Robertson declared at one point: "There's been some very raw stuff going on, I thought we were past that after Watergate. I've learned that George Bush was chairman of the party during 1973 and 1974, and perhaps they learned something from that era that they carried over into 1988. . . . There's no question we're dealing with every sort of underhanded trick you can conceive of to deny me the nomination" (Maralee Schwartz and Charles R. Babcock, "Anti-Christian Bashing," *Washington Post*, 2 February 1988).

127. After Super Tuesday, Bush's victory was a foregone conclusion but the identity of the delegates who would nominate him was still disputed in many places. Some states that had had primaries still had caucuses to pick the actual delegates. Some of the caucus states had only gone through their first round and still had not had the state convention that would choose national delegates.

128. On hiring see Allen Hertzke, "Pat Robertson's Crusade and the GOP: a Strategic Analysis" (paper presented at the annual meeting of the Midwestern Political Science Association, Chicago, Ill., April 1989), 13. Hertzke does not identify *which* state director he is quoting.

Michigan, despite the intensity of the battle that waged there, was marked by widespread incorporation of Robertson leaders into the Bush effort (Michigan Robertson chair Lori Packer, interview with author, 20 April 1989). My interviews in Washington State revealed much less cooperation.

129. Thus the American Conservative Union helped start a group called the "Committee to Save the Reagan Platform." The group "closely monitored and aggressively lobbied to ensure that the 1988 Republican Platform remained consistent with the conservative platforms of 1980 and 1984" (press release by the committee, 9 August 1988).

130. Republican Party, *Republican Platform* (proposed by the Committee on Resolutions to the Republican National Convention, 15 August 1988), 32.

131. See Peter Callaghan, "Robertson Touts Bush-Dole Ticket For Republicans," *Tacoma News Tribune*, 2 July 1988. Kemp information is from Bruce Hawkins, director of Robertson's Washington State campaign, interview by author, 1 January 1989. While Robertson himself opposed Kemp, I found that many of Robertson's supporters were more favorably inclined toward the congressman.

132. This was also a variation on Mario Cuomo's "Tale of Two Cities" speech to the 1984 Democratic convention. Needless to say, the Robertson and Cuomo portrayals of the Democratic and Republican "cities" were strikingly different.

133. See Gary Wills, "The Power Populist," *Time*, 21 November 1989.

134. See James A. Barnes, "Blessing Bush," *National Journal*, 9 April 1988, 940.

135. See Lyman A. Kellstedt and John C. Green, "Knowing God's Many People: Denominational Preference and Political Behavior," in *Rediscovering the Religious Factor in American Politics*, eds. David Leege and Lyman A. Kellstedt (Armonk, N.Y.: M. E. Sharpe, 1993), 64; and *CBS News/New York Times Poll*, 10 November 1988.

136. The most prominent of these claims was made in a work published just prior to the opening of the caucuses and primaries (Hadden and Shupe, *Televangelism*). See Bruce, *Pray TV*, for an extended critique of Hadden and Shupe's analysis.

137. See Michael D'Antonio, *Fall from Grace*, 239.

Chapter 6

1. Pat Robertson, *The Plan*, 177.

2. See Mary G. Brennan, *Turning Right in the Sixties: The Conservative Capture of the GOP* (Chapel Hill: The University of North Carolina Press, 1995); and William Rusher, *The Rise of the Right*, chap. 6.

3. See Steve Bruce, *The Rise and Fall of the New Christian Right*; and Michael D'Antonio, *Fall from Grace: The Failed Crusade of the Christian Right*.

4. See Christian Coalition, *Contract with the American Family* (Nashville: Moorings, 1995), appendix "About the Christian Coalition."

5. See John Persinos, "Has the Christian Right Taken Over the Republican Party?"

6. I conducted over forty-five interviews, ranging in length from forty-five minutes to four hours, in Virginia, Michigan, and Washington State.

7. On differences between Robertson activists and Republican regulars in Virginia, Michigan, and among campaign contributors, see John McGlennon, "Religious Activists in the Republican Party," Corwin Smidt and James Penning, "A House Divided," and John Green and James Guth, "Robertson's Republicans."

8. For the most part, the state-level interview subjects quoted in this chapter will be kept anonymous to protect them from any possible embarrassment. Some well-known activists are quoted by name where specific knowledge of the source would make a difference to the reader's interpretation of remarks.

9. See John McGlennon, "Religious Activists in the Republican Party." See also Jo Freeman, "The Political Culture."

10. Quoted in Terry McDermott and Ross Anderson, "Right-Wing Revolts Aren't New to GOP," *Seattle Post-Intelligencer*, 13 March 1988.

11. Bruce Hawkins interview with author, 14 August 1992. See also Ralph Reed, *Politically Incorrect* (Dallas: Word Publishing, 1994), 3.

12. The first figure of coalition growth is from "Robertson Group Vows to Fight for Sectarian Sex Ed," *Church and State* 43, no. 6 (June 1990): 14; the second is from Frederick Clarkson, "The Christian Coalition: On the Road to Victory," *Church and State* 44, no. 1 (January 1992): 4–7; and the third is from a 14 August 1992 interview with Bruce Hawkins. See membership claims in Christian Coalition, *Contract with the American Family*, appendix. Circulation figures are from Skipp Porteous, *The Freedom Writer* (March 1995), 4.

13. See Matthew Moen, *The Transformation of the Christian Right* on the move from top down to grassroots strategies. See also William Fisher, Ralph Reed, and Richard Weinhold, *Christian Coalition Leadership Manual* (Virginia Beach: Christian Coalition, 1990), esp. section 3.

14. Christian Coalition, "The Road to Victory: Conference and Strategy Briefing" (Virginia Beach: Christian Coalition, 1991).

15. For meeting attendance, see Frederick Clarkson, "Christian Coalition: On the Road to Victory," 4. Conference details are from Joseph L. Coon, "Detour on the Road to Victory," *Church and State* 46 (October 1993); and "Road to Victory '93, The Tide is Turning/Agenda," Christian Coalition press release, 2 September 1993. On the grant see Donna Minkowitz, "Outlawing Gays," *The Nation* 255, no. 12 (19 October 1992): 420–21.

16. Allen D. Hertzke and Robert Booth Fowler, *Religion and Politics in America: Faith, Culture, and Strategic Choices* (Boulder: Westview Press, 1995), 146.

17. See *The Activist's Handbook* (Greater Barrington: Institute for First Amendment Studies, 1993); and Moen, *The Transformation*.

18. The leader was Richard Land, director of the Southern Baptist Convention's Christian Life Commission. See "Evangelicals Offer Uneasy Support to Bush," *Christianity Today* 36, no. 4 (6 April 1992).

19. Phyllis Schlafly, phone interview with author, 29 October 1992.

20. See "Bush Solidifies Support with Pro-Lifers," *Human Events* 52, no. 18, 3.

21. See Family Research Council, "Who Is Gary Bauer?," *Family Research Council—World Wide Web Home Page*. On opposition to the NEA, see Joe Conason, "The Religious Right's Quiet Revival," *The Nation* 254 (27 April 1992), 554. Also from personal interview with Leigh Ann Metzger, 21 August 1994. In the Bush White House's public liaison office, Metzger was in charge of outreach to evangelicals.

22. See Pat Robertson, *The New World Order*, 37.

23. Interview with author, 21 August 1994.

24. The information in the paragraph is based on a 22 July 1994 personal interview with Robert Dugan. On Bush, the Christian Right, and the gay rights issue, see also Thomas B. Edsall, "Gay Rights and the Religious Right," *Washington Post*, 10 August 1992; Ann Devroy, "Bush Faults Special Laws for Gays," *Washington Post*, 22 April 1992; and Kim A. Lawton, "A Republican God?," *Christianity Today* 36 (5 October 1992).

25. See "Why Buchanan Is Running," *Human Events* 51 (7 December 1991): 3. Note that attendance at the meeting did not necessarily imply an endorsement of Buchanan.

26. The 1988 Washington chair, Bruce Hawkins, claims that many ex-Robertson activists were recruited to the Buchanan campaign but that, given a short lead time, Buchanan was unable to build the sort of grassroots organization Robertson had created in 1988. Bruce Hawkins, interview with author, 14 August 1992.

27. Robertson support for Bush is in Ronald Smothers, "Bush Less Than Loved among the Christian Right," *New York Times*, 10 March 1992. Also from Robert Dugan, interview with author, 22 August 1992.

28. See Ronald Smothers, "Bush Less Than Loved among Religious Right."

29. Bruce Hawkins suggested that a desire to build strength within the party and to influence the platform lay behind Pat Robertson's decision to endorse Bush (interview with the author, 14 August 1992).

30. See Donna Minkowitz, "Outlawing Gays."

31. Interview with author, 22 August 1994.

32. The figures for convention delegates and platform committee members are from a 14 August 1992 personal interview with Bruce Hawkins, Christian Coalition's press secretary at the convention. These numbers are difficult to confirm, but I have not heard them challenged. During platform committee hearings, many members were using the rhetoric of the Christian Right. The members from several states were persons I was familiar with from my previous research on the Christian Right.

33. RNC for Life press release, 11 August 1992.

34. Phone interview with Phyllis Schlafly, 29 October 1992. Note that the forty members of the platform committee that her group was on friendly terms with probably included many of the platform committee members claimed by Christian Coalition.

35. Crisp, a former GOP cochair, is from the party's moderate wing. Stone,

with a background in direct mail fundraising, was identified, at least prior to her activism on the abortion issue, with the Right, having raised funds for Jesse Helms and the contras (Martha Sherrill, "The GOP's Abortion Rights Upstart," *Washington Post*, 4 April 1992).

36. The Republican platform committee was officially titled the "Committee on Resolutions," but I will use its informal, more descriptive, title in the pages that follow.

37. Ann Stone, chairwoman of Republicans for Choice, claims that the pro-choice forces were initially looking to propose somewhere between nine and twelve different amendments (interview with the author, 28 October 1992).

38. Phyllis Schlafly phone interview with author, 29 October 1992. I attended the committee hearings and it was clear that there was little support for any consideration of pro-choice measures.

39. Ann Stone, interview.

40. Bruce Hawkins, interview.

41. Ann Stone and Phyllis Schlafly, both of whom had good opportunities to observe the Bush campaign in action, paint very different pictures of its activity. Stone depicts a Bush team active in picking the platform committee, one that orchestrated the votes of many of the platform committee members. During the hearings, Stone says, many of the committee members she knew were pro-choice followed the lead of Bush point man Bo Calloway and voted against their private beliefs. Schlafly, reflecting on her years of involvement with the party, claims that the national party had less control over the platform in 1992 than in any convention she had seen. (Ann Stone and Phyllis Schlafly, phone interview with author.)

42. Arm twisting is one point on which Ann Stone and Phyllis Schlafly did agree—phone interviews.

A *USA Today* poll found that, by a 48 percent to 32 percent margin, convention delegates opposed attempts to remove a call for a constitutional ban on abortion from the platform (Mimi Hall, "Abortion Not a Dead Issue," *USA Today*, 13 August 1992).

43. Unless one counts the conservative tone of the 1988 platform's language on AIDS.

44. The harsh Christian Right criticism the Bush administration had received on this issue may have discouraged Bush administration attempts to tone down platform language dealing with the rights of gays and lesbians.

Mawyer, in phone interview with author 26 October 1992, claimed that the Christian Action Network was the originator of the adoption language and of the clause calling for criminal sanctions against those who knowingly spread the AIDS virus. In phone interview with author, Mawyer voiced surprise at passage of antigay amendments.

45. Page 76 of the platform that calls for changes in the RICO laws to require "proof of all elements by clear and convincing proof" in civil cases. This language was added during the platform hearings; the issue was brought up by an anti-abortion activist (Michael Undseth of Washington State) who pressed for stronger language linking opposition to RICO laws to an explicit defense of civil disobedience.

The school prayer plank began "Mindful of our country's Judeo-Christian tradition and rich religious pluralism" (Republican Party, *1992 Republican Party Platform*, 21). Bruce Hawkins' comment is from his interview. The God and Country rally took place on 17 August 1992.

46. Material in this paragraph is based on my attendance at the events and convention sessions in question.

47. Press release, "Remarks by Reverend Pat Robertson."

48. Press release, "Prepared Text of the Acceptance Address by the Vice President." See also press release, "Remarks by Marilyn Quayle Given before the Republican National Convention on August 19, 1992."

49. See William Safire, "God Bless Us," *New York Times*, 27 August 1992. Bush's comments come from an address to the National Affairs Briefing organized by Religious Roundtable leader Ed McAteer.

50. Ann Stone, interview.

51. A weak economy also hindered efforts to divert attention from social issues. The 1988 platform begins with a section entitled "Jobs, Growth, and Opportunity for All." In 1992 such an opening would have been hard to sell; the platform opens instead with a section entitled "Uniting Our Family."

52. The Clinton campaign was clearly expecting a "family values" attack and used the Democratic convention to define "family" issues on their own terms, stressing economic security over the moral themes favored by the Christian Right.

53. Frederick Clarkson, "The Christian Coalition: On the Road to Victory."

54. Bush-Quayle '92 General Election Committee, "Evangelical Leaders and Laymen Meet with President Bush, Launch Evangelical Coalition for Bush-Quayle," press release, Saturday, 22 August 1992. See also Guth, Green, Kellstedt, and Smidt, "God's Own Party"; and Ralph Reed, *Politically Incorrect*, 199. Reed puts the number of churches used for literature distribution at sixty thousand. As an example of the voter guide design, 1994 Christian Coalition guides listed whether or not candidates supported *special* rights for homosexuals or favored banning *legal* firearms (Allen Hertzke and Robert Booth Fowler, *Religion and Politics in America*, 145). On the role of other Christian Right groups see Guth, Green, Kellstedt, and Smidt, "God's Own Party."

55. On decline in support, see Guth, Green, Kellstedt, and Smidt, "God's Own Party," 173–74. See also John C. Green, James L. Guth, Lyman A. Kellstedt, and Corwin E. Smidt, "Murphy Brown Revisited: The Social Issues in the 1992 Election," in *Disciples and Democracy: Religious Conservatives and the Future of American Politics*, ed. Michael Cromartie (published jointly Washington, D.C.: Ethics and Public Policy Center/Grand Rapids: William B. Eerdmans Publishing Company, 1995); and Guth, Green, Kellstedt, and Smidt, "God's Own Party." Another analysis finds that beliefs concerning "family values" played a significantly larger role in the 1992 election than in previous elections, but is unable to determine whether they helped or hurt Bush (Phillip E. Hammond, Mark A. Shibley, and Peter M. Solow, "Religion and Family Values in Presidential Voting," in *The Rapture of Politics*, eds. Steve Bruce, Peter Kivisto, and William H. Swatos, Jr. [New Brunswick: Transaction Publishers, 1995]). Clyde Wilcox questions the claims of the "Murphy Brown" article, claiming that, properly

analyzed, social issues and the Republican convention together account for a Republican loss of 2 percent of the vote. See "Comments," at the end of "Murphy Brown Revisited," 75.

56. See, for example, Gustav Niebuhr, "Push on Gay Ban Roils Religious Community," *Washington Post*, 29 January 1993.

57. See Ralph Reed, *Politically Incorrect*, 219.

58. See Christian Coalition, *Contract with the American Family*, appendix.

59. A "substantial" force was defined as Christian Right strength above 25 percent but below 50 percent in the state party organization (see Persinos, "Has the Christian Right Taken Over the Republican Party?").

60. Pennsylvania and Maine are in the substantial category; the rest of the states in these regions are in the minor category (Persinos, "Has the Christian Right," 22).

61. This is not to say that control of official state party organizations is of *no* value. For example, in general elections, party resources can be targeted toward party candidates sympathetic to the movement (Christopher P. Gilbert, "Christians and Quistians in Minnesota," *PS: Political Science and Politics* 28, no. 1 [March 1995]: 20–23).

62. John C. Green, James L. Guth, Lyman A. Kellstedt, and Corwin Smidt, "Evangelical Realignment: The Political Power of the Christian Right," *Christian Century* 112, no. 21 (5–12 July 1995): 676–79.

63. See Green, Guth, Kellstedt, and Smidt, "Evangelical Realignment," 678. The poll used for the 1992-1994 comparison is a different one than that used in table 6.2. The 12 percent rise is to 72 percent from a 1992 level of 60 percent support for GOP House candidates. Interestingly, the gender gap that appears among other groups does not appear among evangelicals, perhaps reflecting the religious basis of the GOP's appeal to the generally more devout female half of the evangelical population.

On the voting behavior of evangelicals, see Green, Guth, Kellstedt, and Smidt, "Evangelical Realignment," 677, 679. The 38 percent figure was higher than that for those in other religious traditions, including Black Protestants who have a much longer tradition of using churches for the dissemination of political messages.

64. Green, Guth, Kellstedt, and Smidt, "Evangelical Realignment," 678. From 1992–1994, regular church attending Catholics exhibited a fourteen-point swing in favor of Republican House candidates.

65. The Christian Right had, however, been an enthusiastic backer of North's efforts to aid the Contras and seemed undisturbed by the fact that North's efforts on the Contras' behalf had broken the law.

66. For an account of the early stages of the Virginia Senate campaign, see Sidney Blumenthal, "Christian Soldiers," *The New Yorker*, 70, no. 21 (18 July 1994): 31–37. See also Clyde Wilcox, Mark J. Rozell, and J. Bradford Croker, "The Christian Right in the Old Dominion: Resurgent Republicans or Holy War?" *PS: Political Science and Politics* 28, no. 1 (March 1995): 15–18.

67. The material in this paragraph draws from Christopher P. Gilbert, "Christians and Quistians in Minnesota."

68. See Wilcox, Rozell, and Coker, "The Christian Right in the Old Dominion," 16.

69. See John Green, "The Christian Right and the 1994 Elections."

70. For documentation of Allen's links to the movement, see People for the American Way, "Virginia Governor George Allen's First 100 Days: Payback Time for the Religious Right" (press release—19 April 1994). See also Wilcox, Rozell, and Coker, "The Christian Right in the Old Dominion," 17. On Grams and Quist see Gilbert, "Christians and Quistians," 22. On sentiments of the House freshmen, see Green, Guth, Kellstedt, and Smidt, "Evangelical Realignment," 677. The one fourth figure is not unduly high given evangelicals' proportion of the U.S. population, but it is high given the traditional underrepresentation of evangelicals in Congress.

Conclusion

1. Interview by author, 6 March 1989.

2. Christian Coalition, "Contract with the American Family" (Christian Coalition News Press Release), 18 May 1995. See also Anne Tin and Julianna Gruenwald, "'Contract with Family' Welcomed Cautiously by House GOP," *Congressional Quarterly Weekly Report* 53, no. 20 (May 20 1995): 1148–150. The version of the contract presented on page 1449 is slightly less specific than the version in the press release, but covers the same ten points.

3. Christian Coalition, "Contract with the American Family."

4. See Luker, *Abortion and the Politics of Motherhood.*

5. See "Contract with America," *Electronic Democracy Homepage,* on the World Wide Web.

6. See Richard L. Berke, "Christian Coalition Ends Convention with a Dual Identity," *New York Times,* 10 September 1995.

7. Diamond, *Spiritual Warfare,* 66; and Gary Jarmin, personal interview, 22 March 1989.

8. See Moen, *The Transformation of the Christian Right.*

9. Christian Coalition, *Contract with the American Family,* appendix. On potential exaggeration of coalition membership, see Porteous, *Freedom Writer.*

10. See Christian Coalition, *Contract with the American Family,* 136.

11. In 1994, evangelical leaders (including Pat Robertson) and conservative Catholics put out a statement of common goals. For a copy of the statement, see "Evangelicals and Catholics Together: The Christian Mission in the Third Millennium," *First Things* 43 (May 1994). For discussion of the document, see Rob Boston, "Marriage of Convenience," *Church and State* 47, no. 5 (May 1994): 7–10. Christian Coalition recently launched a new group, "Catholic Alliance."

12. See Ralph Reed, *Politically Incorrect,* chap. 4. The chapter is entitled "The New Amos and Andy: How the Media Portrays People of Faith."

13. See Richard L. Berke, "The 'Contract' Gets New Ally on the Right," *New York Times,* 18 January 1995. See also Anne Tin and Julianna Gruenwald, "'Contract with Family' Welcomed Cautiously by House GOP."

14. See Laurie Goodstein, "Christian Leaders Are Urged to Use Abortion as

'96 Test," *Boston Globe*, 6 July 1995. See also, for example, Carolyn Curtis, "Putting Out a Contract," *Christianity Today* (17 July 1995): 54.

15. See Noll, *The Scandal of the Evangelical Mind*.

16. For the classic statement of this argument, see Robert Bellah, *Beyond Belief* (New York: Harper & Row, Publishers, 1970), chap. 9, "Civil Religion in America."

17. Richard G. Hutcheson, Jr., *God in the White House* (New York: Macmillan Publishing Company, 1988), 51.

18. For competing arguments on this issue, see Stephen L. Carter, *The Culture of Disbelief* (New York: Basic Books, 1993); Jim Castelli, *A Plea for Common Sense* (San Francisco: Harper & Row Publishers, 1988); and Richard John Neuhaus, *The Naked Public Square* (Grand Rapids: Eerdmans, 1984).

19. See Ronald W. Walters, *Black Presidential Politics in America*.

20. See Pat Robertson, *The New World Order*; and Michael Lind, "Rev. Robertson's Grand Conspiracy Theory."

21. See Fitzgerald, *Cities on a Hill*, 170–71.

22. See William G. Mayer "Caucuses: How They Work, What Difference They Make," 122.

Index

About the Author

Duane Murray Oldfield is assistant professor of political science at Knox College in Galesburg, Illinois. He received his Ph.D. from the University of California at Berkeley.

DATE DUE
